OUR PEACE

THE BLACK HISTORY OF SNYDER, TEXAS
1914-1966

Jared Dennis

"For he himself is our peace, who has made the two groups one and has destroyed the barrier, the dividing wall of hostility, by setting aside in his flesh the law with its commands and regulations."

-Ephesians 2:14-15

DEDICATIONS

This book is dedicated to the faculty, staff, and students of the Abraham Lincoln School of Snyder and their families.

And to the memories of Mount Olive Baptist Church founding deacon John Baker and Lincoln School principal Daniel Johnson.

Lincoln High School memorial in Snyder, Texas. July, 2021.
Photo by the author.

ACKNOWLEDGEMENTS

Extra special thanks to the staff of the Scurry County Museum for access to their knowledge and archive.

And to the Texas Tech University Library for digitizing more than fifty years of Snyder's historic newspapers from the original microfilm for this project.

Special thanks to: The Scurry County Historic Commission, The Scurry County Library, The Scurry County Sheriff's Department, The Snyder Chamber of Commerce, The Snyder News, Bell-Cypert-Seale Funeral Home, Community Bank of Snyder, Vernon Clay, Veena Clay, Sam Harrison, Elowese Clayton, Rose Nell Walker, Tony Wofford, Pearl Beverly, Dr. Walter Morris Baker, Mike & Marci Dennis, Jal Dennis, James Dennis, Terri Piel, Drew Bullard, Frank & Elyndabeth Toland, Reid Johnson, Joe Jackson, Nicole DeGuzman, Tessa Holladay, Gerald Corkran, Mary Ezell, Linda Fulton, Magan Wadleigh Thomas, Melody Appleton, Lori Botts, Brent and Lori Wells, Heather Smith, Jack Lewis, Brendan Hutt, Summer Thomas, Josh Ortegon, Sandra Salinas, and Linda Heath.

CONTENTS

INTRODUCTION

We Wear the Mask
By Paul Laurence Dunbar

We wear the mask that grins and lies,
It hides our cheeks and shades our eyes,—
This debt we pay to human guile;
With torn and bleeding hearts we smile,
And mouth with myriad subtleties.

Why should the world be over-wise,
In counting all our tears and sighs?
Nay, let them only see us, while
We wear the mask.

We smile, but, O great Christ, our cries
To thee from tortured souls arise.
We sing, but oh the clay is vile
Beneath our feet, and long the mile;
But let the world dream otherwise,
We wear the mask!

Poet Paul Laurence Dunbar. Namesake of the Dunbar School of Snyder, Texas.

This book will attempt to tell the Black History of Scurry County, Texas from 1914 to 1966. Most of the sources for this history come from the newspapers of the city of Snyder. When possible, written and recorded personal accounts, city and county records, academic publications, museum artifacts, original interviews, historic maps, and old photographs will be used to supplement these stories.

This history did not occur in a vacuum and it will not be presented in one. Instead, it will be woven back into the story of Snyder.

To better understand events within Scurry County, it will be necessary to discuss events beyond it. The story will frequently zoom out to cover contemporary trends in the known Black History of Texas. However, this book is not intended to give the reader a deep understanding of the topic. Doing so would only drown out Scurry County's contributions to that much larger story.

It will occasionally be necessary to address events beyond Texas that are simply too important to ignore. These stories are only included if they provide insight into the economic, cultural, or religious history of Scurry County's African-American community.

It is important to acknowledge that the Hispanic population of Scurry County was also subjected to segregation prior to the 1954 U.S. Supreme Court case of *Hernandez v. Texas*. Their contributions to the history and culture of Scurry County are just as old, many times more complex, and worth the telling. That story will be referenced here, but any attempt to cram a thorough telling of it into the same book would only overwhelm the Black History of Snyder.

■■

For many years, various combinations of apathy, stubbornness, grief, fear, shame, bitter resentment, innocent ignorance, and the limitations of living memory hindered this subject from being studied in the way one might approach any other historical topic. In the 21st century this veil of silence has, for the most part, lifted.

In its place is a historical blind spot that provokes more curiosity than trepidation in the minds of many Scurry County residents.

Living memory was the main motivator for the timing of this book. The Baby Boomer generation is well represented in Snyder's population at the time of this writing. They will be the last to have witnessed the period that is this book's primary focus. Waiting might have calmed passions, but it would have come at the cost of living connections.

The second reason for the timing is technological. When the original microfilm scans for the Snyder Signal and Scurry County Times newspapers were created, only 3 copies were made. If a person wanted to read one of these copies, they would have to be in Snyder or Lubbock and request access to one of West Texas' few working microfilm readers. Thanks to the cooperation of the Texas Tech University Library, anyone can now read digital copies of Snyder's historic newspapers on the internet.

The third reason is the near-universal outpouring of support from the people of Scurry County. They made time, pulled strings, confirmed locations, rummaged through storage rooms, confided old memories, and always insisted on the importance of telling this story.

■■

History is subjective. Every historian, professional or amateur, must sit down before a giant pile of facts and decide which ones tell the story and which ones can be ignored. The act of making those choices will reflect that historian's lived experiences, their familiarity with the topic, education level, social and economic background, political and religious philosophies, implicit and explicit biases, and so on. The inevitable result will be an interpretation of the past that is unique to that historian, shaped by the sources available to them, and influenced by the times in which they are writing.

It is therefore helpful for the reader to understand a few things about the author from the beginning. I am male, white, a born citizen of the United States, cisgendered, and heterosexual. I am an actor and a storyteller. I hold a master's degree. As an adult,

I have never experienced oppression from my society worse than temporary discomfort, embarrassment, or inconvenience. No Supreme Court decision was ever necessary to ensure my rights. In short, I am an imperfect messenger for this story.

I love Snyder, Texas. I represent the fifth generation of a family that has lived in Scurry County since 1924. I was raised on stories of the region's romantic Western tragedies and the explosive onrush of its late 20th century modernity. Most of it was taught to me by relatives who still refer to Western Texas as "God's Country." We have long thought of Snyder's history as an extension of our own.

But there was a story that my grandparents couldn't tell me. Or perhaps wouldn't. A story that was never fully articulated in any of their books and only briefly mentioned in one.

Growing up in Snyder, I was generally aware that it had once been a legally segregated city. Many institutions that had enforced or participated in segregation were still around. The physical evidence, though often subtle, was everywhere. Older white and Hispanic people could recall a few details. Older Black people, when they were willing to discuss it at all, knew significantly more. But there was no place where a curious person could get the whole story, all at once, and presented with the kind of careful thoroughness that had long been applied to other aspects of Snyder's past.

We get to choose what to do with the world that our ancestors handed to us. Future generations will have opinions about our choices. I chose to tell this story so others can learn in a few hours what took years to piece together. I did my best to present it with the honesty, dignity, and care that it deserves.

UNDENIABLE TRUTHS

"We hold, as undeniable truths, that the governments of the various States, and of the Confederacy itself, were established exclusively by the white race, for themselves and their posterity; that the African race had no agency in their establishment; that they were rightfully held and regarded as an inferior and dependent race, and in that condition only could their existence in this country be rendered beneficial or tolerable:

"That, in this free government, all white men are, and of right ought to be, entitled to equal civil and political rights; that the servitude of the African race, as existing in these States, is mutually beneficial to both bond and free, and is abundantly authorized and justified by the experience of mankind, and the revealed will of the Almighty Creator, as recognized by all Christian nations; while the destruction of the existing relations between the two races, as advocated by our sectional enemies, would bring inevitable calamities upon both, and desolation upon the fifteen slaveholding States."

-A Declaration of the Causes Which Impel the State of Texas to Secede From the Federal Union. Signed by William Scurry on February 2, 1861.

Confederate Brigadier General William Read Scurry, namesake of Scurry County. Photo circa 1863.

"The people of Texas are informed that, in accordance with a Proclamation from the Executive of the United States, all slaves are free. This involves an absolute equality of personal rights and rights of property between former masters and slaves, and the connection heretofore existing between them become that between employer and hired labor. The freedmen are advised to remain at their present homes and work for wages. They are informed that they will not be allowed to collect at military posts and that they will not be supported in idleness either there or elsewhere."

-General Order No. 3.
Proclaimed at Galveston, Texas on June 19, 1865. Juneteenth.

"Sixty millions of whites are in no danger from the presence here of eight millions of blacks. The destinies of the two races in this country are indissolubly linked together, and the interests of both require that the common government of all shall not permit the seeds of race hate to be planted under the sanction of the law. What can more certainly arouse race hate, what more certainly create and perpetuate a feeling of distrust between these races, than state enactments which, in fact, proceed on the ground that colored citizens are so inferior and degraded that they cannot be allowed to sit in public coaches occupied by white citizens? [...]

"If evils will result from the commingling of the two races upon public highways established for the benefit of all, they will be infinitely less than those that will surely come from state legislation regulating the enjoyment of civil rights upon the basis of race. We boast of the freedom enjoyed by our people above all other peoples. But it is difficult to reconcile that boast with a state of the law which, practically, puts the brand of servitude and degradation upon a large class of our fellow citizens,–our equals before the law."

-*Plessy v. Ferguson,* 1896. "Separate but equal."
Dissent by Supreme Court Justice John Marshall Harlan.

"The power and authority is hereby conferred upon the Cities of Texas to provide by suitable ordinance for the segregation of negroes and whites in any such city. [...]

"That the governing authorities of any such city shall have the full power to define the negro race, negro community, white race, and white community.

"That the governing authorities of any such city shall have full power to enforce the observance of any ordinance passed leading to or providing for the segregation of the races and to require the observance thereof by appropriate penalties."
-Civil Statutes of Texas, 1948. Title 28, Article 1015b

"No white child can be adopted by a negro person, nor can a negro child be adopted by a white person."
-Civil Statutes of Texas, 1948. Title 3, Art. 46a, Sec. 8

"Any white person [...] may use the county free library [...] and may be entitled to all the privileges thereof. [...] The negroes of said county [may] be served through a separate branch or branches of the county free library, which shall be administered by a custodian of the negro race under the supervision of the county librarian."
-Civil Statutes of Texas, 1948. Title 35, Art. 1688

"No white children shall attend schools supported for colored children, nor shall colored children attend schools supported for white children."
-Civil Statutes of Texas, 1948. Title 49, Art. 2900

"Negro porters shall not sleep in sleeping car berths nor use bedding intended for white passengers."
-Civil Statutes of Texas, 1948. Title 71, Art. 4477, Rule 72

"Every railway company [...] shall provide separate coaches [...] for the accommodation of white and negro passengers."
-Civil Statutes of Texas, 1948. Title 112, Art. 6417, Sec. 1

"If any white person and negro shall knowingly intermarry with each other [...] they shall be confined in the penitentiary not less than two nor more than five years."
-Texas Penal Code, 1948. Title 9, Art. 492

"No individual, firm, club, copartnership, association, company or corporation shall knowingly permit any fistic combat match, boxing, sparring, or wrestling contest or exhibition between any person of the Caucasian or 'White' race and one of the African or 'Negro' race."

-Texas Penal Code, 1948. Title 11, Art. 614-11(f)

"All negro passengers boarding their buses for transportation or passage shall take seats in the back or rear end of the bus, filling the bus from the back or rear end."

-Texas Penal Code, 1948. Title 19, Art. 1661.1, Sec. 1

CHAPTER 1
FIREBRANDS AND DYNAMITE

"There are plenty of ways to rid a community of undesirable people and things without resorting to firebrands and dynamite. A man who will blow up a house and murder human beings is at heart a murderer of the assassin kind. A law abiding community shudders at the thought of a dynamiter in their midst. Human life is in peril, and no man can feel absolutely safe. Such lawlessness is bound to reflect on the good name and prosperity of the community."

-The Snyder Signal. July 9, 1915.[1]

Confederate Days in Snyder, Texas. January 1, 1915. Courtesy Scurry County Museum.

Segregation began in Snyder, Texas at about three o'clock in the morning on Thursday, July 8, 1915, when a bomb exploded on the southwest corner of modern day 26th Street and Avenue Q. The blast shattered the hardwood floor of a two-story hotel, hurling shards of wood and glass toward the walls of First Baptist Church a few dozen yards to the south. Across the street to the north, the shockwave slammed against the side of the First Presbyterian Church, rattling the little wooden steeple that crowned its eastern face. Dust erupted into the air along the horse-trampled roads of Snyder's business district. Echoes of the blast thundered off the windows of the Scurry County Courthouse and went booming out through the sleeping town.

For a moment, the only sound was the Texas wind. Then the shouts came.

■■

The story of Snyder's African-American community began in the Autumn of 1914 when a train on the Santa Fe Railroad came to a stop in front of the Snyder Train Depot. Built three years earlier of intricately molded concrete and terracotta, the depot gleamed a pristine white and blue, mirroring the endless skies of Western Texas that surrounded it.

Dozens of passengers shuffled off the segregated car at the rear of the train and onto the bricks that lined the ground around the depot. They had come by pooling their money to purchase a party ticket. At least fifty passengers were required to qualify for such a ride.[2]

Among them was seventeen-year-old John Baker, a recruiter for the Fuller family. The Fullers ran Snyder National Bank and owned the local cottonseed oil mill southeast of town. John Baker would make Snyder, Texas his home for the rest of his life and bear witness to this entire story.

As Snyder's newest residents gathered under the station's awning, they would have noticed the lack of a segregated waiting area near the building. Their journey had begun far to the east in Waskom, Texas, where the customary infrastructure of segregation had long been in place.

19

Waskom was a community built around cotton. The area's old slave plantations had, by this time, been divided up and leased to sharecroppers and tenant farmers.

These sharecroppers were typically paid two-thirds the value of the cotton they produced in a year. The surplus value went to the landowners, often the same families who had owned both the plantations and the laborers therein prior to the Civil War.

Once the cotton was sold and all outstanding debts had been covered, there was often little or no money left to cover the needs of the sharecropping family. When a bad growing season failed to cover the sharecropper's initial debts, those debts would compound. Consecutive bad years could potentially lead to a lifetime of work with no hope of ever paying what was owed. By the 1910s, this widespread system of debt peonage was contributing to an exodus of African-Americans from the southeastern U.S., known in later years as the Great Migration.[3-5]

The outbreak of The Great War during the summer of 1914 drove up the value of Snyder's cotton products and created an acute labor shortage. Western Texans scrambled to take advantage of lucrative opportunities created by America's neutrality in the conflict. This spike in demand offered the sharecroppers an opportunity to escape the old system by leveraging the only asset they had in abundance: cotton experience.

THIS IS SCURRY COUNTY'S MAJOR INDUSTRY

Fuller Cotton Oil Company, established in 1908, was and continues to be the largest single industry in the county. This picture of the oil mill in Southeast Snyder was made several years ago, and does not include a number of additions and improvements.

The Scurry County Times. December 30, 1937.

The Fuller Cottonseed Oil Mill was located on the south side of modern day 34th Street between Avenues J and L. The city's southern limits ran along 32nd Street at the time, so the mill was located just outside of town along a spur of the Roscoe, Snyder, and Pacific Railway. The mill could be seen from downtown Snyder due to the tall chimney and water tower that dominated the complex.

The new workers were enticed to this place by the promise of eight dollars and fifty cents per week. Housing was provided for them in the form of a few single-room buildings that surrounded the mill. These structures had no amenities other than windows. Multiple families occupied most of the little homes during the busy seasons. A single outhouse was shared by the entire complex. Fresh water had to be retrieved from the mill itself.

Not all of the newcomers were poor sharecroppers. Some had the means to enjoy more comfortable arrangements. Although Snyder was not yet an officially segregated city in 1914, individual hotels could make their own broad policies about who could rent a room and who could not.

One block east of Snyder's public square, on the southwest corner of West Street and Scurry Street (later 26th Street and Avenue Q respectively), sat Jim Percy's hotel. When the city's first African-American residents came inquiring, it was his door that opened to them.

Jim Percy's hotel was a two story wooden structure with a porch and awning that extended out into West Street on its north side. Nestled between a pair of Snyder's most prominent churches, the sounds of two singing congregations overlapped the little boarding house on Sunday mornings. After services, the hotel would respond with music, laughter, arguments, and all the other sounds of secular life.[6,7]

■■

Mamie Dixon had a powerful voice. She also had a passionate disposition and was thoroughly fluent in the obscenities of her time. On a warm Friday evening in April of 1915, someone hurt Mamie so deeply that she shouted her way into history.

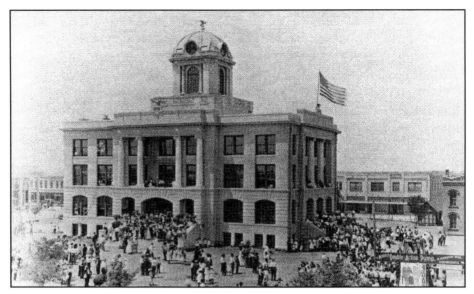

The Scurry County Courthouse in 1912. Courtesy Scurry County Museum.

Ms. Dixon had offended *"another negro woman and from the testimony it seemed that a spirit of jealousy was manifest in the case."* The details of the argument have been lost to time, but a complaint was made to the Snyder Police Department shortly after the event. Mamie found herself under arrest. Her arraignment was set for the following Monday.

As Mamie ascended the stairs at the courthouse entrance and made her way up to the top floor, she passed through a gawking crowd. Taking her seat in the sunny courtroom with its commanding view of the square below, she watched people pack into every seat and available standing space to watch the show unfold. Within this group of onlookers was a reporter from the Snyder Signal's office on the south side of the square. The trial of Mamie Dixon would be the first mention in the local paper of African-Americans residing in Snyder, Texas.

"Negro Woman Tried In The Mayor's Court," announced Friday's headline. The article noted that Mamie was *"arraigned Monday before Mayor Noble. A great crowd of men filled the courtroom for a negro trial has heretofore been unusual in Snyder and men were curious to hear it. There was an evident spirit of*

levity in the crowd, but Mayor Noble suppressed it. He said although the defendant is a darkey, her rights in court are the same as any other person. The crowd then put on a solemn expression and there was no levity."

Having restored order to the courtroom, Mayor Noble heard testimonies from several residents regarding activities at the *"colored people's hotel"*. Mamie asserted that *"she was not guilty and didn't swear,"* but the court was unmoved after hearing stories of her *"loud and vociferous talking and cursing."*

At the end of her very public trial, Ms. Dixon was fined *"one dollar and costs all amounting to $12.25."* It was a sum equal to about one-and-a-half weeks of her labor at the mill. *"Mamie paid the charges and went her way."*[8]

■■

The spiritual needs of Snyder's newest residents had gone largely unmet for the first several months of their time in the city. The established congregations of West Texas were heavily white during this period and among the most ethnically exclusive institutions in the region. This arrangement was enforced by cultural tradition as often as by local law.

Reverend U. S. Mingo spoke in Snyder on June 21, 1915. He had come from Fort Worth at the request of a developing congregation in need of guidance to bring their own religious traditions to Scurry County.

The location of Snyder's first official African-American religious gathering is unknown. It likely happened at Jim Percy's Hotel or near the oil mill grounds but no evidence survives to the present.

Regardless of the location, twenty-two people showed up to the meeting to become charter members of the new church. By the end of the night, a volunteer committee had been formed to look for a suitable building in town for worship.[9]

Sadly, the first attempt to establish a Traditionally Black Baptist Church in Snyder would fail. The summer temperatures were climbing in the little town and welcomes were wearing thin.

■■

Between their work hours at the mill, the lively drama at the hotel, and the recent attempts to establish their own church, Snyder's first Black residents were flourishing and becoming increasingly visible in the city's public life. Their regular gatherings on the square were becoming points of friction to individuals who regarded them as a public safety issue or simply resented the way the city was beginning to look.

One anonymous person took their complaint directly to the Snyder Signal, making a case that *"Snyder is a rapidly growing city and naturally an undesirable element is apt to accumulate right under our noses. Colored people are essential here as the population increases, but caution should be used and a tight ban inaugurated. Trouble might result, so why not begin now and colonize or adopt an agreeable plan that will be permanent pertaining to the government of the negro population. Get busy at once."*[10]

THE NEGRO HOTEL WAS DYNAMITED

TWO BOMBS PLACED UNDER THE BUILDING—ONLY ONE IS EXPLODED

The Snyder Signal. July 9, 1915.[11]

■■

Jim Percy awoke from a dream to find himself hurtling toward the ceiling of his bedroom on the second floor of his hotel on West Street. He crashed back down onto the mattress in a pile of sheets with one of the loudest sounds he had ever heard ringing in his ears, the odor of spent gunpowder in his nostrils, and darkness all around. He looked out his window to see the shards of its glass panes sparkling in the dust of Scurry Street below.

He couldn't hear. He couldn't smell. He could barely see. But he could still shout.

It had already been a particularly difficult week for Mr. Percy. It seemed that the Snyder Police had been watching his business constantly since he first made the choice to accept Black patrons. During the first week of July, 1915, law enforcement had been particularly visible.

On the day before the explosion, Percy had been arrested on one charge of *"keeping a disorderly house."* After paying the fine at the county jail, he walked home and went to bed in a terrible mood.

Now he could hear someone shouting back to him over the high-pitched ringing of his ears. As he made his way down what was left of the hotel's wooden stairs, he was met by the sight of his tenants standing shocked and shaking in the road. Miraculously, there had been no life-threatening injuries.

Snyder's first African-American residents quickly gathered what remained of their belongings and made their way to the cottonseed oil mill housing southeast of town. There would be no Black families residing within the city limits of Snyder, Texas for the next thirty-eight years and four months.

Daybreak revealed the debris of the hotel scattered across the quiet intersection where hoof prints battled with tire tracks for control of the dust. As Mr. Percy surveyed the damage to his establishment, he glanced under the boards of its front porch and noticed the second bomb.[11]

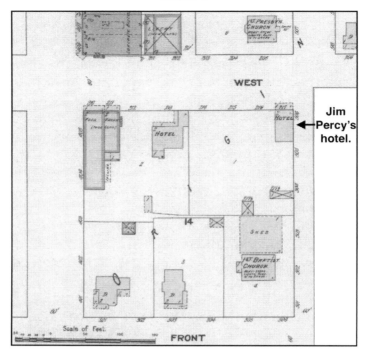

One block southeast of the Scurry County Courthouse in 1911 (above) and 1920 (below).[6,7]

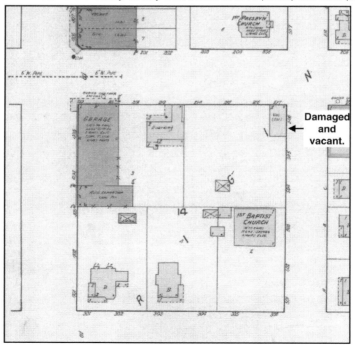

■■

On Friday, July 9, 1915, the front page of the Snyder Signal announced that *"The Negro Hotel Was Dynamited."* Written less than one day after the explosion, the story included the recent development that *"there were two bombs placed on top of the ground under the southeast corner of the house. Only one went off. It shows to have been set off by a fuse about a yard long. The other bomb failed to shoot. It had been thrown further under and was immediately under a bed where it is said a man and a woman were sleeping. This bomb is dynamite and is being kept."*

The article noted that *"No negroes have ever lived in Scurry County until last year when they were brought here to pick cotton. There has been a general feeling that they were not wanted, but many people have employed negro help and their numbers have increased.*

"There have been murmurings of dissatisfaction because of the location of their hotel in the business district and reports have been circulated regarding the conduct of the people there.

"It is supposed that the attempted dynamiting came as an expression of objection of some person or persons to the presence of these people.

"It is understood the dynamite case is being investigated and furthermore that steps may be made to localize the negro population in something like a specified district."[11]

News of the attack beeped out from the Snyder Signal's new telegraph office. The story was picked up by the Associated Press. Small towns featured the shocking story on their front pages with splash headlines. *"Negro Hotel At Snyder Blown Up,"* blared The Abilene Reporter. *"Negroes Leave Town Following Explosion,"* shouted the Brownsville Herald.

In the big cities of eastern Texas, where the regularity of such violent reports was becoming increasingly embarrassing, the story was buried in a more discreet font. *"Negroes Flee From Snyder"* was the headline on page four of The San Antonio Express. *"Negro Hotel Blown Up,"* admitted The Houston Post on its own fourth page.

Coverage of the Snyder hotel bombing. July, 1915.[12-32]

Within two days of the explosion the story was appearing in newspapers as far away as Joplin, Missouri and Hutchinson, Kansas.[12-32]

The following week's issue of the Snyder Signal contained no mention of the hotel bombing. No newspaper ever received a follow-up from Snyder. The story was never mentioned again.

Scurry County's first experiment with an integrated society had lasted less than one year. In time no one would remember. But the vacant wreck of the little hotel on West Street was still standing as a silent reminder five years later in 1920. By June of 1927 it had been pulled down, built over, and forgotten.[7,33]

The people of Snyder would never learn who planted the devices that resulted in more than half a century of segregation in their city.

CHAPTER 2

THE LIMITS LAID OUT

"There are those of them who are pleased to do right and it is unfortunate for them that any of their race should make trouble for their kind by going beyond the limits laid out for them by the people who live here, but the affair of last Monday night is apt to bring on a condition very hurtful to the welfare of all the quiet and law abiding negroes."

-The Snyder Signal. March 19, 1920.[1]

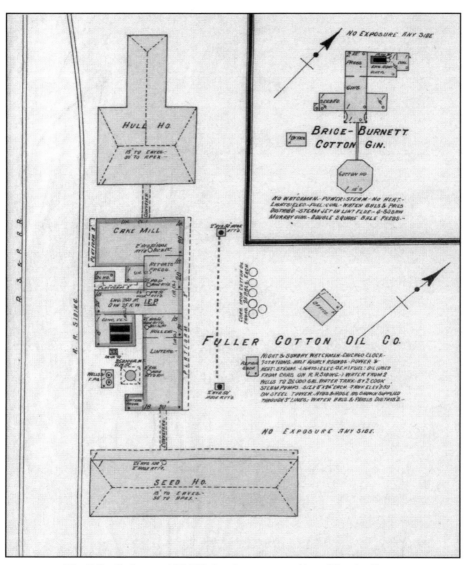

*The Fuller Cottonseed Oil Mill. Southeastern outskirts of Snyder, Texas.
Sanborn Maps. January, 1920.*

A fist slammed into the side of Loy Ramsour's head on the chilly evening of Monday, March 15, 1920. Loy, the white superintendent of the Fuller Cottonseed Oil Mill, had been in an argument with one of his Black employees. That argument was now a fight. As fists flew between the two men, a second worker joined in the fray. A blow from an unexpected direction rattled Mr. Ramsour's skull and he tumbled onto the stony soil where the RS&P Railroad tracks shone in the new electric lights of the mill.

The stars overhead gazed indifferently back at Loy as the sounds of work boots went crunching furiously across the gravel of the mill yard.[1]

■■

I n the years following the bombing of the little hotel on West Street, the Snyder Signal did its best to ignore the attack and the community that had been its target.

On December 16, 1916, the residents of the oil mill complex decorated their homes with Christmas ornaments while the wealthy landowners of West Texas decorated Snyder's courthouse square with blood. About one block west of the bombed-out hotel on West Street, Ed Sims was shot several times with a pistol and once with a shotgun within view of hundreds of holiday shoppers. The thirty-two-year-old heir to a profitable cattle ranch was hustled into a nearby storefront where he bled to death.

The Signal reported on the ensuing trial into the early months of 1917. The bloody feud that resulted in the killing of Ed Sims would eventually be romanticized in the collective memory of Snyder as one of the last legendary events of its early history. The tale even included appearances by Frank Hamer, a young Texas Ranger who would become legendary in his own right for his involvement in the Sherman Riot of 1930 and his ambush of Bonnie Parker and Clyde Barrow in 1934. Similar events to the south of Snyder would seldom be elevated to comparison with Shakespearean tragedy.[2]

The deadly Johnson-Sims feud began its journey from current event to local legend on April 6, 1917 when the United States finally entered The Great War. About 380,000 African-Americans would serve in the war effort. The conflict brought on a rush of patriotic nationalism that flooded the first few pages of the Snyder Signal with riveting news from the front, ads for war bonds, and beautifully illustrated propaganda from the Wilson Administration week after week.

President Wilson would have been particularly resented at the oil mill. The first southerner to win the White House since 1848, Woodrow Wilson brought his cultural traditions along with him. The Wilson Administration had ordered the segregation of the Railway Mail Service back in 1913. By 1917, Wilson's custom of racial separation was quickly spreading to every aspect of the federal bureaucracy. The war and the emergency powers it provided accelerated this transformation.[3]

The Great War finally came to an end on November 11, 1918. The little city of Snyder had dutifully sent its sons to *"make the world safe for democracy,"* in the words of President Wilson. At least seventeen of them never came home.[4]

Millions of young men with combat experience began to flood back across the Atlantic and into the United States. They were greeted by a quickly crumbling wartime economy, numerous immigrant laborers who fled to the U.S. during the conflict, and a Great Migration of African-Americans fleeing the cotton fields of the southeast.

The value of Scurry County's cotton and cattle plummeted as the war ended. With demand for its products collapsing and jobs in short supply, Snyder's overall population underwent a sudden and steep decline.[5,6]

■■

By the early summer of 1919 even remote cities like Snyder began to notice that something had gone terribly wrong.

At the time of this writing, 1919 is frequently described by American historians as the worst period in the nation's race relations since the Civil War. Fueled by widespread economic hardship and cultural resentments, countless incidents of white supremacist terrorism and dozens of "race riots" broke out nationwide. The monstrous climax came during a period that author and civil rights activist James Weldon Johnson dubbed The Red Summer.[7]

Like most Southern newspapers of the period, The Snyder Signal consistently portrayed African-American communities as guilty. Armed with a weekly newspaper and shielded by anonymity, the white population of Scurry County battled their anxieties in the editorial pages.

"A negro rebellion in the United States," said one Snyder resident, *"could become a dreadful condition because of the number and the nature of negroes. A war would disorganize business in all lines, would interfere with the labor market, and would expose families everywhere to the sneaking viciousness of the blacks. The government should take steps at the very outset to protect business and society against thieving, arson, assassination, outrages, and such other crimes as negro fiends are apt to resort to. Unless the authorities organize efficient machinery to meet the conditions, the white people are apt to take the matter into their own hands."*[8]

"Northern people have thought for fifty years that the folks in the south were cruelly hard on negroes because once in a while a coon was waited on by a mob and lynched for criminal assault. Now the negroes are giving the north a chance to see what effect that unspeakable crime has on the feeling of northern people," scoffed another writer in The Snyder Signal.[9]

"A general race war in this country would be a national tragedy," wrote another anonymous resident, *"and the negro would resort to all sorts of outlawry but a determined American spirit will win out to the utter ruin of negro interests. The better class of negroes will stand pat for Anglo Saxon supremacy."*[10]

A riot began in Longview, Texas on July 10th that lasted for three days, killed four people, and destroyed most of the city's Black district. The Texas Rangers and elements of the Texas National Guard confiscated more than 6,000 firearms in Gregg County during the ten days of martial law that followed the Longview Race Riot.[11]

Five days later, a Black man smoking a cigarette too close to a white woman caused a brawl involving more than sixty people in Port Arthur, Texas.[12]

On July 19th, four days after the violence at Port Arthur, the chaos of The Red Summer came to the nation's capitol. Rumors propagated about the questioning and release of an African-American man accused of sexually assaulting the wife of a white Navy sailor. A white mob marched through southwestern D.C., beating the residents with metal pipes and wooden clubs as they went. The crowd was even larger on the following day. Attacks occurred across the city with police turning a blind eye.

By Sunday, the third day of the violence, the Black population of Washington had armed and organized themselves, firing on any white person who approached their neighborhoods. Near the end of the fourth day of havoc in D.C., President Wilson ordered the National Guard to end the unrest. The weather got there first. After about 40 deaths and more than 150 reported injuries, a heavy rain ended the Washington D.C. Race Riots.

"In Washington City a negro outrage leads to race antagonism. Down here in Texas it leads to a few dead niggers," said one reader in the Snyder Signal.[13]

Other letters attempted to offer more nuance.

"White people throughout the South are not condemning the peaceable, law-abiding negroes on account of race riots. The southern people know the negro. There are many good, quiet negroes, who know their limits and are strong in condemning the recklessness of the younger negroes in their attitude toward social conditions. The solid, reliable negroes attend to their own affairs and are content to put in their efforts for the betterment of their race. The young negroes who get obsessed with a spirit of race equality are the trouble makers. Leading negroes can make it possible for their people to live in peace if they will teach their race to accept such social code as the South has always approved, but if negro speakers and preachers side with the obstreperous negroes, they are apt to arouse popular feeling against the whole race.

"Fifty negro preachers in Washington City preached last Sunday on the recent riots and some of them charged that white people brought on the race clash. They say that in the face of recent criminal assaults on white women by negroes. That is one crime that white men will punish for and any negro who seeks to defend such criminality is inviting a just wrath down upon him."[14]

The most notorious event of the whole deadly summer began to unfold in Chicago on July 27th. When a raft full of Black teenagers drifted toward an unofficially white beach, someone began throwing rocks at them. Seventeen-year-old Eugene Williams was struck in the head and drowned in Lake Michigan.

An officer of the Chicago Police Department refused to arrest the stone-thrower, handcuffing one of the Black men who complained instead. Six days of rapidly escalating violence followed that killed 38 people, wounded more than 500, and left thousands of Black Chicagoans homeless.[15]

Eleven hundred miles away in Snyder, readers reacted to the news with shock and disgust.

"Chicago is in the throes of a race riot. It may be the carrying out of a pre-ordained plan, but any how the unrest now among the negroes is apt to lead to practical extermination of the race, whereas if they will stay in the negroes' place the present and future generations will find the Southern people their best friends."
[16]

The violent reports of 1919 seemed like novel events to the young people of Snyder, but the older generations still carried memories from the last time the terrible cycle had played out. On the first day of August, one older writer attempted to put the problem into context for a generation growing up with automobiles, radios, and electricity.

"About 15 or 18 years ago there came on what seemed to be a wave of negro fiendishness all over the South and for a while there was hardly a week passed without a negro outrage. It seemed the black brutes had a mania for assaulting white women and the people throughout the country were compelled to resort to drastic means to protect their wives and daughters.

"No woman or girl dared to venture out alone from her home in a negro inhabited settlement. They were not safe in their homes when the men were away. It required a few lynchings and strenuous watching to put a check on the wave of criminality, but for several years now we have heard less of it until within the last few weeks.

"It is now recalled that that period of criminality followed soon after the Spanish American War. In that war there was a good

deal said complimentary of the negro soldiers and it is probable that they came back puffed up and clamoring for a degree of social consideration, and failing to get that, tuned their deviltry to forcing attention on defenseless white women.

"Recently we have read of rape, slander, arrogance and insolence of negroes in Gregg county resulting in riot and race war and the establishment of martial law. Then there was race trouble at Port Arthur, and in Washington City, where seven white women were criminally assaulted and a war ensued between whites and negroes. [...]

"There is a cause for this renewal of negro criminal insolence, and Texas Rangers who have been investigating believe they have found the seat of the trouble. While in France, the American negroes were honored by the French people as part of the American army that had come there to save France from German dominion.

"The French gave honor to uniform and admired the fighting qualities of the negro soldiers. They have not had occasion to look upon the negro as an inferior race and the less enlightened French extended a degree of social equality that has turned the negro's head and has prompted him to want the same consideration in America and in his natural condition, ignorance, insolence, and lecherous inclination he resents the American line of social caste and in his spirit of envy, hate, and beastly nature he proposes to have the consideration shown him as abroad to run riot in crime as a means of expressing resentment.

"The ignorant negro is urged on to criminality by those more enlightened. Although such crimes will continue to call for speedy and positive punishment just as long as there are white men enough in the south to defend southern homes and the honor of Southern wives and daughters."[17]

■■

Mount Olive Baptist Church, originally known as First Negro Baptist Church of Snyder, was founded some time in 1920. Their first worship service, a significant moment in the cultural history of Scurry County, went unnoticed by the Snyder Signal. The story would not be mentioned in a local newspaper until 1956.

Snyder's oldest Traditionally Black Congregation was organized, at least in part, through the work of John and Mary Baker. John Baker was born in Waskom, Texas on August 21, 1897. Drafted for service during The Great War, Private Baker was inducted at Marshall, Texas on September 25, 1918. The young Mr. Baker served his country as a laborer at Camp Bowie near Brownwood, Texas until receiving his honorable discharge on January 2, 1919. John returned to Snyder shortly thereafter.[18]

Together with his wife, twenty-three-year-old homemaker and future journalist Mary Baker, John transformed a one-room house on the cottonseed oil mill grounds outside of Snyder into a sanctuary.

Left: John Baker in 1918. Courtesy Dr. Walter Morris Baker.
Right: John Baker. Date unknown. Courtesy Scurry County Museum.

37

Worshiping with the Bakers on that Sunday morning were fellow founding church members Prince Curr, Hattie Umphrey, Alice Ellis, John Ellis, and Octavie Anderson. The service was lead by Reverend Will Anderson.

The First Negro Baptist Church of Snyder adopted a new name shortly after its founding. The precise date of the change is unknown, but by 1925 they were already referring to themselves as Mount Olive Baptist Church.[19]

■■

As the sun rose on March 16, 1920, it revealed two sets of boot prints in the dust along Texas Highway 7. Known in later years as US 84, Highway 7 ran southeast from Snyder toward the nearby community of Hermleigh. The bootprints abandoned the main road just north of town and plodded eastward toward the Fisher County line. It was there that the tracks finally caught up with the work boots that had created them.

The two mill workers had been running all night. Their feet ached after marching through eighteen miles of darkness. Their heads were dizzy from dehydration and a lack of sleep. Their knuckles throbbed faintly from a recent encounter with Loy Ramsour's head.

A distant glint of chrome came gliding up behind them, churning the boot prints into a narrow line of dust that billowed out over the lonely farm-to-market road. Deputy Sheriff Thrash brought his Ford Model T to a gentle stop near the two exhausted men. Dust overtook the sputtering vehicle. The conversation that followed, presuming a conversation happened at all, was short. The deputy's car went speeding back toward the Scurry County Jail with two extra passengers.

On March 19, 1920 the lead headline in The Snyder Signal said *"Negro Laborers Assault White Mill Superintendent Here Monday Nite."* The newspaper admitted that the two laborers had only *"beat Loy up somewhat"* but the breach of the local social code was not to be forgiven. After describing the incident to their readers, The Signal opined on the situation in a subsection titled *"Negroes Make Race Trouble."*

"The development of the cotton industry in West Texas brings with it such work as people have found it suitable to employ negro labor. The picking season and the compress and oil mill can furnish a great deal of work for that class of labor and many here have been employing negroes and there have been more of them here than in former years. The negro has been assured that so long as they attend to their business and stay in their place they will not be molested and for the most part those that are here have behaved very well and paid well for their work.

"There are those of them who are pleased to do right and it is unfortunate for them that any of their race should make trouble for their kind by going beyond the limits laid out for them by the people who live here, but the affair of last Monday night is apt to bring on a condition very hurtful to the welfare of all the quiet and law abiding negroes."[1]

With the hotel bombing only five years past and barely a few months since the unrest of 1919, this message was received by some in the town as a call to action and by others as a deadly serious threat. It was certainly a threat to local cotton interests. Rumors buzzed and tensions mounted for more than a week.

Then something unexpected happened. One person walked a full circuit around the Snyder square with a petition and gathered enough signatures to not only change the tone of the local newspaper, but potentially prevent a catastrophe. The name of the organizer was not disclosed in the original document and may never be known for certain.

"Owing to the serious nature of the labor situation, Snyder is in imminent danger of losing the compress and oil mill. Unless these two institutions are allowed to employ negro laborers they will be forced to move to other locations. The compress has already closed down for the season on account of inability to keep laborers, and the oil mill has only been able to operate on half time.

"We believe that such industries as the compress and oil mill should be encouraged, they being the only payrolls we now have. We feel that they are essential to the success of our town, and knowing that it is impossible to operate them without negro labor, we think it would be a serious mistake to not permit the

negro laborer to remain here during the cotton gathering season and while the oil mill and compress are operating.

"We have noticed in a newspaper of recent date that there is some resentment against the negro laborer. Knowing that negro labor is absolutely essential to the farmer during the cotton picking season, and to the oil mill and compress in all cotton growing countries, we feel that we should urge the negro who behaves himself be allowed to stay, and that our newspapers refrain from publishing articles that would tend to frighten the negro away."[20]

The statement was published in The Snyder Signal on April 2, 1920. Signatories came from a broad spectrum of Snyder's society including entrepreneurs, educators, bankers, firemen, ranchers, dry cleaners, the local coroner, World War veterans, a future state treasurer, and Snyder's future mayor and Towle Park namesake Howard Garfield Towle. Several local businesses signed on collectively.

The backlash was a terrible embarrassment for the Snyder Signal. Fearful of being blamed for any future violence in retaliation for the oil mill incident, the newspaper responded with a clarification.

"Referring to the well signed article in this paper regarding publications recently appearing in a newspaper in Snyder, the Signal will say, it fully endorses the purpose of the citizens and business firms signing the protest against the propagation of any sentiment calculated to drive away a class of labor so much needed here. The policy of the Signal is well known here at home on that point. The development of any town and country requires all kinds of labor that will build up legitimate and profitable industries.

"There are certain lines of work where promoters find it difficult to keep white labor, and as in other sections they have found that negro labor is almost necessary to successfully operate their business.

"The Signal has always favored the importation of such labor as necessary for industrial, material, civic and moral upbuilding. The Signal has never indulged in inflammatory expressions. The Signal is for white supremacy, and for promotion of law and order.

"At the time of the recent trouble at the oil mill the Signal said it was unfortunate for the better class of negroes. There are those that want to work and behave themselves and keep in their place and any breech is apt to reflect on all the representatives of the race, yet the Signal knows that the people here will protect the law-abiding negroes while they work and conduct themselves right.

"Just last week the Signal called attention to the dearth of domestic labor. The women of Snyder need help in house cleaning, laundering, and other work and cannot get it. They are not above doing this work themselves, of course, but many are not physically able and they have other things to do. If we had a supply of that class of labor to do the menial work the Snyder women would be better contented and happier."[21]

The crisis had been averted. Other than the arrests of the two unnamed laborers, there would be no retaliation for the fight at the oil mill. The Snyder Signal would never again suggest collective punishment for individual violations of the city's social code.

**TO THE CITIZENS OF SNY-
DER AND SCURRY COUNTY**

Owing to the serious nature of the labor situation, Snyder is in imminent danger of losing the compress and oil mill. Unless these two institutions are permitted to employ negro laborers they will be forced to move to other locations. The compress has already closed down for the season on account of inability to keep laborers, and the oil mill has only been able to operate on half time.

We believe that such industries as the compress and oil mill should be encouraged, they being the only pay-rolls we now have. We feel that they are essential to the success of our town, and knowing that it is impossible to operate them without negro labor, we think it would be a serious mistake to not permit the negro laborer to remain here during the cotton gathering season and while the oil mill and compress are operating.

We have noticed in a newspaper of recent date that there is some resentment against the negro laborer Knowing that negro labor is absolutely essential to the farmer during th cotton picking season, and to the oil mill and compress in all cotton growing countries, we feel that we should urge that the negro who behaves himself be allowed to stay, and that our newspapers refrain from publishing articles that would tend to frighten the negro away.

A. N. Epps.
C. R. Buchanan.
Gay McGlaun.
J. Monroe.
J. W. Fesmire.
H. W. Harless.
H. P. Brown.
John Gladson.
J. E. Johnson.
J. D. Norris.

H. W. Waterman.
J. T. Bridgman.
M. E. Rosser.
Jim Harless.
W. U. Telegraph Co.
Caton & Codson Dry Goods Co.
C. G. Hailey.
W. L. Gross.
Hugh Boren.
Manhattan Hotel.
R. M. Stokes.
F. T. Wilhelm.
G. W. Bynum.
Blackard Hdw. o.
Snyder Natl. Bank.
J. H. Byrd.
P. Brady.
S. J. Casstevens.
G. A. Glen.
Allen Warren.
Lon McNeil.
O. L. Wilson.
P. M. Chambers.
C. J. Sims.
Buckhorn Tailors.
R. L. Johnson.
J. R. Strayhorn.
R. G. Davenport.
W. E. Doak.
E. C. Mil's.
E. L. Darby.
Roy H. Brown.
N. M. Harpole.
T. E. Jenkins.
J. D. McClanahan.
J. O. Dodson.
Geo. J. Parsons.
G. W. Hatcheson.
Baker Grayum & Aderson
Olin Johnson.
E. C. Neeley.
L. & H. Economy Store.
W. S. Beaucamp.
O. F. McClinton.
E. E. Matthews.
T. B. Ware.
J. W. Templeton.
G. B. Clark.
Geo. Eppley.
L. T. Stinson.
Harvey Schuler.
T. C. Hoy.

B. A. McPherson.
C. S. Perkins, Jr.
G. W. Brown.
R. L. Terry.
Guy Paxton.
W. A. Martin
Zac Evans.
Earl Brown.
J. H. Sears.
W. M. Morrow.
W. L. Bishop.
J. W. Grayum.
H. G. Towle
J. W. Stinson
Wade Winston.
Oran G. Wilson
Walter J. Leach
Sed A. Harris.
W. H. Cauble.
T. C. Watkins.
W. G. Ralston.
A. M. Herrin.
W. C. Wenninger.
H. L. Davis.
S. D. Clower.
W. S. Adamson.
W. B. Lee.
W. D. Sims.
J. C. Jurick.
J. O. Stinson.
G. W. Boswell.
Frank Darby.
Hugh Taylor.
T. J. Blackburn.
R. H. Curnutte.
Joe Strayhorn.
D. Anderson.
A. D. Erwin.
R. L. Burditt.
C. F. Neel.
Bert Baugh.
J. J. Taylor.
G. M. Garner.
J. L. Waskom.
J. H. Fondy.
Neil Gross.

The Snyder Signal. April 2, 1920.[21]

CHAPTER 3
IF KARE SHOULD INTERFERE

"High School Notes:

"The girls have selected the name, motto, and colors for their club. The name is the K.K.K. motto 'If kare should interfere, kill it.' [*] Color: Sky blue and rose. Of course the boys are all wondering whether this club is another branch of the Ku Klux Klan."

-The Snyder Signal. November 18, 1921.[1]

* The Ku Klux Klan often changed the letter "C" to "K" in their promotional materials. "Care" becomes "kare", etc.

Klansmen
Klanswomen

AND THEIR FAMILIES

DON'T FAIL TO BE ON HAND AT OUT BIG

Chicken Fry

TO BE GIVEN IN PASTURE ABOUT 2 MILES NORTHWEST OF THE
SANTA FE DEPOT, NEAR THE HIGHWAY. REMEMBER THE DATE

Thursday, July 17

LET EVERY KLANSMAN AND KLANSWOMAN IN SCURRY COUN-
TY BE PRESENT, AND, IF YOU WISH, PLEASE BRING A WELL-
FILLED BASKET OF KNICK-KNACKS.

MRS. MOORE of Lubbock

WILL SPEAK FOR US AND SHE SURE LIKES THE BASKET
LUNCHES. DON'T BE LATE. WE WILL BEGIN EATING PROMPT-
LY AT 7:00 P. M. MRS. MOORE SPEAKS IMMEDIATELY AFTER
THE FRY.

GET ALL THE DETAILS AT THE HALL THURSDAY NIGHT (TO-
NIGHT) OF THIS WEEK.

ATTEST: Kligrapp. Signed: Exalted Clyclops

The Scurry County Times-Signal. July 10, 1924.[22]

Combs and brushes went swooping around the overflowing pews as the churchgoers did their best to recover hairstyles ravaged by the incessant wind. It was the morning of November 24, 1921, the Sunday after Thanksgiving, and the congregants at the First Baptist Church of Snyder had much to be thankful for.

The postwar economy was showing signs of recovery. Prohibition had quieted the region's once-rowdy saloon culture. And the women of Scurry County who could afford the state's poll taxes were celebrating the first anniversary of their enfranchisement.[2,3]

Mayor Fritz R. Smith led the opening prayer. Psalm 107, *"Give thanks to the Lord for He is good; His love endures forever,"* was the weekly scripture and the focus of the sermon. Reverend Jeff Davis, pastor at First Baptist, conducted services for one of the largest holiday crowds ever hosted by the church.

The offering that day was to be donated to the United Charities of Snyder. The charity was an organization of *"five or six men represented by the different denominations of the city."* The money would be used for *"alleviating distress in destitute conditions and all worthy causes"* according to the Snyder Signal.

"At this time Bro. Davis said he had a letter with the request not to open until the collection started and it was found to be an offering of $50.00 to the United Charities of Snyder from the Invisible Empire of the Ku Klux Klan of Snyder. Total offering amounted to $1,120.75. [...]

"Bro. Davis in closing the service said he had been at many thanksgiving services where offerings were made, but this was the best one that he had ever seen, for a city the size of Snyder."[4]

This was the first official public act of the Ku Klux Klan in Scurry County. The origins of the Snyder Klan are mysterious by design. The rest of the city would be introduced to the Invisible Empire three weeks later on December 16th when the following message was posted in the local paper.

"(Editor Snyder Signal: Kindly copy the following, destroy this the original, and publish verbatim in your next issue of the Snyder Signal.)

"Conditions have arisen in our county that demand an expression from us on many subjects. We take this method of touching on some of the more important ones now.

"Recently, notices purporting to be by the Ku Klux Klan have been posted or communicated in Snyder, the public being aware of the existence of a Klan in Snyder, may be led to believe in some of these wild statements that have gained currency recently, hence, we wish to state that the Klan makes no threats, we have not posted or caused to be communicated any words written or spoken to any one. We do not know that we will do so, but should one receive a communication from us in the future, they will have no reason whatever to doubt its authenticity.

"To the law abiding citizens, regardless of race, in our midst: This Klan offers you every support to make this community a decent one in which to maintain your home and bring up your family in peace and happiness.

"We know what is going on in our midst. It is difficult, if not almost impossible for the evil doer to hide his actions from 300 picked men who resolve that all laws of our land, and those of nature, be vindicated and not broken. Without regard to honor or integrity, and with no respect for the virtue and chastity of our womanhood, the bootlegger, gambler, thief, high-jacker, whoremonger, and profane swearer in the public places, have run wild and loose long enough. We say here and now, get you a job or move on, be a man or be minus. Heretofore you have known where to stop in order to evade the law but now BEWARE. We will not overlook proper investigations of night auto rides and clandestine meetings between men and women and certain pandering.
"-Snyder Chapter Ku Klux Klan"[5]

■■

In the early summer of 1921, only seventeen years after its construction, Snyder Public School was being pulled down. It is unlikely that any non-white child ever saw the building's interior.

The southwestern corner of modern day 26th Street and Avenue M had been the educational heart of Snyder since a simple wood frame schoolhouse was constructed there in 1882. The little town's population quadrupled over the following two decades and in 1900 the Snyder Independent School District was formed.

In 1904 a two-story brick building on the same site became the first to bear the name of Snyder Public School. The city had already outgrown the facility by the time of its completion. A concrete annex known as *"the chicken coop"* was quickly slapped together to handle the overflow of children. By early 1921, Snyder was in need of a more capable space to educate its youth. In the meantime, the 1921-'22 and '22-'23 school years would be taught in the city's churches.[6]

■■

At the time of this writing, there are three known sets of Snyder's newspapers on microfilm. None of these sets contain any issues from 1922 or 1923. All information about Scurry County during this period comes from later or outside sources.

■■

John Baker looked good in a suit. The twenty-five-year-old deacon always had a sharp appearance on Sundays as he welcomed the members of Mount Olive Baptist Church into their makeshift sanctuary.

Nobody wore a suit to the cottonseed oil mill. On weekdays the mill yard was filled with the constant racket of machinery, the shrieks and hisses of freight trains, and the sounds of playful children darting between the wooden seed carts and along the mesquite-shrouded banks of Deep Creek. Early on a February morning in 1922, John Baker tucked his freezing hands into the pockets of his Sunday suit and walked into town.

Mr. Baker's quickest route to the square on foot was to follow the railroad tracks. Luckily for his clothes, the wet winter of 1921-'22 still held down the dust along the unpaved streets of downtown Snyder.

After 8 years as a recruiter for their cottonseed oil business, the Fuller family rewarded John by bringing him into the team at Snyder National Bank. With his days of commuting between Waskom and Snyder now behind him, the charismatic Mr. Baker would serve as the bank's custodian for the next fifty-four years.[7,8,9]

■■

exas, 1923, Article 309a stated that *"in no event shall a Negro be eligible to participate in a Democratic Party primary election held in the State of Texas."* By 1923 two decades of poll taxes had severely limited Republican Party activity in Texas. The Democratic primaries had become the only way to choose representatives for the House, Senate, and most state-level offices.

This new law barred all Black Texans from any meaningful participation in state level politics. Although white-only primaries would eventually be declared unconstitutional, legislation enacted between 1923 and 1944 would ensure the dominance of a white, conservative Texas Democratic Party majority until the 1970s.[10]

J.J. Moore No. 1, the first producing oil well in Scurry County, was drilled in February of 1923 near what is now the intersection of Highway 350 and Farm-to-Market Road 1606 in Ira, Texas. Although production was modest and low oil prices in the 1920s discouraged further exploration, petroleum would eventually replace cotton as the county's most important industry.[11]

The newly completed Snyder Public School (later Snyder High School/Travis Jr. High) held classes for the first time in September of 1923. A new football field was built on Snyder's southern border, encompassed by modern day Avenues L and M between 30th and 32nd Streets. More than one thousand white students reported to the new school on the first day.[6]

Great War veteran Roy Jennings moved to Scurry County in 1924 and became the first African-American to own property there. Mr. Jennings purchased the old Charlie Reichart cotton gin block near the Fuller Cottonseed Oil Mill and built his home on the site. Roy briefly worked at J. G. Lockhart's barber shop in Snyder before being hired as a custodian for the First State Bank & Trust Company. He bought and sold livestock as a side business. Less than five years after his arrival, Mr. Jennings opened Snyder's first

Black-owned business: The Blue Jacket Shoe Shine Bar on the east side of the courthouse square.[12]

■■

By the beginning of 1924 The Snyder Signal had become The Scurry County Times-Signal. The name change and partial new ownership had done little to shield the paper from intimidation by the Snyder Klan. One such threat appeared on the front page on April 17th. Written in the intentionally vague language common to the Klan, the title was simply *"Resolution"*.

"Be it resolved by Scurry County Klan No. 180, in Klonklave assembled, that all concerned may understand and know that this Klan does not look with approval upon the violation of any proper contract between men; and further, that with reference to the establishment and publishing of a paper in Scurry County, which should be in contravention of right and justice and proper contract between the Editor of the Scurry County Times and any other party, this Klan goes on record as opposed to it.

"Be it further resolved that a copy of this resolution be delivered to the Editor of the Scurry County Times, and that a copy be recorded with the record of the Klan.

"Done in Klonklave assembled this April 14th, 1924.

ATTENTION KLANSMEN!

Special meeting of the Scurry County Klan No. 180 called for Monday night, March 17th, at 7:30 o'clock.

All Klansmen urged to be present.

The Scurry County Times-Signal. March 13, 1924.[21]

Attest: Kligrapp. Signed: Cyclops."[13]

1923 had been the high water mark of the K.K.K. in Texas. October 23rd was declared Ku Klux Klan Day at the State Fair in Dallas. The event drew an army of robed Klansmen and more than 5,000 new members joined the organization. Meanwhile the Dallas Klan was building an infamous reputation for dealing out vigilante "justice" with wet ropes, boiling tar, and jars of acid in secluded areas along the Trinity River.

The efforts of the Invisible Empire elected numerous judges, sheriffs, legislators, and district attorneys across the state. The 1924 election cycle would see their biggest push for influence to date. The greatest impediment to the Klan's political rise was press coverage of racial violence committed by its members.[14]

Dallas-area dentist Hiram Wesley Evans was elected Imperial Wizard (national executive) at the Klan's first national convention in November of 1922. Evans set out to reform the organization's image by placing stricter controls on local chapters. By early 1924, regalia was only to be worn at official Klan-sponsored events and a heavy focus was placed on getting members elected to important political offices.[15]

■■

The Grand Dragon of the Realm of Texas dispatched his Kleagle from Ft. Worth to Snyder on May 13, 1924. Mr. S.W. Arms was a gifted speaker and one of the highest ranking Klansmen known to have visited Scurry County.

A lonely thunderhead in the west cast its welcome shade on Snyder's City Auditorium where a large crowd had gathered for the speech. Legions of insects darted in and out of the electric spotlight beams above the crowd as the Kleagle approached the podium. There to greet him with warm handshakes were the Exalted Cyclops of Scurry County and Mrs. Moore of the Lubbock Lady Klan.[16]

"Mr. Arms' first part of the lecture", wrote a reporter for the Scurry County Times-Signal *"was along the lines of good citizenship, national affairs, and a favorable commendation of Protestantism as against Catholicism. His remarks were intensely interesting and were such that all classes could heartily endorse,*

Klan and anti-Klan alike. He spoke of the recent enacted immigration restriction laws and stated that the Klan was behind this restriction of immigration from the old world. [...] He stated that hundreds of thousands of the ignorant and criminal classes of citizens from the old world were fixing to dump themselves upon American soil. This law with restriction and exclusion of some nationals would preserve America for Americans.

"The Times-Signal will not undertake to give the lecture a thorough covering at this time, but will say that Mr Arms is a forcible speaker, and brings a message of momentary importance. [...] He stated that the first prerequisite to Klan membership was a belief in the tenants of the Christian religion, and if a man believed in evolution he had no place in the Klan, as that organization did not initiate or fellowship monkeys."

As the applause subsided from the Kleagle's joke, a torrent of rain suddenly fell upon the crowd. The boot-churned earth of the auditorium turned into a thick mud as the spectators hurried back to their cars. Wet, hooded men in white robes scrambled to unplug the spotlights.

"The lecture had only proceeded for something like a half or three-quarters of an hour," noted the Times-Signal, *"when the cloud dispersed them.*

"The writer was present and was disappointed in not hearing the gentleman through his lecture, but left with the rest of those who ran from the cloud.

"Mrs. Moore, of Lubbock, representing the Lady Klan, was present and was to address the ladies after the main lecture on Klanism. The rain interfered with her program."[17]

Mrs. Moore would eventually get her chance to speak more than two months later on July 17th during the Klan's big chicken fry. The Times-Signal was pleased to run ads for the event, but never reported on the substance of Mrs. Moore's speech.[18]

■■

Miriam Amanda "Ma" Ferguson was an openly anti-prohibition and anti-Klan candidate. In July of 1924, she trailed behind her tea-totaling, Klan-supported opponent Felix D. Robertson but managed to stay in the runoffs. Ferguson's advancement to the second round of the Democratic primaries set off alarm bells among the leadership of the Texas Klan.

Her campaign came with plenty of baggage. Miriam's husband, James Edward Ferguson, was the first Governor of Texas to be impeached. The charges were misappropriation of public funds and failure to enforce the state's banking laws. If "Ma" was going to win the governorship for herself, she would need to keep the conversation focused on solutions to Klan violence and stirring public resentment of strict federal alcohol laws.

The prospect of a Texas government under the Fergusons would have been a nightmare for the Klan. Their national office in Atlanta recognized this fact immediately. The Klan's Department of Education began buying up space in newspapers across Texas to promote favorable opinions of Klansmen and help the chances of Fritz Robertson in the August runoffs.[19]

One such article appeared in the Scurry County Times-Signal on July 17, 1924. The headline was *"The Attitude Of The Ku Klux Klan Toward The Negro."*

PUBLIC LECTURE!

Will be delivered at the City Auditorium next Monday night.

September 29, at 8 o'Clock

This lecture will be delivered by Mrs. Cora Megrail, a speaker of national reputation. Mrs. Megrail was one of the leading speakers for national prohibition and is now one of the national Lecturers for the Knights of the Ku Klux Klan. Mrs. Megrail's message Monday night will be on the

Objects and Principles of the

Knights of the Ku Klux Klan

Everyone is invited to hear this wonderful message. It is Free to everyone.

COME EARLY AND GET A GOOD SEAT

AT THE

City Auditorium

SNYDER, TEXAS

The Scurry County Times-Signal. September 25, 1924.[23]

"The Knights of the Ku Klux Klan is not anti-Negro; neither does it foster racial hatred. We do not intend to harm the Negro in any way whatever; but will protect and defend his rights just as freely as we will our own. We have no fight to make on his race or any race; but will aid him in every possible way to enjoy his rights as a citizen, and improve his condition physically, mentally, morally, and spiritually - even to the keeping of his racial blood pure. The Klan is by far the Negro's best friend, if he will stay in his place.

"As a citizen of the United States the Negro has certain inalienable rights which are guaranteed to him by the Constitution, and should not be denied to him under any circumstances. [...]

"[H]e has a right to the society of his own people, and should be encouraged in his social relations. There should be no social relations between the negro and the white, and the honest, sensible negro does not desire such relation. [...]

"[H]e has a right to have his own secret orders and exclude all other races and colors. He has a perfect right to name "Black" as a condition of membership in his organizations. No one ever accused him of fostering racial prejudice or stirring up racial hatred, although he has barred whites from his orders from their beginning. It was only when the white man began to exercise the same right that had been conceded to the negro that the fanatical Jew and Catholic set up the howl of 'racial hatred' and 'religious prejudice.'

"Be not deceived and misled by the enemy's propaganda, the Klan is not anti-negro; but is the good negro's best friend, and the avowed enemy of all law violators whether white or black.

"All these rights and privileges that we have granted to the negro, belong also to the white man; the right we have granted to the Jew, belong also to the Gentile; the rights we have granted to the Catholic, belong also to the protestant. We cannot see how any fair-minded, honest man can deny this position. This is the Klan's unalterable position, both on races and religions. In all fairness, we cannot understand why any sane man should object to, or find fault with such a policy.[...]

"We do not seek to exterminate, deport, or enslave the negro; but to protect him in his rights, give him a square deal, and improve the condition of his race. The law-abiding negro need have no fear of the Klan; but woe be unto the criminal, white or black. We have sworn to get him into the clutches of the law if we can.

"Many negroes have been saved from lynching during the last two years by reason of the Klan's protection, and guarantee of a fair trial by jury. Lynchings in 1923 were 50 per cent less than they were in 1922. Magazine articles and the associated press have extolled this fact; but none of them have given the real reason for this reduction of mob violence. The cause is simply this: Previous to 1922 the Klan was confined to small sections of the country. By the beginning of 1923 more than 2,000,000 men had sworn to uphold and enforce the law through constituted authorities. During 1923 more than 2,500,000 more did the same thing. [...] This tremendous army of men scattered throughout America was the force and direct cause of the decrease in lynchings.

"At this writing, April 22, 1924, we have just read of the second lynching for the present year. At that rate they will be reduced about 75 per cent this year, under the record of 1923. The subsidized press will never give the Klan credit for the reduction; but the Klan is doing it just the same. Every honest negro in America ought to stand by the Klan, and we firmly believe they would if they were properly informed and free of the lying propaganda that has been dished out to the public by our enemies.

"This is the Klan's attitude toward the negro, and we submit that it is fair, honorable, just, and equitable; the lying propaganda of Jews, Catholics, and negro-social-equality advocates to the contrary notwithstanding. Keep the racial blood pure, defend each other's rights, protect each other's interests, and deal honorably with each other is the doctrine of the Klan in regard to races. Certainly no fair-minded man can object to such a policy."[20]

But most fair-minded men in Texas were aware of the Klan's terrible reputation for violence by the spring of 1924. Anti-Klan voters united behind "Ma" Ferguson in the August gubernatorial runoffs and she became the Democratic Party candidate. The Klan's last chance was to pull off a seemingly impossible feat: convincing a significant portion of white conservatives in Texas to vote for a Republican. That Republican was former University of Texas Law School dean George Charles Butte.

When "Ma" Ferguson won the general election in November of 1924, the free fried chicken and long columns in the newspaper came to a sudden end. In January of 1925, shortly after being sworn in, Governor Ferguson passed an anti-mask law that prevented the Klan from operating anonymously in public.

As the first few months of 1925 dragged on, Klan meeting announcements in the Times-Signal became infrequent. The last mention of the organization in the local paper came on April 16th. By the summer of 1925, Scurry County Ku Klux Klan #180 was dead. Although "Ma" Ferguson's mask law would eventually be overturned, by 1927 the Invisible Empire's Realm of Texas had been reduced to a marginal influence in state politics.

The most visible and lasting legacy of the Texas Klan would be the numerous like-minded public officials they helped to elect. Some of these politicians and lawmen were already publicly distancing themselves from the organization by the late 1920s.[14,19]

The Exalted Cyclops of Scurry County was the first and last member of Texas K.K.K. #180. The local newspaper never revealed his identity.

Klansmen

JOINT MEETING

Monday Night, March 16th.

Come and bring one or more friends. Mrs. T. J. Moore of Lubbock will lecture for us.

Klanswomen

The Scurry County Times-Signal. March 12, 1925.[24]

CHAPTER 4
HEARTILY IN SYMPATHY

"A move is on foot in Snyder to segregate the negroes. The Times-Signal is heartily in sympathy with the movement. Snyder is a white man's town and let's keep it that kind. Negroes are all right, if you like 'em, but let's see to it that they are kept in their place, and one of their places is a negro district clear away from white residents."

-Scurry County Times-Signal. May 21, 1925.[1]

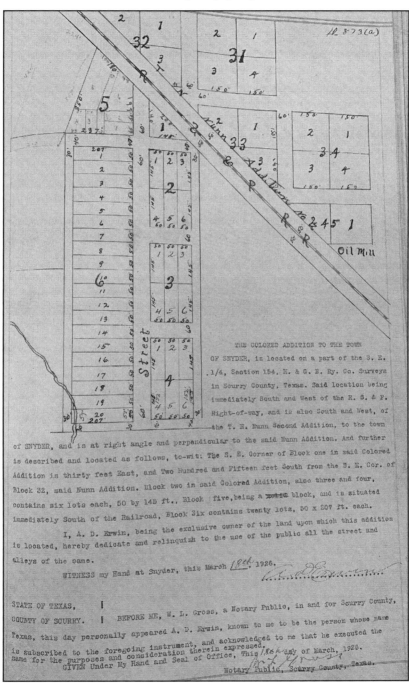

Snyder's "Colored Addition" founding document. Courtesy Scurry County Clerk.[12]

The grounds of the Scurry County Jail had never looked more beautiful. Colorful dresses and sunbonnets milled about the building as the Altrurian Club of Snyder busily replaced clumps of weeds with fresh flowers.

The club, mostly populated by the wives of Snyder's most notable business owners, had embarked on a project to beautify the city with as many visible improvements as possible. On October 10, 1924, while working on the jailhouse project, the ladies were interviewed by a local reporter. Mrs. Thrane, chairwoman of the club's civic committee, commented that *"no city can be what we would always be proud of unless we first clean up and then beautify with flowers, trees, and shrubbery. It is the wish of this committee to be able to make steps toward civic improvements and to interest wide awake men in beautifying their homes."*

At the end of the interview, one of the Altrurians asked the reporter: *"As we have the negroes among us, is it not possible that we could build or help build a school house, also combine with it a church? We should in some way take the matter up and show the negroes we are at least interested in their schooling."*[2]

■■

On January 13, 1925, one week before "Ma" Ferguson was sworn in as governor, the 39th Legislature of Texas began their regular session. They quickly amended the state penal code to declare miscegenation a felony. All interracial marriages performed in other states were instantly nullified in Texas. This was followed by a series of new statutes that mandated racial segregation in public accommodations like schools, libraries, bus stops, and train stations statewide.[3,4,5]

The RS&P Railroad's old Snyder depot was a humbler building than its Santa Fe Railroad counterpart. Originally built to handle freight instead of passengers, the ground floor of the wooden structure was a single room. A narrow staircase ascended to a small office perched on the second floor. More than a dozen glass windows flooded the little building with light, offering views of the trains that rumbled by on their way to and from the cottonseed oil mill southeast of Snyder.[6]

Depot of the Roscoe, Snyder, & Pacific Railway, early 1920s.
Courtesy Roscoe Historical Museum.[6]

Sometime in the first half of 1925 the RS&P decided to construct a larger facility that would comply with state passenger segregation laws. The new depot would be built on the same site as the old one: the south side of modern day 26th Street, east of Avenue Q. R.O. Dobbins, manager of the RS&P, told the Scurry County Times-Signal that the new building *"will be built of brick and tile and will be 80 x 200 feet. It will contain passenger and ticket office, two waiting rooms, one for whites and one for negroes, baggage room, freight office, and a large concrete shipping platform. Work on the new building will begin about January 1 [1926]."[7]*

Once complete, the new station would be the first building in Scurry County designed from the start to accommodate racial segregation. The old wooden depot was moved southeast along the tracks and placed just beyond the city limits near the oil mill.

One morning in the early autumn of 1925, the old depot began its first day as the Dunbar School of Snyder. The school was named in honor of late-nineteenth century African-American poet Paul Laurence Dunbar. The name was chosen by Mr. Jesse Carruthers, the first person hired to teach at the new school.

A small sum was set aside in the county budget for the education of African-American children. Most of the money went toward paying the salary of Mr. Carruthers. On the first day of classes at the new school, Mr. Carruthers was teaching twenty-five students in grades one through seven. High school-level classes were taught exclusively to white students in Scurry County, a policy that would continue for the next thirty-two years.[8]

The Scurry County Times-Signal. April 2 - 23, 1925.[25-28]

The first day of formal education for African-Americans in Snyder's history went unreported in the Scurry County Times-Signal. The editor finally noticed at the end of the winter break in January, 1926, noting that *"There has been a negro school started in Snyder down near the oil mill. Now the negroes will have a chance to learn a little something if they will just take it. Apparently the school is progressing very nicely."*[9]

The building had no water and no electricity. Materials used to educate the children at Dunbar were mostly donated secondhand from Snyder Public School. There was seldom enough paper or chalk, and geography lessons were accompanied by outdated maps. All twenty-five students shared a single pit toilet with the workers at the nearby oil mill.[10]

■■

Hill Street, known in later years as Avenue M, ran in a straight line south from Snyder Public School until it met the RS&P Railroad line near modern-day 33rd Street. In the early spring of 1926, Hill Street began to creep southeast along the tracks. After a few dozen yards, the road workers crossed the railroad line and resumed their march southward toward the Dunbar School.

The plan to create a segregated colony for Scurry County's growing Black population began to take shape in early 1926. *"For some time the ministers of Snyder and some of our enterprising people have felt that the negro was not receiving proper attention along religious and educational lines,"* wrote Reverend H. J. Manley in the Scurry County Times-Signal. *"We are willing enough to have their services during the special busy seasons but then they may go after the rush. This seems to be the attitude as some view the situation.*

"There is now on foot a movement by the churches of Snyder to secure a plat of ground and have it designated as 'Negro Section', where they will have their own school and church. It is our purpose to build a chapel for all denominations of the colored people with the privilege of using the same building for school purposes. We are also of the opinion that these, our neighbors, should have their rights of autonomy preserved to them in their own community life.

The Scurry County Times-Signal. April 30 - May 21, 1925.[29-32]

"Since the women seem to have sponsored and first gotten behind this idea in this worthy enterprise, they are given their rightful place on committees to work out plans for the future destiny of our beautiful Snyder. Along with the Ministers' Association, we have the following appointed to assist in this most worthy cause:"[11]

The first person to sign the announcement was Mary Towle. Mrs. Towle was a Sunday school teacher, cofounder of the Altrurian Club of Snyder, president of the Women's Society for Christian Service, secretary of the Northwest Texas Methodist Conference, and chairwoman of the Texas Federation of Women's

Groups. She was also the spouse of Snyder's Mayor H.G. Towle. Clare Dodson Smith, wife of county judge and former mayor Fritz Smith, also signed. Ten other women, each identified in the paper by their husband's names, joined in the effort.

Scurry County's first designated neighborhood for African-Americans was officially drawn out on March 18, 1926. Six weeks later, at the end of April, the committee announced the end of its work.[12]

"Some weeks ago" wrote Reverend H.J. Manley to the Times-Signal, *"the Ministerial Association of Snyder appointed a committee of twelve members from the six churches represented by said association. These twelve [...] made up a committee to assist the Colored people of Snyder in securing an addition where the negroes might have their own church and school.*

"The committee met last Monday and reported that the addition had been set apart, a lot donated for a church and school purposes. Also it was reported that a committee had been appointed among the colored people to build a Mt. Olive Baptist Church and that they have the work well in hand.

"This being true, the committee [...] proceeded to close out its work and disband."[13]

The new neighborhood would officially be called *"Colored Addition"*. In time it would become known colloquially as *"The Flat"* (pluralized as *"The Flats"* after 1950), *"Colored Town,"* and many other less flattering names.

It would be another five months before the new Mount Olive church was complete and homes could be built. The Times-Signal never elaborated on the reasons for the delay, but by August of 1926 the paper's impatience was beginning to show.

"We see where some of Texas' largest cities are making arrangements to segregate the negroes from the whites" wrote Times-Signal editor J. L. Martin. *"We thought Snyder had a movement started in that direction. Has the proposition failed utterly? Or have the people lost interest in this very important movement? Negroes are better satisfied in exclusive negro districts, and so are the better class of whites better satisfied when negroes and whites are segregated."*[14]

The Scurry County Times-Signal. June 4 - June 25, 1925.[33-35]

Mr. Martin was not alone in his sentiments. The Times-Signal noted that the *"editorial last week on segregating the negroes from the whites brought considerable favorable comment. But comment alone will never put the negroes of Snyder in a district to themselves. Who will take the initiative step in this important matter? By all means, it ought to be done."*[15]

The first church to occupy the northeast corner of modern day 34th Street and Avenue M was completed in the late autumn of 1926. On Sunday, November 6th, the congregation of Mount Olive Baptist worshiped together in their own building for the first time. Everyone was invited.

"*Special announcement extends to the white citizens of Snyder a special invitation to come and worship with us Sunday evening Nov 6 at 3 p.m. Sermon by State Missionary, Dr. Miles W. Jenkins. Come and hear the famous East Texas Conference quartet sing special selections of ancient negro folk songs. Something you will enjoy.*"[16]

The services were well attended. The following week's issue of the Times-Signal included a *"Card Of Thanks."*

"*We the members and friends of the Mt. Olive Baptist Church (Colored) wish to extend to the white citizens our appreciation for their liberal contribution paid in our financial effort and their presence in our great services Sunday afternoon.*"[17]

■■

Snyder enjoyed the blessings of mild temperatures and plentiful rainfall throughout most of 1927. The broader American economy was at the peak of its post-war boom, creating plenty of demand for Scurry County's beef and cotton products. Tire tracks had now fully conquered the muddy streets of Snyder and the residents of the city began to express their good fortune with generosity, vanity, and celebration.

Jeweler, amateur aviator, cofounder of the Snyder Volunteer Fire Department, president of the Texas State Board of Examiners in Optometry, and future Towle Park namesake Howard Garfield Towle became the mayor of Snyder in April of 1927. He would hold this office for the next twenty years. H.G. and Mary Towle had long been one of Snyder's most visible couples. The Towle family's home at modern day Avenue U and 30th Street was already a social hub for Snyder's most influential residents and prominent visitors.

That summer saw *"the finest Fourth of July that was ever attempted in Snyder."* Ten thousand people were expected. Fifteen thousand showed up and crammed themselves into Snyder's Wolf Park.

Fifty-five hundred pounds of beef were barbecued for the celebrations along with pork, mutton, chicken, and bread. The barbecue quickly ran out and impromptu hamburger stands were set up to feed the rest. The day was such a success that a city-wide Fourth of July celebration became an annual event in Snyder.

The Snyder Black Tigers were to play the Colorado City Black Tigers in a baseball game, but the opposing team cancelled on short notice. Snyder's event committee scrambled to find a replacement team. Rotan was available but they had to walk most of the way and didn't arrive until after 6pm. After only three innings Snyder was in the lead 6-3 when the game was cut short to allow the Post Junior Cowboy Band to close out the day. This was the first known sporting event in Scurry County's history to feature all-Black teams.[18]

A new high school wing was added to the southern end of Snyder Public School just in time for the 1927-'28 school year. Meanwhile, plans were being made to move the students at The Dunbar School into a more suitable building.[19]

"Snyder's colored colony," wrote the Times-Signal in March of 1928, *"is happy over the dedication ceremonies to be held Sunday afternoon at their new church home, the Mt. Olive Baptist Church, which is located one block east of the city ice plant, in the colored addition. [...]*

"White folks are invited to attend the dedication Sunday afternoon and assist the congregation in liquidating their church debt. Plans are also being made to establish a colored school here and to engage a young pastor."[20]

Dedication ceremonies were held for the Mount Olive Baptist Church building on Sunday, April 1, 1928. Reverend Jenkins of Mount Olive *"asked the Times-Signal to thank the white folks for helping in the good work here. The local committee, John Baker, Roy Jennings, and J.J. Smith, also want to add their thanks to that of Rev. Jenkins."*[21]

■■

In the autumn of 1928, after two years in the old train depot, the Dunbar School of Snyder held classes in a new single-room building for the first time. The little schoolhouse stood on the south side of modern day 34th Street, just west of Avenue M.[8,19]

The Snyder Signal's 1915 dream of a *"segregated colony"* on the outskirts of Snyder had finally become a reality. Real estate

Left: John Baker in 1925. Courtesy Scurry County Museum.
Right: Mary Baker in Snyder, circa 1920s. Courtesy Dr. Walter Morris Baker.

transfers in the new neighborhood began to be announced in the paper.

"A. D. Erwin to Mt. Olive Baptist Church, block 1, colored addition, consideration $400." "A. D. Erwin to John Baker, lots 1 and 2, block 2, colored addition, consideration $215." "A. D. Erwin to Bill Miles, lot 3, block 6, colored addition, consideration $75." "A. D. Erwin to Harry Flannagan, lot 2, block 3, colored addition, consideration $75."[22,23]

The muddy streets of the Snyder Square were covered over with red bricks in the early summer of 1929. These were the first paved roads in Scurry County. Unfortunately, no copies of Snyder's 1929 newspapers survive to the present.[24]

■■

October of 1929 brought numerous bank failures and a global market panic. At the time of this writing it remains the largest sell-off of stocks in US history. President Hoover's cabinet insisted on minimizing government involvement with the financial crisis. Increased foreign production, lack of demand, and a surplus of cotton in Texas were already driving down the value of Scurry County's crops.

The entire developed world was slipping into a Great Depression and the people of Snyder were being dragged down with it.

CHAPTER 5
1930 HOWLING

"If I could do nothing more than to judge the future of Snyder and Scurry County by the past year, I must admit that I would be a bit discouraged. But we have a new year before us- a future that promises to become gradually brighter and burst into the bloom of prosperity before another year has come. [...]

"The leading business men and financial giants of the country cannot be wrong when they predict a period of renewed prosperity for the coming year. With them, I believe the height of the depression wave has been reached and passed, and that in a few months we will be wondering what all our 1930 howling was about."

-Mayor Howard G. Towle. January 8, 1931.[1]

The Scurry County Times. April 14, 1932.[2]

A panic broke out in Hermleigh, Texas on a cold, windy afternoon in late February of 1930.

Work had begun on grading Texas State Highway 7 (now US Highway 84) from Nolan County toward Snyder. The first effects of the Great Depression were already being felt in the area and the state had hired many newly unemployed West Texans to do the work. As the tractors lumbered slowly toward the little community of Inadale, one of its sixty residents noticed that some of the workers who followed along with the machines were Black. A message was carried a few miles up the road to warn the more than five hundred residents of Hermleigh.[3]

"When our road construction began near Inadale early last week", wrote local newspaper The Hermleigh Herald, *"a petition was circulated and signed by nearly a hundred men asking for employ of our own unemployed men. Undoubtedly on the part of those circulating and signing the petition mention was made of the few negroes who were brought into the county by the contractor. Owing to prevailing race prejudice and the fact that negroes are not allowed in certain communities in Texas, fear was generated and the work on the road was closed down for two days."*

Some in Snyder expressed fear that their neighbors in Hermleigh would do something rash to intimidate the road workers. *"When the situation was made known and people who signed the petition came to see that the petition was interpreted to have a different meaning than that intended, mass meetings were held in Snyder and Hermleigh in which the misinterpreted meaning of the petition was retracted."* Although no specific threat was ever articulated, the Herald stressed that *"Mr. Shillings, road contractor, acted wisely in closing down the work for the time being."*

The peoples of Snyder and Hermleigh eventually came up with a solution. The Scurry County Times-Signal announced that *"sub-contracts have been let on two parts of the road, and many of our home men will likely find employment. [...] The work of grading is to be completed in 90 days."* While these *"home men"* spent the spring of 1930 grading the little stretch of highway that passed through the town, the state's workers would detour around and pick up their slow march toward Snyder on the other side. No

African-American laborers were allowed to set foot within the community limits of Hermleigh.[4]

By 1930 Snyder had grown to a population of 3,008. At the urging of Mayor Towle, the city's old street names were changed to a simple grid of letters and numbers. Scurry County's total African-American population at the beginning of the 1930s was 147. Almost all of them lived in The Flat.[5]

May 8th was graduation day for Dunbar's eighth grade class of 1930. *"A play and other closing features will be held at the colored school house"*, said the local paper, *"to which whites have been extended a cordial invitation. A 'Tom Thumb Wedding' will be the headliner in which the 23 pupils will take part."*[6]

This was the earliest known performance of a play by an all-Black cast in the history of Scurry County. No admission fee was charged to the Depression-stricken people of the city. Instead, donations were discreetly taken after the show.

■■

On May 9, 1930, roughly 5,000 people participated in the lynching of George Hughes for his alleged sexual assault of a white woman near Sherman, Texas. After failing to take Mr. Hughes alive, the crowd went on a rampage known in later years as the Sherman Riot. Local law enforcement declined to intervene. The Texas Rangers, lead by Captain Frank Hamer who had been involved in Scurry County's own Johnson-Sims Feud, fled from the city. The Texas National Guard stood idle until the damage was done.

Before the late spring of 1930 The Snyder Signal and Scurry County Times often framed lynching as a rare and necessary evil in places where law enforcement was scarce or nonexistent. But the Sherman Riot was so destructive and so impossible to ignore that it changed the way incidents of lynching would be covered by the press in Snyder forever.[7-9]

"At Sherman, where a negro had confessed to the most heinous crime in the books," wrote the Times-Signal, *"an infuriated mob usurped the prerogatives of the law, murdered a prisoner in custody of officers of the state, burned the court house, sacked*

and pillaged a large area in the negro quarter, and terrorized a large percentage of the negro population.

"Not one Texas editor lifted his pen in defense of the Sherman mob, and practically every editor in the state urges that leaders and members of the mob are convicted and punished."[10]

On June 5th, after almost a month of constant press coverage, one anonymous person in Snyder complained that *"many a newspaper editor, throwing a few thousand verbal stones at Texas on account of the recent riotous doings at Sherman, will overlook the rottenness in his own front yard."* George F. Smith of the Times-Signal fired back that, *"as an editor, speaking frankly, we don't care a hoot whether you agree with what we say or not, but if we are wrong, don't wait for somebody to tell you. Think it out yourself."*[11]

The Snyder News. April 11, 1930.[40]

Of the thousands who participated in the Sherman Riot only thirty-two were initially charged with crimes. The number quickly shrank to fourteen. In the end only a single person was convicted. Eighteen-year-old J.B. McCasland was sentenced to four years in prison for rioting and arson. No one was punished for the lynching of George Hughes.[12]

■■

When the State of Texas made Juneteenth an official state holiday in 1980, Scurry County's own traditions were already half a century old.

Snyder's Wolf Park was located northwest of the modern-day Scurry County Library, extending west from Avenue T along the south side of 22nd Street. The park had long been the county's primary recreation area for hosting rodeos, 4th of July celebrations, and outdoor baptisms in the cool waters of Deep Creek. It was in this place that Snyder's city-wide Juneteenth traditions began in the summer of 1930.

"More than a thousand visitors are expected at Wolf Park next Thursday when the colored folks celebrate Emancipation Day", wrote the Scurry County Times-Signal.

"The committee composed of Bill Miles, John Baker, and Bill Clay promise free fish, chicken, beef, and pork with all the trimmings and a dance at Wolf Park at night to top off the day's festivities. One of the highlights is a baseball game between Amarillo and Dallas, the winner to play Snyder for state honors. Both games come in the afternoon."

"White folks of the section have been invited to witness the ball games and enjoy the free entertainment that will be provided."

Unfortunately Dallas and Amarillo cancelled at the last minute. Only a single baseball game was played between Snyder and a team from Littlefield. A seven piece orchestra provided music for the dance at sundown.[13-16]

Meanwhile, on the opposite side of town, Hardy Hill was celebrating the 65th anniversary his people's freedom in a pasture. A hot, dry June had baked the grass around his little tent to a sickly brown-gray. After a decade of mild summers and plentiful rains, Western Texas was beginning to slip into an unusually dry period in the summer of 1930. The area would not see another year of above average rainfall until 1941.

Back in 1924, District Judge Fritz Smith of Snyder wrote to the prison at Huntsville, Texas to request that *"a negro worker"* be sent to him on parole. Twenty-four-year-old Hardy Hill was bussed to Snyder where he moved into the Smith family's servant quarters.

Originally from Pittsburg, Pennsylvania, Mr. Hill had been imprisoned at Huntsville for selling a mortgaged bale of cotton. He was described by his employers in Snyder as a *"white man's negro"* and they praised his industriousness, noting that *"when he worked, he worked."* After two years serving the Smith family, Hardy Hill received a pardon in 1926. Finally free, Hardy married a woman from Snyder and had one child with her.

Mr. Hill was diagnosed with tuberculosis in the summer of 1929. The county provided him with a tent in which he spent the last year of his life quarantined in a pasture outside of Snyder. During that time Hardy was visited only by his family, doctors from the nearby hospital, and the cattle that grazed around his new home.

Hardy Hill would finally lose his long battle with the disease on Monday, June 23, 1930. His grave in the Snyder Cemetery is unmarked at the time of this writing.[17,18]

In 1937 the Kerrville State Sanatorium would become the first medical facility in Texas to admit African-American tuberculosis patients.[19]

■■

P rior to the summer of 1930, the more affluent people of Snyder still clung to hope that the Great Depression wouldn't be so bad. After all, they had experienced difficult economic times before and always weathered the storm. But in the summer of 1930 their resources and resolve were put to the test when the Texas beef market began to collapse.

Quickly crumbling demand in the financial centers of the American northeast and the Hoover Administration's new tariffs on trans-Atlantic goods caused the price of Scurry County's cattle to suddenly plunge from twelve cents per pound to five cents.

Meanwhile, the value of cotton continued its steady decline and was now worth only one third of the 1929 price.[20]

The pain of the Depression was detectable on almost every page of Snyder's newspapers in the second half of 1930. Local grocery stores promised *"depression prices"* to anyone who still had money left to spend. A new weekly column, *"The Town Doctor, Doctor Of Towns"*, began to appear in the Times-Signal, spreading comforting folk wisdom like *"talk business up and it will pick up"* or *"business depression is largely a state of mind"*.[21,22]

The Scurry County Times. May 12, 1932.[41]

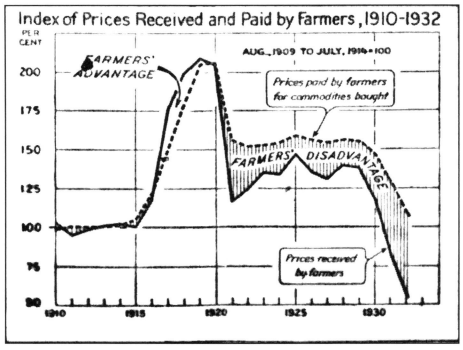

The Scurry County Times. June 29, 1933.[42]

As 1931 dawned, the city's business, religious, and civic leaders did their best to bolster the morale of a people whose quality of life was declining by the day. They appealed to *"the undying spirit of West Texas - to the kind of spirit that brought courageous men and women to West Texas and kept them here"*, while also admitting that the cries of the poor *"are many and some of them pitiful."* A.A. Bullock, president of the Snyder Chamber of Commerce, suggested that everyone's 1930 experiences *"should be forgotten as speedily as possible."*[1]

As the winter of 1930-'31 dragged on, the effects of the Depression continued to deepen. The Altrurian Club of Snyder bought several railway freight cars and converted them into warming stations called *"Hobo Boxes"* to shelter the county's many newly evicted families. The Snyder Parent-Teacher Association organized thrift lectures to educate the public on austerity and sustainability. School taxes were divided into three installments instead of one to give people more time to pay.

Lawns throughout the city transformed into vegetable gardens. Donations were taken to convert the basement level of the Scurry County Courthouse into *"hot room"* serving daily breakfast and supper to Snyder's most vulnerable. By March of 1931, the American Red Cross was feeding more than 300 families in greater Scurry County.[23-26]

In the spring of 1931, as news of bank failures across the nation began to appear in the Times-Signal, the shadow of an airplane raced across the brown expanse of the Texas plains toward Snyder. Seated behind the roaring propeller was M.A. Fuller, owner of the Fuller Cottonseed Oil Mill and president of Snyder National Bank. The rest of the plane's interior was loaded with bags of cash. Or maybe it wasn't. What mattered was that people believed that it was.

John Baker was dressed in his customary suit in the quiet foyer of Snyder National Bank when his employer of eight years slipped through the door. Mr. Fuller had sent a telegram before him to Snyder announcing the arrival of the cash and inviting anyone to withdraw their accounts if they must. In a few minutes the bank would open and the two men would know if the stunt had convinced the people of Snyder that their accounts were secure. Mr. Baker would tell the story of this day to his family for many years.

"Do you have a cigar, John?," inquired Mr. Fuller with his eyes fixed on the clock. *"Cigars make us look like we have everything under control."* John Baker produced a pair of cigars from his pristine suit coat and lit a match for Mr. Fuller. Tendrils of smoke coiled and drifted among the tall columns of the bank foyer as the two men counted down the minutes. *"I won't forget this, John."*

More than seven hundred financial institutions failed across the USA in the first ten months of 1931. Another nine thousand, nearly half of all the banks in the country, would fail before the end of the decade. Thanks in part to Mr. Fuller's stunt, Snyder would endure the Great Depression without a run on its banks.

Mr. Fuller kept his word. *"After that we were blue chip negroes"*, Mr. Baker would recount to his family. By the end of the decade, the Baker home at 1204 34th Street was the most comfortable house in The Flat. For the rest of their lives John and Mary Baker drove nice cars, kept their closets full of fashionable clothes, and gave generously to the collection plate at Mount Olive Baptist Church.[27,28]

The people of Snyder endured the deprivations of the Great Depression for eighteen agonizing months before receiving any kind of assistance from the federal government. In May of 1931 the Hoover Administration's drought relief program finally loaned Scurry County a total of $123,000. Out of the roughly 1,500 farming families in the county, 730 immediately signed up for federal aid. The rest of the money would be used to dramatically expand cotton and feed acreage. If everything went according to plan, Scurry County would produce the largest crop yield in its history in 1932.[29,30]

■■

Dock Wells burst out of the murky water at the 9-R Ranch about twenty miles northwest of Snyder, coughing and gasping for air. He jumped out of the stock tank. Water gushed from his overalls and squirted from his shoes as the ranch hand struggled to catch his breath. Dock's son, two-year-old Collis Wells, was missing. The two dogs that always accompanied the boy had returned without him hours ago.

Ella D. Wells, mother of young Collis and head cook at 9-R, was walking in circles around the main house, shouting the boy's name name into the wind. Her panicked voice was beginning to fail. Meanwhile Dock went from one stock tank to the next, groping blindly with his hands and feet in the lukewarm water for any sign of his son. The desperate search continued all night. At dawn, messengers rushed to the nearby towns to plead for help.

"Two days and nights of continuous searching by posses of white and colored men," wrote the Scurry County Times-Signal, *"have resulted only in the finding of tracks, believed to be the child's, seven miles southwest of the 9-R ranch houses. The tracks, which were found Wednesday afternoon about 4:00 o'clock, indicated that the child was still wandering in the opposite direction from his home. Other tracks nearer the house, some on the edge of a water tank, had been found earlier.*

"Hundreds of men from Snyder and other parts of Scurry County and adjoining counties have joined in the search, the posse numbering more than 100 at times, with most of the searchers alternating. A plane from Big Spring, piloted by Don Teel, circled the ranch country practically all of Wednesday afternoon without finding a trace of the missing child. A number of men on horseback have been involved in the posses. [...]"

"Snyder has been half deserted since Thursday morning," wrote the Times-Signal, "when practically every available man from here joined the posse which had grown to more than 50 men."

On July 30, 1931 the Times-Signal reported the grim news that "the lost child's body was found this morning at 11:00 o'clock, 16 miles northwest of the 9-R ranch houses. Death had apparently come about three hours earlier from exhaustion, hunger, and exposure. The body was brought to Snyder shortly after noon and is being prepared at the Odom Funeral Home."[31]

A followup article in the next issue praised the white residents of Snyder for their generosity and quick action. "Dock Wells, the father, and Ella D., the mother, declare that they had always known the white man to be the colored man's friend, but that the search for little Carlos [sic], brought the lesson home stronger than ever.

"Nathan Reynolds, owner of the Nine-R Ranch, on which the child was lost, says Dock and his wife are faithful workers, and ranch hands throughout the Nine-R country will tell you that Carlos [sic], the only negro child in the whole section, was one of those playful little fellows that everybody liked."

"The other Wells child, a little girl of seven years, was visiting at Waskom, Texas whence the family moved a few years ago. The body of Carlos [sic] was returned there for burial.[32]

Seventy miles away in Tahoka, Texas, the Lynn County News reported that "a fine demonstration of human kindness and sympathy was given at Snyder a couple of weeks ago when hundreds of men and boys spent the major part of two days and nights searching for a negro child two-and-a-half years old who had wandered away from home and become lost. [...]"

"It was a sad incident and the entire population of the town and county genuinely sympathized with the parents, though they were negroes. Southern white people are hard on the negro criminal and they are bitterly opposed to any suggestion of social equality among the races, but they never fail to hear the cry for help from an innocent child though his hair is kinky and his skin as black as night."[33]

■■

By the fall of 1931 the Great Depression had been grinding on for two painful years. The symptoms of the collapsed economy in Snyder had become impossible for even its most affluent residents to ignore. The local paper still insisted that the economy would quickly recover if only the readers would overcome their fears, dig their remaining money from under the mattress, and buy something. Anything. Right now.

"If we could read a history of the great depression of 1931, as written in 1950, we would probably want to hide our heads in shame," wrote one anonymous resident in early September. *"Don't you suppose a paragraph from that history would read something like this: 'Never before had this modern world been touched with a wave of pessimism quite so general, or half so ominous. With plenty on every hand, people of all nations became panicky with a fear of tomorrow. After the debris of doubt and uncertainty was removed, and the economic glories of 1933 and the succeeding years were unravelled, leaders recognized that 50 percent of the depression was a state of mind, a hallucination. Now, 19 years later, the people as a whole see that they groaned beneath puny loads, and cried over milk that was never spilled.'"*[34]

Meanwhile the Snyder school board was scrambling to accommodate a $6,000 slash in funding. Superintendent Wedgeworth *"voluntarily asked for a reduction of $600 in his own salary. In addition to the reduction in his salary, it is understood that he expects to take certain teaching assignments, which practice has not been followed heretofore."* The total budget for the segregated Dunbar School, already scraping by on $200 per year, would remain unchanged.[35]

In the bitter December of 1931 the Scurry County Times-Signal asked local children to mail in letters to Santa Claus for publication. At least one of the students at Dunbar responded. Her original spelling is preserved:

"Snyder, December 7, 1931

"Dear Santa Claus:

How are you today? I hope you are well. I am a little girl at the age of 8 years old. Will you please bring me somethank for Xmas? I will be please at anythang you give me if it is just some fruit but will you please sir send me somethang I will thing you so much the teacher say I am next to the best one in our Sunday School Class. So by by. We are having a program at the colored church Christmas Eve night. The think I wont most is a pair of shoes for school. I wear No. 2 1/2.

"-Dorothy Mae Williams."[36]

■■

On a calm, cool morning in early April of 1932 a pair of shovels stabbed at the dry soil along Avenue M. One of the shovels belonged to Snyder shoe shine parlor entrepreneur Roy Jennings whose cattle trading side business had been ruined by the Depression. The other was wielded by a young man named Jeff Davis.

The little trench in the shadow of Mount Olive Church was filled with seasoned cuts of meat over smoldering mesquite coals, covered with a lid, and left to cook through the night until the entire Flat was saturated with the irresistible smell of beef brisket. Jennings and Davis announced the beginning of their new business venture in the local paper.

"Old Time pit-cooked barbecue", announced the Scurry County Times, *"35¢ pound, lower than ever; cooked daily: barbecue your chickens 25¢ each. We deliver. -Jennings and Davis, colored addition."*[37]

Business was good from the beginning. Throughout the Depression years Roy Jennings would procure the meat and make deliveries while Jeff Davis built a reputation as a gifted pit master. Barbecue would become an important ambassador between the two parallel societies of Snyder. Within a few years, white families who had never visited before would be racing to The Flat after church to try the best brisket in the county.

But luxuries like beef brisket were already beyond the means of many people in Scurry County in 1932. Most of the businesses that managed to last this long could barely afford to stay open. The cotton harvest, despite being almost three times larger than the previous year, was practically worthless due to overproduction throughout the Great Plains.

The Scurry County Times. December 29, 1932.[43]

The local government in Snyder was grinding to a halt. Total expenditures for the county general fund in 1930 had been $41,385. In 1931 it was reduced to $23,082. By 1932 Scurry County was barely scraping by on $15,456.[38]

Salaries were reduced again and again. City services were scaled back in every category. The position of Snyder's City Manager was completely eliminated. One of the few public services that remained unchanged was the $200 allocated for the Dunbar School. With only one room, one teacher, and one chalkboard, there was simply nothing to cut.

When the people of Scurry County voted in November of 1932, 93.8% of them spent their poll tax dollars to elect Franklin Roosevelt. At the time of this writing it remains the greatest political consensus in the county's history.[39]

CHAPTER 6
TWO GAUNT HORSEMEN

"The last week of June the two gaunt horsemen of the plains, drought and insects, began to ride the prairies in a range covering two thirds of the nation.

"By July 25 the two gaunt horsemen had parched and ravished a vast area of America from the Panhandle and Rockies to the Atlantic Seaboard, leaving 4,500 people dead from heat and heart failure and marking up a damage total of $750,000,000."

-The Scurry County Times. July 30, 1936.[1]

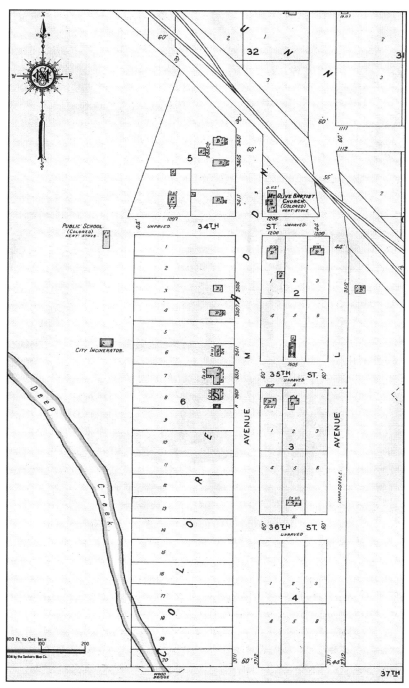

"The Flat." Southeastern outskirts of Snyder, Texas. January, 1936.[2]

In the fall of 1932 the Great Depression was approaching its fourth year. The cotton growing season had been the most productive in Scurry County's history by a significant margin. There was no shortage of work to be done but demand remained stubbornly low. An opinion piece in the Scurry County Times with the title *"Thanksgiving- And Depression"* captured the general spirit of the time.

"Scurry County has an ideal cotton picking season for which to be thankful. We worried and fretted about too much rain early in the fall, and threw up our hands in childish horror when the picking season was delayed a month. Will we pause Thursday to give thanks for for the bountiful crop that has come forth in spite of these discouraging prospects?

"The cotton price has dropped to a ridiculously low level, but five or six cent cotton with a 45,000-bale crop is much better than five or six cent cotton with an 18,000 bale crop. Are we thankful that we have the largest crop in history while most of the cotton belt has suffered reverses of various sorts? [...]

"Our debts have piled up to almost unbearable proportions, and our taxes have dealt us misery from January through December. In the meantime, nation has gone deeper in debt to nation, and taxes in many foreign countries are double our own.

"The depression has prevented our schools from expanding as we would like for them to expand. It has kept our places of worship less modern than we might have wished. [...] A very small percentage of the folks you see on the streets are poorly clad. Do you suppose 20 per cent of them will pause between bites on Thanksgiving Day to give thanks for their well-clothed bodies?"[3]

As the general economy of Scurry County wilted, illicit alcohol sales soared. This was particularly true in The Flat, where the white people of Snyder could discreetly purchase a bottle of beer with their barbecue beyond the watchful eyes of the Snyder Police Department. The sheriff was almost certainly aware of all this as arrests tended to only happen after dark.

A new national debate over prohibition was raging and momentum was building in favor of repeal. *"The trouble with the extreme prohibitionist"*, wrote Scurry County Democratic Party Chairman F.I. Townsend, *"is that he cannot view the liquor* question as it really confronts us. [...] He fails to realize that a law that is not vigorously supported and upheld in public sentiment is worse than no law. Take, for instance, the fourteenth and fifteenth amendments to the constitution of the United States giving the negro the right of citizenship and giving him the privileges and status of white people: How has that worked?

"In the South the negro is practically disenfranchised - they are not allowed to marry whites or attend the same schools as the whites or ride in the same cars with whites. And why not? Because public sentiment is against it and the people of Texas and other southern states found ways and means to circumvent and override the constitution of the United States.

"There is a fundamental error involved in national prohibition. It was never intended that the federal government should take over the police powers of the states, and the sooner we recognize that fact and get back on the track laid out for us by our forefathers the better it will be for us."[4]

In June of 1933, five months after Franklin Roosevelt was sworn in as president, the people of Snyder began to see the changes that they had voted for. The local newspaper announced the arrival of *"far-reaching events for Scurry County."*

"Headlines are blaring about the New Deal, and most of us have come to realize that unparalleled economic recovery is breaking the shackles from a distraught people.

"Now come two events of such stupendous proportions that one needs a fertile imagination to grasp their possibilities.

"The cotton curbing plan is without doubt the most remarkable experiment, in many respects, that has been undertaken by Roosevelt. What effect will it have on Scurry County if the drought claims a major portion of our crop? And what effect will it have if we have another bumper crop? In either case, the Scurry County farmer, and all who depend on him directly or indirectly, will benefit.

"Consider the public works plan. It is possible that Scurry County will receive a sum that reaches into the hundreds of thousands of dollars. [...] Can you imagine several hundred working on a hospital, an auditorium, a giant irrigation project, a park plan, a gymnasium, a school improvement project? Can you *imagine them joining the army of the employed rather than shifting from hand to mouth, often without the law's boundaries? Can you imagine the the farmer's child, the laborer's child the merchant's child, enjoying the privileges of which they have been deprived these three or four years of doubt and perplexity? [...]*

YES, MR. PRESIDENT

We're glad to tell you that we're joining in with all Snyder and Hermleigh in the chorus:

"We'll Do Our Part"

In conformity with the National Industrial Recovery Act, formulated to create employment, increase our purchasing power, to restore business generally, and to conform with the forty-eight hour week plan for employees, the undersigned grocery stores and meat markets of Snyder and Hermleigh have agreed to the following opening and closing hours . . . effective, Tuesday, August 1st, and continuing until a permanent code becomes effective in our business:

WEEK DAYS:
Open at 8:00 a. m.–Close at 6:00 p. m.
SATURDAYS:
Open at 8:00 a. m.–Cloee at 9:00 p. m.

The undersigned stores will open and close promptly at the hours indicated above. Those inside a store at closing time will be waited on, but no one will be admitted for purchase of any item after the doors are closed. Telephone orders will not be received before or after the hours indicated, but any orders received prior to the closing hour will be delivered the same day.

WE EARNESTLY REQUEST OUR PATRONS TO CO-OPERATE WITH US BY DOING THEIR SHOPPING AS EARLY AS POSSIBLE!

J. S. BRADBURY GROCERY	PARKS MEAT MARKET	W. W. EARLY, Hermleigh
BROWN & SON GROCERY	PICK & PAY GROCERY	
COCHRAN BROTHERS	PIGGLY-WIGGLY No. 1	FARGASON BROTHERS, Hermleigh
CROWDER MEAT MARKET	PIGGLY-WIGGLY No. 2	HERMLEIGH GRAIN CO., Hermleigh
CITY MEAT MARKET	HENRY SHULER GROCERY	
FARMERS EXCHANGE	HUGH TAYLOR & CO.	PAY & TAKE IT, Hermleigh
N. M. HARPOLE GROCERY	J. J. TAYLOR GROCERY	
HANDE-DANDE GROCERY		VAUGHN GROCERY, Hermleigh

The Scurry County Times. August 3, 1933.[41]

"*Heaven deliver us from a siege of inter-community friction that might put a heavy damper on the entire program that looks toward recovery of full pocketbooks and open souls.*"[5]

The summer of 1933 brought many sudden changes to civic and economic life in Scurry County. The Roosevelt administration paid local farmers a total of $275,000 to reduce cotton output by planting native grasses in their fields. More than 130 businesses in Snyder, including The Scurry County Times itself, flew the blue eagle of the National Recovery Administration in their windows.

The New Deal dominated the headlines of the Snyder paper throughout 1933 and 1934. But ominous coverage of events overseas began to creep into the conversation.[6,7]

The Times observed that "*recent events in Europe are effecting us quite perceptibly. As The Texas Weekly points out, Hitlerism's rapid rise meant new uniforms and new flags by the hundreds of thousands. Since Germany is one of our leading cotton buyers, this new demand for our staple crop undoubtedly helped the market to continue its climb upward.*

"*Strange as it may seem, it is no doubt true that new uniforms for soldiers of the swastika meant new dresses for the wives of Scurry County cotton farmers.*"[8]

■■

On Monday, June 4, 1934 Snyder National Bank remained closed in observance of the 126th birthday of Confederate President Jefferson Davis. Ironically, bank custodian John Baker was free all day.[9]

Mr. Baker's steady job at the bank had insulated him from the worst privations of the early 1930s, but the Great Depression was always just outside the door. The Flat was always among the first communities to suffer in the bad times and the last to recover in the good. These particularly bad times had put Mr. Baker in the unusual situation of being more affluent than some of his white neighbors. While they were tightening their belts during the hungry winter of 1932-'33, John Baker could have ordered his lunch from the back door of any restaurant in town.

The Flat was already showing evidence of recovery in 1934. A series of choir concerts led by Mrs. S.L.F. Wilson, teacher at the Dunbar School, raised enough money to purchase a piano for the students. Boxing promoters The Townsend Brothers staged the first all-Black public boxing match in Snyder's history in March but poor attendance discouraged future bouts.[10-15]

President Roosevelt's National Recovery Administration had stabilized the local economy in Snyder for now, but the weather threatened to bring it all crashing back down. Five consecutive years of drought and overproduction had made life more difficult for local farmers than ever before.

The thermometer at the Scurry County Times office on the square reached 114.5 degrees on the afternoon of June 21, 1934. It was the hottest day in county history since records began in the 1880s. The following day saw 111 degrees. The month of June brought only 0.4 inches of rain.[16,17]

Federal drought relief poured into Scurry County throughout the summer of 1934. Thousands of cows were bought up and destroyed by the government. Farm acreage was further slashed throughout the county. The federal government began to hire Snyder's unemployed men to pave dozens of city streets and alleys in the blistering summer heat.[18,19]

In July, Dr. Lawrence Nixon of El Paso brought a lawsuit against the Texas Democratic Party for its racially discriminatory voting rules. Texas Attorney General and future Governor James Allred responded by issuing an opinion that endorsed the legality of white-only primary voting.[20]

"What about the negroes?", asked a dissenting voice in the Scurry County Times. *"The state's Democratic chieftains showed a decided lack of conviction and justice when they left the negro voting question in the air, so to speak. They just followed the old American custom of passing the buck on to county and precinct officials, who are left to largely determine the negro's status in Saturday's election. The party is only too glad to let the negro pay poll taxes and other taxes, but it is too narrow to let him vote his convictions in the manner of other men. Is the North's condemnation of the South as a hotbed of race prejudice entirely true, after all?"*[21]

In late November of 1934, the United States Public Health Service awarded a certificate of merit to The Dunbar School of Snyder for their outstanding observance of National Negro Health Week. Activities necessary to win the award included *"health talks in school and church, posters, songs, general house and yard beautification, hauling of tin cans and rubbish, installation of pit toilets, fighting the fly, special attention to the bath, toothbrush, clean finger nails, hands, face and clothing."*[22]

■■

A darkness that threatened to consume the whole world came rolling and boiling across the plains on the unseasonably warm Saturday afternoon of February 23, 1935. Temperatures rapidly dropped as a mountain of suffocating dust swallowed up helpless cattle on the ranches of Scurry County. The bright afternoon skies over Snyder turned a dark brown. Streams of gritty particles blasted through every crack and crevice of the little houses in The Flat.

Occasional dust storms have been a part of life in western Texas since before recorded history began. But this was something new. Something far worse.

Scurry County Times editor Leon Guinn described the event as *"a three day sandstorm that did not completely let up until Monday. All day Sunday the dust filtered through the air and at night it settled in swirling masses that reminded old-timers of days gone by."*[23]

It was only the beginning. On March 3rd, J.W. Roberts of Snyder gave an account of another storm that *"swooped down upon us from the southwest, and within 30 seconds from the time it struck it was as dark as any night at midnight that I have ever lived through. Some white people were frightened, and there were negroes in The Flat who made ready for the judgement. It had old-timers scratching their heads trying to recall another such storm. It was one of those things that happens once in a lifetime".*[24]

It happened again two weeks later when a dust cloud *"descended almost like a pall. The wind was moderate, but visibility was as short as two or three blocks."*[25]

The Scurry County Times identified the heart of the problem early on. *"Very likely sandstorms in West Texas are just sandstorms like they have always been with this important addition: that the farmer has come along and plowed up thousands of acres of land, giving the winds access to loosened soil that was not available 'away back when-.'*

"Seemingly in these latter years the sandstorms are more awe-inspiring, because the cloud of dust and dirt which they gather makes pillows and billows hundreds of feet into the air that settle down and sift through cracks and crevices. On highways and adjacent to fields, when a heavy storm hits, traffic stops for a few minutes at least."[26]

In April of 1935, an opinion piece in the Snyder paper entitled, *"Wanted: An Inventor"*, captured the desperation of the moment. *"Wanted— By a country that is being blown away by degrees; an inventor who can construct dust-proof houses and blow-proof fields; price is no object; what we want is results- r-e-sults- and damn the consequences and cost. Apply before the next duststorm to any Northwest, Mid-West, or Southwest farmer or housewife."*[27]

Snyder's Church of God In Christ congregation in 1935. Courtesy Scurry County Museum

There was plenty of blame to go around.

"In many hill country Southern counties soil destruction has reached the proportions of a calamity," said one anonymous writer in Snyder. *"While statute books and court procedures are severe on negro crap shooters and chicken-stealers, white land owners who let their soils wash away commit a far greater crime against humanity.*

"When we destroy the soil fertility which the Almighty intended should nourish not only you and me but all those who may come after us for a million years to come, we white land owners commit a crime far greater than that of any ignorant negro who steals a chicken or ham or sheep. Those petty thefts affect only individuals today. But when we destroy essential soil fertility we sin against the human race not only today but for the tomorrows. Yet our so-called statesmen in the legislature of the South for years and for generations have been formulating statutes and setting up court machinery to punish chicken stealing and crap shooting while the destruction of the Almighty's greatest gift to our section- destruction which ensures disaster alike to this generation and to all future generations- has been treated as a matter of no public concern."[28]

Federal assistance continued to flow into Scurry County as the Dust Bowl worsened. The Agricultural Adjustment Administration sent a total of $522,000 to Snyder in 1934 alone. Another $44,553 in farm relief came in the first 3 months of 1935.[29,30]

In the spring of 1935 the Roosevelt administration began an ambitious plan to contain the Dust Bowl. *"Scurry County will be included in the 1,000-mile shelter belt of trees that is being planted by the federal government from the Canadian border to the South Plains of Texas"* wrote Leon Guinn of the Scurry County Times. *"With 3,250,000 acres of sterile land in Texas caused by drought and dust and 75,000,000 sterile acres in the United States, one of the most intriguing fields of endeavor for the next 20 years will be soil conservation and erosion work. Static electricity with severe dust storms has adversely affected seed germination in many states, burning up soil energy in large areas, and in places it will take all the skills of science to make sub-soil acres profitable again."*[31,32]

The people of western Texas endured a dust storm of regional size forty times in 1935. Another sixty-eight would come in 1936. In 1937, the worst year of the Dust Bowl, there were at least seventy-two. Roughly one third of all farming and ranching families abandoned the Texas Panhandle during this period.[33]

■■

On a hot Sunday morning in June of 1935, the congregation of Mount Olive Baptist came together in the shadow of their little church to begin a religious revival that would last for eight days. Dozens of hands, recently washed but already gritty with dust, gripped each other in a circle. Urgent prayers for rain flew into the Texas sky. Hymns echoed through eastern Snyder, attracting white neighbors in numbers that grew each day. By the end of the week the crowd had grown so large that the revival was relocated to Wolf Park. Deep Creek became the scene of scores of baptisms. The air was thick with powerful sermons and fine dust.[34]

The first phase of New Deal aid in Scurry County had not been evenly distributed. The federal government was consistently responsive to the needs of local farmers, ranchers, and businesses. But a concession to Southern conservatives in Congress by President Roosevelt in 1933 resulted in domestic workers and landless farm hands being exempted from most benefits. This policy, indirectly but deliberately targeted at African-Americans in the South, directed most of the money received by Scurry County away from The Flat.

The Works Progress Administration, founded in May of 1935, attempted to address the problem of unequal aid distribution. In August, the W.P.A. announced a $283,000 plan to hire all 472 of Scurry County's eligible unemployed men. This broad hiring policy benefitted many families in Snyder's Black section during the remaining New Deal years.[35]

Most of the money from the W.P.A. in 1935 was spent on grading and paving the dusty streets and alleys of Snyder. Local officials set aside $75,000 for expansions to Snyder Public School. These included a garage, a workshop, and *"numerous other* changes to beautify the campus and grounds." The most visible and expensive of these improvements would be a modern gymnasium built with native stone. Similar but smaller gymnasiums would be constructed in the nearby towns of Ira and Dunn.[36-38]

Construction on The Snyder Gymnasium, known in later years as Travis Gym, began on the chilly Friday morning of November 1, 1935. The entire school was in attendance.

"After a brief dedication ceremony", wrote the Scurry County Times, *"25 men began moving dirt, digging ditches, and hauling materials. Now, five days after the work started, 40 men, working in two shifts have been employed. [...]*

"John E. Sentell made the principal address Friday morning. Mayor H.G. Towle and president H.L. Davis of the school board also spoke briefly. Superintendent C. Wedgeworth presided. The Tiger Band played several numbers. [...]

"The project will be far more than a gymnasium. The three-way basketball court may also be used for special gatherings and for other sports. Built-in bleachers to accommodate several hundred people will be afforded. Two dressing rooms will be provided for the convenience of players.

"An outstanding feature will be the band room, where the musicians may practice without disturbing classes. This room and another large room in the building will be used for physical education work, now provided for all students.

"School officials expect the building to be completed and ready for use in early 1936."[39]

The county planners continued to lavish W.P.A. funds on the students at Snyder Public School throughout the late 1930s. During the same period, no federal money would be allocated for the children at the nearby Dunbar School.

■■

Jeff Davis' barbecue was now so famous that it had become a tourist draw for Snyder. His delectable brisket taught the "respectable" people of Scurry County how to find The Flat back in 1932. Now, three years later, it was joined by a pork sausage so delicious that residents of nearby Colorado City were driving through thirty miles of dust for a plate. One afternoon in the autumn of 1935, Jeff Davis was approached by Snyder restaurateur Bob Gray.

Mr. Gray was the owner of The Tavern, a restaurant he had established on the southeast corner of the Snyder square in March of 1934. Scurry County had voted to remain dry after the end of prohibition, so The Tavern was a tavern in name only. To cement his restaurant's status as the best in town, Mr. Gray attempted to assemble the finest restaurant team that Snyder had to offer. The most important part of the plan was to lure the pioneer of Scurry County's barbecue scene out of The Flat by offering him the position of head chef in an otherwise segregated restaurant.

The plan worked.

"In the kitchen, which is in the charge of that experienced colored chef, Jeff Davis, several improvements have been made to speed up service and to make cooked foods more appetizing than ever before. Jeff and his wife, by the way, make open pit barbecue just a block east of The Tavern. This same barbecue, just like they made in the good old days, is served on Tavern lunches."[40]

Jeff Davis. The Scurry County Times. November 28, 1935 (damaged microfilm).[40]

The Tavern was so eager to promote their acquisition of Mr. Davis that they included an image of him with their announcement in the Scurry County Times. This was the first time that a photo of an African-American resident of Scurry County appeared in a Snyder newspaper.

CHAPTER 7
ACCOMPLISHED BY VANDALS

"Buffalo hunting opened up a vast empire of territory for occupation, put the Indian forever out of Texas, changed him from a blood-thirsty savage to a meek, submissive ward. [...]

"Magazine writers and others who claim that the killing of the buffalo was a national calamity and was accomplished by vandals simply expose their ignorance, and I resent such an unjust judgement upon us."

-Josiah Wright Mooar, 1933.[1]

He Followed the Thundering Buffalo Herds

J. Wright Mooar. The Scurry County Times. May 7, 1936.[2]

The old hunter sat tall and proud in his weathered saddle. An antique .50-caliber Sharps rifle, allegedly designed at his own request, rested silently across his lap. Little puffs of dust followed the hooves of the arrogant horse as it carried one of the last living legends of the West toward the Snyder square one last time.

Row upon row of horses added their own prints to the sand as a little army of cowboys bore witness to Josiah Wright Mooar's last ride. Hundreds of children cheered from the sidewalks. A camera crew from the Scurry County Times scrambled onto a roof in the square for a better view. Ghosts of the Comanche watched silently from the banks of Deep Creek.

Behind this glorious scene, a 1936 Chevrolet Master Deluxe 2-door Town Sedan rumbled impatiently along.[2]

■■

On the day that Scurry County was established, Black Texans were already there. They had likely come as buffalo skinners, harvesting carcasses in the wake of the commercial hunters that scoured the area. With support from the U.S. 4th Cavalry during the Red River War, the hunters had made western Texas uninhabitable for the Comanche that had long resisted their presence. By 1876, there was nothing left to stop the hunting teams from driving the American Bison to regional extinction.[3-5]

The personal accounts of Scurry County's first African-American inhabitants do not survive to the present. Barely a decade after their emancipation, it is probable (but by no means certain) that they were illiterate.

The decision to name the new county after William Scurry was made hundreds of miles away in Austin. Bitter from the pain of civil war and impoverished by the destruction of their slave cotton industry, the Fifteenth Texas Legislature began to name pieces of the former Comancheria in honor of Confederate leaders.

It was a prolific trend. Counties were named for Matthew Ector, Robert Foard, Peter Gray, John Gregg, John Hemphill, John Hood, Jefferson Davis, Robert E. Lee, Thomas Lubbock, Benjamin McCulloch, William Ochiltree, William Oldham, Horace Randall, George Reeves, John Reagan, James Starr, William Scurry,

Alexander Stephens, Thomas "Stonewall" Jackson, John Sutton, Alexander Terrell, Benjamin Terry, Thomas Green, William Upton, Clinton Winkler, and Henry Wise.

Their names would serve as perpetual reminders to anyone who could read a map that, despite Emancipation and Reconstruction, the old powers of Texas were still in charge.

Land in the newly-minted Scurry County was to be distributed according to federal homestead laws. However, the Texas Black Codes of the late 1870s forbade the transfer of public land to Black Texans. Instead, the lands of the Comanche would be handed out to Anglo-Texans and European immigrants. This policy ensured that the county would be under the exclusive control of its white inhabitants from the beginning. Their Black and Tejano neighbors would start with nothing.[6]

In the beginning, Scurry County was Confederate in name only. Vermont native, former Chicago streetcar operator, commercial buffalo hunter, and Scurry County's first white permanent resident J. Wright Mooar introduced industrial capitalism to the area. Shooting and skinning methods developed by Mr. Mooar and his hunting team brought the Great Plains buffalo population from somewhere between thirty-five and seventy-five million in 1871 to near extinction by 1884. Mooar claimed to have personally shot more than 20,000 of them.[7]

Pennsylvania native, commercial buffalo hunter, and former Union Army Private William Henry "Pete" Snyder founded the county's first white-owned business on the banks of Deep Creek. The spot was a hub for hide wagons bound to and from the nearest railroad station. By late 1878, a tent city of buffalo hides and mesquite limbs had formed around Mr. Snyder's shop. This is the traditional telling of how Snyder, Texas began.[8,9]

In 1874 the plains of Scurry County had been so full of buffalo that herds sometimes stretched between horizons. By the fall of 1878, the area was littered with countless carcasses and heaps of bones.

Cleaning up after the buffalo hunters became an industry unto itself. "Bone picking", the practice of gathering and selling buffalo remains for fertilizer, would be a staple activity of poor West Texans until the late 1930s. It would take more than fifty years to rid Scurry County of the tragic mess left behind by four years of commercial buffalo hunting.[10]

Scurry County appeared in the U.S. census for the first time in 1880. The county's total population was 102. Eight of them were Black. A decade later only two remained. By 1900 the number of Black Texans in the county had fallen to zero.[11]

As Snyder flourished into a town and J. Wright Mooar settled into his life as a rancher, the economic and political power of Black Texans was steadily increasing. Norris Wright Cuney was elected national committeeman and chairman of the Texas Republican Party in 1886. Born into slavery, Cuney held the highest political position of any Black person in the American South in the 19th Century. The period from 1883 to 1896 would later be known to Texas Republican Party historians as The Cuney Era.[12]

The end of that era coincided with the *Plessy v. Ferguson* decision in May of 1896. The U.S. Supreme Court ruled that African Americans can be served separately from the white population if they are provided with accommodations of equal quality. The ruling, commonly known as "separate but equal", reinforced existing racially discriminatory laws across the United States and paved the way for many more to come.

Buffalo bones litter the Great Plains circa 1890.

On November 4, 1902, the Texas Legislature passed a law requiring a poll tax receipt in order to vote. State lawmakers had promoted the idea as a way to regulate elections and prevent voter fraud but the practical effect was to discourage political participation among Tejano, Black, and poor white Texans. Black voters in Texas had numbered more than 100,000 in the 1890s. By 1906 there would be less than 5,000.[13,14]

■■

Festivities to mark a century of independence from Mexico were held in countless cities and towns across Texas in April of 1936. Snyder's own celebrations spanned several days, culminating in the Heart of West Texas Centennial Parade. The presence of J. Wright Mooar at the head of the procession momentarily tore the attention of the Texas press away from the World's Fair in Dallas.[15-16]

The Ft. Worth Star-Telegram wrote *"J. Wright Mooar, 85, who headed the pioneer section of the Heart of West Texas Centennial Parade in Snyder April 21, undoubtedly has been a vital part of more West Texas history than any other living person.*

"Woven into the life of the veteran buffalo hunter are tales of almost fictitious adventure and trail blazing. [...] His first winter's hunt out of the Deep Creek camp was a remunerative one for the Mooar brothers, 4,500 hides and 62,000 pounds of cured meat being sold at the end of four months."[2]

The centennial celebration would be one of J. Wright Mooar's last public appearances. After the conclusion of the parade, the State of Texas presented the City of Snyder with a new plaque to commemorate the occasion. The simple bronze plate tells of William Scurry's actions during the Civil War and how the county came to bear his name. The plaque was fixed to the side of the Scurry County courthouse where it hung for many decades before being moved in the 1970s. At the time of this writing the old 1936 Scurry plaque is bolted to a granite stone at the northeast corner of the town square.

■■

Temperatures in Snyder exceeded 100 degrees almost every day in August of 1936. The city set a new all-time record of 115 degrees on the 13th. After seven years of drought and blowing sand, western Texas had never looked so bleak and dead.

Rainfall in 1936 had been only 22% of normal. Hardly a week passed without a dust storm. In early August, the Agricultural Adjustment Administration gave Scurry County $603,965.75, their largest drought aid package to date.[17,18]

As the miserable summer drew to a close, a poem by Snyder resident W.P. Bolin titled *"The Drought"* appeared in the Scurry County Times.

> *The Gulf clouds drift athwart the sky,*
> *The raven goes a-croaking by,*
> *And everything is surely dry*
> *In Scurry County, Texas.*
>
> *To find the maize, you need a writ;*
> *The cotton's opening - every bit.*
> *You have to prime yourself to spit*
> *In Scurry County, Texas.*
>
> *The drought, it seems, is here to stay.*
> *The sun shines hotter every day,*
> *And Hell's not half a mile away*
> *From Scurry County, Texas.*[19]

Published on the same day, in the same paper, on the same page, and under the same title, a separate opinion piece by E.C. Ralston noted that *"the drought has caused the green leaves to turn brown and fall and all fruitful vegetation withers and decays.*

"It is more destructive to the animals and vegetable life than the ravages of war, or a desolating tornado, or the withering winds of the desert.

"It strips the land of all fruitful vegetation. It stops the onward march of prosperity. It spreads with an ever increasing

rapidity, want, misery, and woe. It robs mouths of food, backs of clothes, and the soil of moisture and vegetation.

"Gray hairs, desolate homes, widows, and orphans are the price of victory and some die from hunger. Add that to the ghastly picture.

"After the drought is over I will venture to say that there will be some whose names will be missing from the newspapers, as they have dragged themselves to die beneath the shade of a tree where the birds of the air have picked out their eyes, the vultures of the air have eaten their flesh, and their bones have molded into dust."[20]

Through all of these hardships, the Works Progress Administration remained committed to Snyder's survival. In September of 1936 they provided the funding to pave every remaining street and alleyway in the city with caliche and asphalt.[21]

At 10:30 AM on Friday, October 9, 1936, a crowd of more than 1,000 people gathered on the south side of Snyder Public School. They had come to witness the official dedication of the Snyder Gymnasium, known in later years as Travis Gym. Constructed entirely by the hands of local laborers, the building was one of Snyder's most visible New Deal projects. A reporter from The Scurry County Times was on hand to record the occasion.

The Scurry County Times. October 15, 1936.[23]

105

"*Admitted by school people and builders to be one of the most modern and attractive gymnasiums in West Texas, the native-stone building will be officially presented by C. Wedgeworth, superintendent, and received by King Sides, high school principal.*" [22]

"*The program was not only one of praise for those who are behind the project, but also one of hope that the giant building may prove to be of outstanding worth to the students of the school. [...] The Tiger Band gave several selections.*"[24]

Four weeks later, 91.3% of Scurry County voters spent their poll tax dollars to elect Franklin Roosevelt to a second term.[24]

As the 1936-'37 winter break drew near, the students at Snyder Public School celebrated with live entertainment. "*Shows may come and shows may go, but the old-time negro minstrel will long be a favorite with show-going people,*" predicted Scurry County Times editor Leon Guinn.

"*So say members of the American Legion Auxiliary, who are presenting Tuesday night, 8:00 o'clock, in the school auditorium, the 'Dixie Blackbird Minstrels,' an array of home talent.*

"*The minstrel is a black-face show in five acts, and is declared by the sponsors to be one of the most unique minstrel arrangements of the day. The cast is composed of 50 Snyder performers, selected for their ability in singing, dancing, and wise-cracking. Rehearsals are being conducted with the directorial assistance of Miss Charlsy Morrow, a professional play director for the Sewell Lyceum Company of Atlanta, Georgia. [...]*

"*Proceeds will be used by the Auxiliary to supplement its milk fund for needy children and for other worthy purposes.*"[25]

In early 1937 the Roosevelt Administration rolled out its Emergency Education Program to provide adult learning opportunities to underserved communities. The project was initially met with suspicion by many white southern conservatives for its obvious benefits to racial minority groups. After a brief investigation, The Scurry County Times began to push back against this sentiment.

"*So much misguided opinion has adversely affected the emergency education program in Texas, The Times (by special request) is glad to present herewith the program's highlights- as gleaned by field observations.*

"To know what the emergency education program division of WPA is doing for Texas, one must consider what this federal project is doing for your county and mine, who through adversity's lean years have been denied the public school education you and I were fortunate in securing. [...]

"A source of interest is the Mexican class, with 15 enrolled. Adult Mexicans, whose ancestors trekked across the Texas plains with Coronado, are not only learning the king's English, but are translating 'centavos y pesos' into American dollars and cents. Interviewed, one student 'wanna learn count weights in ingles multiple de uno, dos, tres, keep cotton weighted para mi amigo y mi (my old friend and me).

"In the oil mill section of Snyder the negro class, with 20 on roll, is socially important. Several negroes have been taught to read and write, and the more advanced pupils have been taught arithmetic, hygiene, and better citizenship. After all, one writer says, 'the negro race has learned a lot of its meanness from white folks,' the emergency program is aiming to instill [in] the chocolate race all the good points of white civilization, crowd out some of the meanness learned from white people."[26]

After two years of improvements to Snyder Public School at the direction of local officials, the WPA had finally found a way to bring some of its benefits to The Dunbar School.

The value of cotton and beef rebounded significantly in the second half of 1937. The local paper maintained a cautious tone, but hopes for an end to the Great Depression began to stir in Snyder. Drought conditions in Scurry County still persisted, but the Dust Bowl was beginning to recede from western Texas.[27]

In February of 1938 The Flat looked much the same as it had in February of 1932. The tire ruts in Avenue M had worn a little deeper. Hymns still rang out from Mount Olive on Sundays. The Dunbar School piano still filled the weekday air with music.

Meanwhile, across the railroad tracks to the north, The City of Snyder had been transformed by the New Deal. *"I will say, in reference to improvements in Snyder, that they all have been of the permanent type,"* said Snyder mayor Howard Towle in February of

1938. *"The Snyder School Gymnasium, valued at $30,000, has a garage built on the east side, gymnasium and garage materials being of native rock and concrete.*

"We have completed 24 blocks of asphalt paving, with an estimated value (based on contract paving) of $158,400. Curb and gutter has been completed on 16 more blocks which are ready for topping. Curb and gutter has practically been completed on 15 more blocks. [...]

"[WPA officials] have been pleasant to work with, our improvements will serve the city for generations to come, and this WPA work has provided a livelihood for some sixty families. In all, WPA work has been quite successful in Snyder."[28]

■■

Snyder Public School sat empty and silent on the night of March 10, 1938. The teachers and students had rushed home hours earlier to relieve their exhaustion of one another. The first indication that anything had gone wrong was the smell of smoke drifting eastward down 26th Street.

The fire started in the auditorium. By the time the Snyder Fire Department arrived, the entire north wing was ablaze.

"Snyder hearts were burned last Thursday as the school plant crackled and became an outlined ghost in the night", lamented Leon Guinn of The Scurry County Times.

"But if one is a pronounced Pollyanna, one who sees good In everything, one can readily conceive that the disastrous fire will make Snyder a better community In which to live and rear children.

"Tragedy makes the world akin. It brings neighbors together. It levels old bitternesses. It sends jealousies and backbitings to the grave. It unites strength and ability, bodies and minds.

"The city is carrying on in a manner little short of miraculous. Only two days of school were missed. Many thousands of dollars went up In smoke, but money can be created by willing hands.

"Snyder, where man's humanity to man often sleeps but never perishes, has converted burning hearts into plowshares of reconstruction."[29]

As It Looks at the Time of Publication After the Tragic Fire

1938 school yearbook. Courtesy Scurry County Museum

With most of Snyder Public School in ruins, the white children of Snyder needed new spaces to continue their education. First and second graders would be taught in the basement of First Baptist Church during the 1938-'39 school year. Third grade was held in the Methodist sanctuary while the fourth graders were hosted by the Presbyterians. Junior high classes were held in the Snyder Gymnasium. The high school students were able to remain in the relatively undamaged south wing while repairs were underway.

Plans to reconstruct Snyder Public School began almost immediately after the fire was out. In September of 1938 the Public Works Administration provided $65,455 to help cover the school's restoration. Total costs would be about $146,000.[30-35]

In early April of 1938 the Dunbar School observed Negro Health Week. The five-day event included lectures on hygiene, first aid, healthy living conditions, and methods of acquiring healthcare in segregated societies. The week's activities briefly caught the attention of the local paper.

Times writer Leon Guinn marked the occasion, writing that *"last week was the twenty-fourth annual National Negro Health Week in America, but the Southern press failed to get mad about the situation just because it was 'nigger' week. Started by that profound negro scholar, Booker T. Washington, founder of The Tuskegee Institute, this week was set aside by colored folks for racial observance, just as Clean Up Week or any similar occasion is observed by white races. It seems as though a chief point of concern right now revolves around whether to say 'colored folks,' 'darkies,' or 'niggers.' 'Niggers' is the Yankee rendition, but most Southerners lean to the same expression."*[36]

Two weeks after pondering the appropriate slur to apply to his neighbors, Mr. Guinn found himself standing in the heart of their neighborhood. On April 28, 1938, twelve years after the founding of the Dunbar School, the Snyder newspaper finally covered a graduation ceremony in The Flat.

The event was held inside the one-room schoolhouse at 8 p.m. with two seventh graders receiving diplomas. A commencement ceremony was held at Mount Olive Baptist Church with a Boy Scouts of America executive from Sweetwater delivering the opening address. The audience sang "America" and "Peace Shall Reign At Last." The evening ended with the presentation of diplomas across the street at Dunbar. The Scurry County Times failed to mention the names of the two graduates.[37]

██

During the 1938-'39 school year, as Snyder Public School was being rebuilt, Dunbar would receive more attention from the local paper than ever before.

October 10, 1938 was the first day of school and the first day of work for new teacher Myrtle C. King of Rotan. As she finished her commute to the dead end of 34th Street just west of Avenue M, Miss King found twenty-three children waiting with their parents in front of the Dunbar School.[38]

Among those children was seven-year-old second grader Vernest Newsome, later Vernest Tippens. In a 1984 interview with the director of the Scurry County Museum, Mrs. Tippens recalled her experiences as a child going to school in The Flat.

"[Dunbar] had an outhouse probably less than fifty feet from the school and about twenty feet to the south was [the city incinerator]. When the city would pick up dead animals they would come down and burn them in there, even when we were having school. It smelled stinky. We had one teacher and she taught all the grades and all the subjects. [...]

"Two or three kids would be assigned to go [to Snyder Public School] and get the lunch for the Black kids. We had to bring it in syrup buckets. It would look like mush and the teacher would divide it between the kids. [...] You couldn't eat in the restaurants or anything like that.

110

"Sometimes you had separate restrooms. If it was really, really an emergency you might could go at the courthouse if you were caught uptown but there wasn't anywhere else for the Blacks to go unless you was near the bus station or something like that. In the restaurants you always had to wait out back. It was something that we just accepted because there was nothing you could do."

When the museum director asked if she resented this unequal treatment as a child, there was a short pause. After a thoughtful moment, Snyder City Councilwoman and Scurry County NAACP Secretary Vernest Tippens responded, *"I think maybe I did."*[39]

The Scurry County Times reported on Halloween festivities at Dunbar for the first time in 1938. They came back again for Thanksgiving.[40,41]

In early December, the Chamber of Commerce hired Santa Claus to circle the Snyder square in his airplane. All the white children of the town age 10 or younger were invited to gather on the east side of the courthouse at 3 PM to watch the spectacle. After landing nearby and handing out candy to the gleeful youngsters, Santa was driven one mile away to Mount Olive Church where he distributed the remaining sweets to the other children of Snyder.[42]

Tired of driving all over town to report on a student body scattered by the recent fire, The Scurry County Times asked the students of Snyder to send samples of their own writing for publication in the paper. The first such report from The Dunbar School, written by student journalist Dorothy Baker, appeared on February 9, 1939.

"Snyder Colored School is doing splendid work this term under the supervision of our teacher, Miss King. Semester examinations are out of the way, and pupils are burning the night oil over their studies.

"We want to thank C. Wedgeworth, superintendent, and the school board trustees for use of the gymnasium Friday, January 27. The colored boys' team of our school won both games played.

"We are in hopes we'll be able to win at the West Texas Plains district tournament at Slaton March 4. We want some of our white friends to go if possible.

"We appreciate the visits paid us occasionally by Hadley Reeve, junior high principal of Snyder Schools. We invite our white friends to visit the school any time."[43]

■■

Hot swing music blasted out across the dusty lawn of Winston Park southeast of Snyder. Rats Brown and his Swingsters found their tempo. Dancers in sharp suits and summer skirts rushed to the stage for the 1939 Scurry County Juneteenth Jitterbug Contest.

It had been a full day of celebrations. The morning began with a short prayer and an outdoor breakfast. The weather was pleasant and cloudy when the Snyder Black Tigers played the Wichita Black Sox on the Winston Park baseball diamond. A post-game picnic filled the air with the irresistible smell of mesquite-smoked barbecue and the sweet sounds of gospel music.[44]

At sunset, with the dance contest just getting underway, the Texas skies opened up in a torrent of rain. Partygoers in dance shoes scrambled to save musical instruments and platters of beef brisket. Hailstones battered the little park southeast of Snyder.

The most destructive rainstorm in Snyder's history raged throughout the night. The town square got 7.5 inches of rain in 10 hours. Other parts of the county reported almost twice as much. As flood waters reached the 3-foot mark near Snyder's American Legion Hut, the building lifted off of its foundations, floated downstream, and smashed into a private residence at 25th Street and Avenue V. Many other buildings, including the West Side Grocery Store, were washed down the overflowing banks of Deep Creek.

More than 300 Scurry County residents were made homeless and 100 families requested emergency assistance from the government. About 40,000 acres of cotton were destroyed. Roughly 1,000 head of cattle and 800 sheep drowned.

Adjacent to Deep Creek and downstream from the square, the damage to The Flat was some of the most severe. Not a single home was undamaged and many were destroyed.

Mayor Towle of Snyder would spend the rest of the summer coordinating recovery efforts with the Works Progress Administration and the American Red Cross. As of this writing, the Juneteenth Flood Disaster of 1939 remains the heaviest rain event in Scurry County's history.[45-49]

■■

As the flood waters receded and the residents of The Flat began to rebuild their shattered neighborhood, the world was drawing closer to the edge of catastrophe. On the last day of August in 1939, Leon Guinn of The Scurry County Times wrote the following.

"War clouds are hanging oppressively low over Europe this week, with hopes for avoiding a major conflict on Old World soil seemingly on the wane, although Germany's recent non-aggression pact with Soviet Russia was considered by European observers to be a master stroke of strategy. The marching sound of 10,000,000 men under arms this week on Europe's blood-stained battlefields of yesterday almost drown out any appeals made for peace by even President Roosevelt or Pope Pious. Just in case the road ahead does lead to war- which many assert it will sooner or later- the United States will find herself in an almost unavoidable quandary whether to again lend foreign nations money for war materials, or be blamed for not aiding the cause of democracy- or whatever the present appeal for aid may be based on if war overtakes madcap Europe."[50]

War overtook madcap Europe on the following day.

Ten days later, as the Polish Army battled the Nazis in the streets of Warsaw, the first day of school began at a fully restored and modernized Snyder Public School. New features included fireproof brick construction throughout, additional exits with panic bars, modern electrical wiring, additional restrooms, steam heat, and electric lights in every room.[51,52]

Meanwhile, at the hastily reconstructed Dunbar School, musician E.M. Watson began his first day as teacher. In his introductory speech to the Snyder Lions Club, Mr. Watson said *"we believe the colored people of Snyder have an important mission ahead of them in seeing that their children are properly educated. We feel that in properly educating our people we can drastically cut down the element of crime some folks connect with our race."*[53]

Truancy would be significantly reduced during Mr. Watson's first year. Attendance at Dunbar increased from twenty-nine to thirty-eight and a new pit toilet was installed at the teacher's expense.

The Scurry County Times. September 7, 1939.

As Mr. Watson taught his second day of class in 1939, more than 200 gallons of solidified nitroglycerine exploded fifteen miles southwest of Snyder and 2,400 feet below the surface. Several seconds later, a black fountain of crude oil leapt up from the shattered rock beneath the plains. Magnolia Oil, owned by Scurry County resident C.T. McLaughlin, was now the first major petroleum company to begin active operations in the area. This demonstration of the county's first flowing oil well would prompt increased exploration throughout the following decade.[54,55]

■■

First Methodist Church was so packed with people that there was barely room to breathe. The crowd spilled out the door, filled the church grounds, and wound its way along the nearby sidewalks. Snyder's total population in 1940 was 3,815. On May 2nd of that year a crowd of more than 3,000 came to witness the funeral of J. Wright Mooar.

"We had in Mr. Mooar a man who witnessed in the passing of the bison the close of a colorful chapter in Southwestern history. He was ever a community and Scurry County booster," remarked Reverend I.A. Smith during the eulogy. Rites were performed later that afternoon at the gravesite in Snyder Cemetery by members of Scurry County Masonic Lodge 706.[7,56]

When confronted with the ecological and cultural damage caused by the profession he pioneered, Mooar remained unrepentant to the end. In a 1933 interview with McMurry University president James Hunt, Mr. Mooar addressed the controversy.

"Because he has been criticized as a destroyer, a ruthless killer, and wastrel of a great game resource of a nation, the buffalo hunter appeals to the bar of history for his vindication. [...]

"Buffalo hunting was a business and not a sport. It required capital, management and a lot of hard work. [...] If it had not been for the work of the buffalo hunters, the wild bison would still graze where Amarillo now is, and the red man would still reign supreme over the pampas of the Panhandle of Texas. Any one of the families killed and homes destroyed by the Indians would have been worth more to Texas and to civilization than all the millions of buffalo that

ever roamed from the Pecos River on the south to the Platte River on the north."[57]

The death of *"Scurry County's first citizen"* was a milestone in the cultural history of Snyder's white population. It severed the origins of their society from living memory forever and represented, in the minds of some, the death of the Old West itself.

■■

Plentiful rainfall throughout the early spring had made the plains of western Texas as lush and green as the valleys of central Ireland. The most destructive drought in Scurry County's history was coming to an end. On the beautiful spring afternoon of May 5, 1940 the Snyder Black Tigers beat Anson 15-2 at the Winston Park baseball diamond.[58]

Five days later, the German Army invaded France.

CHAPTER 8
DON'T RAISE CANNON FODDER

"Our Schools Don't Raise Cannon Fodder!"

"In London the school children are being moved out by the hundreds of thousands, as the threat of German raiders grows with the progress of this generation's second major war. In Berlin the young Nazi is taught only what Hitler wants taught, and he learns more about the goose step than he does about the three R's. In Russia the youthful Stalinites follow a strictly supervised routine of work and play and study that conforms to the infamous five-year plan.

"In Snyder, as in thousands of other American communities, school bells have no such sinister meanings. The bells that have been calling Scurry County children to classrooms for two or three weeks have truly called them to study, to think for themselves, to learn the God-taught difference between right and wrong. [...]

"So Scurry County's excitement this month grows not out of the fear of air raids, not out of the notion that war is just around the corner, not out of the belief that might makes right. Rather, we are excited because Billy and Susie and Sally and Buster are going back to school!

"Ain't it a grand and glorious excitement?"
-The Scurry County Times. September 7, 1939.[1]

The Scurry County Times. November 9, 1939.[2]

Henry "Peg Leg" DuBaugh saw the flash of chrome and his heart sank. The deputy's car rattled across the little wooden bridge that spanned Deep Creek at 37th Street, then turned to straddle the muddy ruts that sliced The Flat in half along Avenue M.

The patrol car rolled gently to a stop. Its steel door swung open with a little squeak. Boots pressed into the damp earth. Both men had long known this moment was coming. Neither wanted it to happen.

No record exists of a conversation between them. There may not have been one. The wooden prosthesis that gave Mr. DuBaugh his nickname pressed into the porch as he rose from his chair. The deputy's car turned around in the shadow of Mount Olive Baptist, rumbled back across the bridge, and carried "Peg Leg" to the Scurry County Jail.[3]

■■

German planes attacked London for the first time on September 7, 1940. Almost 2,000 people were killed on the first day of The Blitz. As the London Fire Brigade scrambled to save whatever they could, the children of Snyder, Texas were preparing for the first day of the 1940-'41 school year.

"With the formal opening of Snyder Schools Monday morning for the new school year, faculty members plan a term that will serve all the students of the Snyder community", said Snyder Superintendent E.L. Farr. *"Emphasis will be placed on art, music, literature, and other creative activities. The school accepts the responsibility for stimulating intellectual curiosity and appreciation of the treasures of knowledge, and the joys of personal intellectual conquest. [...]*

"Before our young friends end their formal schooling at the secondary level, their school experiences should not only provide social understanding and knowledge of what democracy is and how it works, but also should stimulate emotional drives which should condition future behavior in defense of democratic ideals."[4]

Teacher E.M. Watson of the Dunbar School spoke to The Times on the same day. *"During our new school term that starts Monday at the local colored school, we plan to make classroom*

119

work more appealing to students than it's ever been before. We plan to keep our students interested in school work as something to enjoy along the royal road to higher learning."[5]

A few days later, Times writer Leon Guinn found himself sitting in the pews of Mount Olive Baptist Church with a Bible balanced on one knee and a notepad on the other. An unusually diverse crowd of worshipers filled the tiny sanctuary with music. It was an interdenominational service and attendance was high. During the calm of the sermons, Mr. Guinn recorded a few quotes for the paper.

"Never in our generation have we seen the time when people needed to go to church more than in these fast-changing days," said Mount Olive guest preacher W.M. Carrington of Brownwood. *"If we can educate our people to the point where they will be self-sustaining, we feel that, with the help of our white friends, we can create a lasting amount of goodwill between the races that will result in a decrease of friction between the two peoples."*

Leads in Drive for Good Will Funds

Shown in this picture are Mr. and Mrs. John Baker (colored), who have bought and paid for a home in the colored section of town as an indication of their intention to live here permanently. Baker, a civic and community booster, placed first in the recent money raising contest conducted among his colored brethern to care for expenditures of the good will meeting brought to a close last Sunday by Rev. W. M. Carrington of Brownwood.

The Scurry County Times. September 19, 1940.[56]

Reverend I.A. Smith from First Methodist Church was the next to speak. *"There is no color line where God's kingdom work is concerned. The history of America is a history where religious toleration has been the order of the day. The war raging in Europe today is a result of certain leaders forsaking God, and trying to place greed over morality.*

"People of all religious denominations are more in sympathy with the colored people of our land who are trying to better their positions in life, and live upright Christian lives. The white people will respect the colored folks for living Christian lives and will see that the colored race is offered greater possibilities for advancement than ever before if they adhere to the teachings of Jesus."[6]

The Selective Training and Service Act, the first peacetime use of conscription in US history, was signed into law on September 16, 1940. All men ages twenty-one to thirty-five were required to immediately register with their local draft board. Six weeks later, 89.2% of eligible Scurry County voters helped reelect Franklin Roosevelt to a third term as president.[7,8]

In early November of 1940, with the federal government increasingly shifting its focus to war preparations, the Works Progress Administration was winding down in Scurry County. They had built or improved seventy-three miles of highways, farm-to-market roads, streets, and alleys. Snyder now had more paved streets than any other city of comparable size in Texas. In the counties that comprised the Lubbock District, the New Deal created forty-two public buildings including seventeen gymnasiums, and thirteen schools.[9]

■■

L eon Guinn was sitting in his office at the Scurry County Times when the word came in that "Peg Leg" DuBaugh had been arrested.

Mr. DuBaugh had a good reputation in Snyder. The Times noted that he *"has been consistently keeping out of trouble with law enforcement officials up until now."* But when Selective Service was announced, the thirty-year-old "Peg Leg" was the only eligible resident in Scurry County who failed to register.

That was back in September. It was November now. The board's patience had run out.

Mr. Guinn rushed to the Scurry County Jail. There he was met by members of the draft board who *"refused to comment on this strange case- the case of a colored man who isn't, intentionally, a draft dodger, but a person who has entirely the wrong conception of just what the Selective Service Act means."*

The sheriff led Mr. Guinn upstairs and placed a chair opposite the cell that held Henry DuBaugh. When asked by the journalist for a statement in his defense, "Peg Leg" offered the following response.

"Take, for example, a person what becomes guilty of going out and shooting someone. He is locked up and sent to prison for a long, long time. But when they comes after a person to serve in an armed force, give him a uniform and a gun, he is allowed, when necessary, to shoot all the people he can.

"This being the case, I just waited for Uncle Sam to come after me. I don't feel, however, that the Scurry County draft board holds my viewpoints against me, but had to comply with them laws what are made in Washington."[3]

About a month later, on December 19th, The Scurry County Times paused to reminisce about the last world war as a new one continued to escalate.

"Historians rate it as an amazing fact that during the World War days, German propagandists tried in vain to undermine the loyalty of American Negroes, even going so far as to promise the colored folks special territory In the United States where they could rule themselves. This fact Is brought to light by certain investigators, at a time when Nazi agents find the loyalty of our 13,000,000 Negroes is as strong as ever.

"Members of the colored race are often accused of nearly every kind of misdemeanor under the sun, but they have never been and are not now lacking In loyalty to the nation which emancipated them after a period of forced servitude, and allowed members of the race to gain for themselves a secure position in our social and economic setup."[10]

■■

At the time of this writing there are three known sets of The Scurry County Times on microfilm. None of them contain the years 1941, 1942, 1944, or 1945. No physical copies are known to have survived to the present.

■■

Founded in 1925, The Brotherhood of Sleeping Car Porters was the first labor union led by African Americans to be granted a charter by the American Federation of Labor. In January of 1941, with the United States preparing for a war that seemed increasingly inevitable, Sleeping Car Porter President A. Philip Randolph called for a demonstration to desegregate the U.S. military and ban racially discriminatory hiring in war-related industries. The first March On Washington Movement received a groundswell of support from Black communities nationwide.[11]

As the date of the demonstration drew near, President Roosevelt requested a meeting with the movement's leadership. In a 1968 interview for the U.S. Library of Congress, A. Phillip Randolph remembered: *"I was called to a conference with [President Roosevelt]. The president made, as his first comment, 'Mr. Randolph, we can't have 100,000 Negroes marching on Washington. If anything such as that were to occur, we wouldn't be able to manage them. We'd have bloodshed and death. Now let us get down to business here and find out what can be done.'"*[12]

The two men reached a compromise. On June 25, 1941, President Roosevelt signed Executive Order 8802. The order mandated that *"there shall be no discrimination in the employment of workers in defense industries or government because of race, creed, color, or national origin."* The March on Washington, originally scheduled for the following week, was cancelled. Twenty-three years later, some of the language in Executive Order 8802 would be incorporated into the Civil Rights Act of 1964.[13]

While the March On Washington Movement may have won a victory for nondiscrimination in government hiring, its goal of an integrated military was unsuccessful. Shortly after Roosevelt's executive order was issued, Secretary of War Henry Stimson clarified his department's position.

"It is the policy of the War Department that the services of Negroes will be utilized on a fair and regular basis. In line with this policy, provision will be made as follows:

"The strength of the Negro personnel of the Army of the United States will be maintained on the general basis of the proportion of the Negro population to the country. [...]

"The policy of the War Department is not to intermingle colored and white enlisted personnel in the same regimental organizations. This policy has been proven satisfactory over a long period of years and to make changes would produce situations destructive to morale and detrimental to the preparations for national defense."[14]

■■

Cottonseed oil is extremely flammable. On Monday, November 16, 1942, The Fuller Cottonseed Oil Mill southeast of Snyder burst into flames. The fire burned for several days. With the geographic and economic heart of Snyder's Black section in ruins and many of its residents now out of work or fighting overseas, The Flat would experience an escalating cycle of poverty-driven crime and reactionary policing throughout the middle 1940s.

The Fuller Cottonseed Oil Mill burns. November 16, 1942. Courtesy Scurry County Museum

Anderson Davis Sr. was among those left unemployed after the fire. In November of 1942, "Big Anderson" would be arrested for possession of liquor in a dry county for the first time. Over the next decade, "Big Anderson" Davis and his teenage son "Little Anderson" Davis Jr. would become two of the most notorious bootleggers in the history of Scurry County.[15]

██

When the Scurry County Times microfilm picks back up in early January of 1943, the people of Snyder had been at war for one year and three weeks. Teacher E.M. Watson announced that he would be leaving the Dunbar School in the fall for a new job in Big Spring.[16]

The Navy's Guadalcanal Campaign ended with the Battle of Rennell Island on January 30, 1943. The cost of victory had been 7,100 Americans killed, 7,700 wounded, 615 aircraft destroyed, and 29 ships lost.

Two weeks later, on February 17th, the US Navy recruiting station in Big Spring announced that *"as many 17-year-old boys of Scurry, Kent, Borden, Fisher, Howard, and other counties of this area who can be recruited will be enlisted in the US Navy. [...]*

"Only requirement for immediate enlistment of 17-year-olds is a birth certificate and consent papers, properly signed and notarized by the applicant's parent or guardian."[17]

On March 4th, 24-year-old domestic worker Sidalia Hutchinson became *"the first Snyder colored girl- and one of the first in this trade zone- to be accepted by the WAACS, Women's Army Auxiliary Corps."* The Corps, created in May of 1942 as an official all-volunteer women's branch of the U.S. Army, began active duty in July of 1943.[18]

As a reaction to war rationing, the Depression-era custom of planting food at home was revived and rebranded by the federal government as "Victory Gardens." By 1943 rows of potatoes and squash had replaced the grass in many front lawns and back yards of Snyder.[19]

In early April of 1943 Mount Olive Baptist Church began holding daily prayer services for the safety of local boys in military service. Every afternoon at 3 p.m., a rotating roster of pastors and deacons tended to the spiritual needs of worried parents, children, and spouses in The Flat. The white residents of Snyder were invited and some services were well attended. Church officials at Mount Olive announced their intention to continue the regular prayer meetings for *"as long as the Lord leads."*[20]

At 3 a.m. on April 8th, bootlegger "Big Anderson" Davis was arrested for the fifth time in six months. Two hundred and ten quarts of beer and three gallons of wine were taken from his home in The Flat by Scurry County Constable J.G. "Pop" Galyean and two men from the Texas Liquor Control Board. The law enforcement officers described the raid as a *"real haul"* and said that Mr. Anderson paid out one hundred dollars in fines and court costs *"like a slot machine."* Mr. Davis went home, slept off the rough night, and went on another beer run.[21]

When the 1942-'43 school year drew to a close, the Scurry County Times counted 900 students attending Snyder Public School and thirty-eight at Dunbar. One hundred high school boys from Snyder had already been drafted for military service. At Dunbar, where classes did not exceed the junior high level, attendance was unaffected.[22]

On May 13, 1943, the last Thursday before graduation, the *"Dixie Land Negro Minstrel Show"* premiered at the Snyder Public School Auditorium. Blackface minstrelsy was a popular form of live entertainment in Scurry County throughout the early 20th Century, but this production by the Snyder Lion's Club was the best selling show of its kind in the town's history. It was also the first to be photographed for the local paper.[23,24]

The Scurry County Times. May 6, 1943.[25]

Tickets sold for twenty-five and fifty-five cents at the door or twenty cents in advance at Stinson Drug No. 1. The show grossed $418 during its first performance.[25]

■■

It is uncertain when the Nite Spot first began to serve customers in Snyder's Black district. But by 1943 the restaurant was already a widely known speakeasy where customers from Snyder could enjoy a cold glass of illicit beer with a hot plate of barbecue. Booze-to-go could be purchased from the front porch of "Big Anderson" Davis just down the street.

Will Clay, founder and proprietor of Snyder's Nite Spot Cafe, had a golden tooth that would shine bright enough to make a person squint. Born with pale skin and blue eyes, Mr. Clay could pass for white in cities where he was not well known.[26]

The sheriff rarely busted anyone in the daytime when the more respectable people of Snyder dropped by to enjoy the best pork sausages in the county. But after dark the little cafe in The Flat was notorious for its private rooms where the more taboo vices of gambling and prostitution were available to those on Mr. Clay's good side. The Nite Spot was routinely mentioned or alluded to in Snyder's crime reports throughout the 1940s.

One night in February of 1943, thirty-six-year-old Erma "Horse" Hardrick got into a fight with with "Big Anderson" Davis near the old bootlegger's home in The Flat. Hardrick, *a negro of good reputation* according to the Scurry County Times, *"conked"* the old bootlegger in the head with a beer bottle. The reason for the scuffle is unknown. Four months passed with no further incidents reported between the two men.

During the 1943 Juneteenth celebrations at the Nite Spot, "Little Anderson" Davis Jr. took revenge on his father's behalf. The nineteen-year-old bootlegger shot "Horse" Hardrick multiple times, leaving him dead on the floor of the Nite Spot. There were dozens of witnesses. *"Considerable disorder resulted throughout the entire colored section when shots were fired,"* noted the Snyder paper, *"and the full story of the killing is expected to be unfolded Monday before members of a district court grand jury."*[27]

JUNETEENTH CELEBRATION . . .

Barbecued Chicken, Beef and Pork. White folks will like this fine cooking.

Nite Spot Cafe

Just South of Old Ice Plant   Will Clay

The Scurry County Times. June 17, 1943.[26]

"Little Anderson" was taken to the Scurry County Jail to await trial. "Horse" Hardrick was brought to the Odom Funeral Home and then to Snyder Cemetery where his grave remains unmarked as of this writing. Sheriff John Lynch resigned within days of the incident.[28]

On June 24th, five days after the shooting at the Nite Spot, an anonymous letter was published in the Scurry County Times.

"Gentlemen:

"I think it is time there was something done about this Negro killing, and Negroes running night spots. A good hard-working Negro killed by a young smart Negro bootlegger that has never worked a day in his life; and lots of others that are doing the same as he is, loafing around bootlegging. And lots of Negro women ruining our young boys, and lots of our men too.

"But they will let him go free, and white men will go on his bond so he will be free to kill and bootleg so our men and boys can buy what they want.

"Can't there be something done about it?

"*-Anonymous of Snyder*"[29]

A response appeared in the following issue.

"Editor, The Times:

"In many ways I agree with the letter printed in last week's Times concerning the negro killing. Yet in my opinion there is one statement demanding a rebuff. It's entirely up to the white man whether the negro today is white or whether he stays black and the way he was in the beginning and the way he should stay. The boys and men who are being ruined by the 'lots of negro women' haven't had very far to go in immorality. They had no morals to begin with.

"The citizens of Scurry County should wake up to the corruptness that exists in our local government. The bootlegging mess in Snyder and Scurry County is a blot on it that will take a long time to erase. Why can the negro population, as well as some of the white, continue this practice? Of course it is because a certain class of white people support it.

"The majority of the whites do not support it, however, and these are the people who should question the resignation of a sheriff who has done everything in his power to rid the county of this lawlessness. Also it should make people ashamed that their own home officer couldn't carry on on the salary he was receiving. If you wonder why he could not when others did, perhaps it was because he did not play into the hands of the minority of negroes and white trash who insist on booze-fighting.

"*-Miss Anonymous of Fluvanna.*"[30]

Anderson Davis Jr. was indicted by a grand jury for the "*murder, with malice aforethought*" of Erma Hardrick. Mr. Davis, who was known to brag about having been a bootlegger since the age of eight, was returned to the Scurry County Jail.[31]

As the summer of 1943 came to a close, Scurry County Times staff writer Leon Guinn lamented the unrest on the home front in an opinion piece.

"There has not been an editorial column in many papers that has not contained comment on the recent trouble between the colored and white people on the home front. Detroit, Michigan, was the scene of a disgraceful riot. There has been more comment on race discrimination since the war began—with the colored boys fighting as nobly as the white ones, for their country's cause.

"Foreign countries do not look upon the race problem as do we, and they have not understood the American segregation of the colored; the fact that the colored people mainly are confined to menial labor; and extra propaganda pushed by our enemies is making a ticklish matter worse in the eyes of our Allies. The strike, disorders in California, and two recent lynchIngs are all adding up to some embarrassing moments for us.

"Perhaps we should refrain from criticism of England's policy toward India and figure out how to handle our domestic difficulties."[32]

■■

Dentist Lonnie E. Smith of Houston sued Harris County election official S.S. Allwright for his right to vote in the 1943 Texas Democratic Party primaries. The US Supreme Court agreed to hear the case. On November 19th, the Scurry County Times offered their opinions.

"Texas, traditionally rich in political history and native land of some of the nation's most unusual political characters, will get a considerable amount of publicity during the coming weeks if the U. S. Supreme Court declares the so-called Texas 'white primary' unconstitutional. The case, according to veteran Supreme Court observers, hinges on the right of the Democratic Party Convention in Texas to determine who shall vote in primary elections. Negroes, barred under primary rules, claim It amounts to a denial of suffrage since the Democratic Party Is virtually the only party in Texas.

"Fact that the Supreme Court has accepted the case for review, although it upheld the law several years ago, indicates it will probably reverse itself and is causing a number of Democratic

Congressmen to worry about the probable decision—pointing out that it will add to the administration's troubles in the Lone Star State.

"Despite the rumors rampant in other states, including such neighboring places as Oklahoma and Arkansas, Texas has a lot less trouble with racial affairs than the average outsider might believe. What few racial riots have occurred In the state this year, including a few at army camps over colored soldiers, have been of a minor nature and nothing to cause undue alarm."[33]

The Supreme Court decided the case of *Smith v. Allwright* on April 3, 1944. Racially exclusive primaries in Texas and across the nation were declared unconstitutional. Poll taxes would continue to curb the political participation of Black Texans for decades come, but twenty-one years of total exclusion from state-level power had finally come to an end.

■■

S adly, the Scurry County Times microfilm sets from 1944 and 1945 do not survive to the present. Their absence amplifies the importance of the 1943 newspapers as a partial chronicle of Snyder's wartime experiences.

Most issues of the 1943 Scurry County Times included a list with the name, classification, and draft number of men examined by the county draft board. Residents of The Flat were easy to identify by the mandatory inclusion of the word *"colored"* next to their names.[34-53]

■■

I n the late spring of 1944, seventh grade student and future Snyder city councilwoman Vernest Newsome graduated from the Dunbar School. It would have been illegal for her to attend the high school less than one mile away where the draft had left many desks sitting vacant. Instead Miss Newsome would live with her aunt and uncle in Dallas while she earned her diploma.[54]

■■

Victory in Europe finally came on May 8, 1945. All monuments and public symbols of the Nazi government were to be destroyed or removed from public view.

World War II ended with the surrender of Japan on September 2nd. Some 257,798 Black Texans registered for Selective Service during the conflict. About 80,000 of them were called to serve. Much like their parents' generation in the previous world war, those who served in Europe were exposed to societies that treated them as equals.[55]

In the second half of 1945 the wartime economy gradually returned to civilian hands in Scurry County and throughout the USA. The Great Depression was indisputably over and the boys from The Flat began to come home. Across the railroad tracks to the north, the City of Snyder was entering a period of uninterrupted economic growth that would continue for the next sixteen years.

CHAPTER 9
BREWED IN THE CAULDRON

"Stop Racial Strife In Time"

"While there is yet time to nip the movement in the bud, not only our Texas lawmakers but every Texas citizen should be on the alert for eruptions of racial strife now being brewed in the cauldron of the Communists and those who would arouse civil warfare in this state and the South.

"Unless we take the proper steps in time—be they drastic or not—we will one day be faced in the South with civil warfare that could indeed prove serious.

"The fomenters of racial strife are going about their unholy business behind darkened curtains, and in the cheap atmosphere of back rooms in many more communities than the average citizen thinks. If we allow this scum of our generation to continue sowing seeds of discord we will reap a whirlwind that will not be easily or bloodlessly stopped.

"Those who plan only strife and teach hatred for the American way of life and for our present legal status for the colored people would promptly be executed as traitors and criminals in any other country except easy-going America. It will take unity on every front to pull us safely through the days of economic upheaval and readjustment which lie immediately ahead."

-The Scurry County Times. November 21, 1946.[1]

To the Socialists of Scurry County

I hereby call a meeting of the Socialists to be held in Snyder, Saturday, August 19, at 1:30 p. m.

J. W. GLADSON,
Co. Chairman, Socialist Party.

The Snyder Signal. August 11, 1911.[2]

The political rhetoric of the Second Red Scare began to creep into The Scurry County Times in the fall of 1946. As foreign relations quickly deteriorated with the Soviet Union, a nation-wide panic began to spread that communist infiltrators were working to subvert education, entertainment, religion, and the federal government of the United States.

One tactic of this supposed conspiracy was to promote racial equality as a means of destabilizing society in the American south. Newspapers in the US during this period frequently portrayed civil rights advances for African Americans as victories for Soviet interests. For many white conservatives, Jim Crow-style segregation became regarded as an important bulwark against the creeping advance of communism in America.[1]

It was a tune that the people of Scurry County had heard before.

The Socialist Party of Scurry County was founded in the summer of 1911 by J.W. Gladson of the Dunn community. By December of that year, they had more than forty members. The socialists' ideas appealed to tenant farmers advocating for better labor conditions, Protestant groups promoting liquor prohibition, and educated women from Snyder pushing for their right to vote. Anyone in favor of higher taxes on industrialists and landlords to counter the wealth inequities that had developed during the Gilded Age was also welcome. The socialists held regular meetings in Snyder where they distributed their party's newspaper, The Rebel.

All of that changed in 1917. The Bolshevik Revolution in Russia created widespread fears that radical groups would attempt a revolution in America. Leftist organizations of the period were frequently conflated with Bolsheviks in the press.

President Wilson used his wartime powers to suppress The Rebel by filing criminal charges and refusing to accept any socialist newspapers at US post offices. The paranoia of the period helped to enable the rise of nationalist and nativist organizations like the second Ku Klux Klan. By 1919, the old Socialist Party of Scurry County had fallen silent.

Three decades later, during the onset of the Cold War in the late 1940s, a second Red Scare panic emerged. But this time the alleged domestic enemies were concealing their identities. Anyone could be a secret communist.

There were real Soviet spies in the US during this period, but an avalanche of accusations from the public made actual subversives more difficult for US intelligence agencies to detect. Snyder's socialists of the 1910s and its progressives of the 1930s were all mature adults in 1946. Their neighbors remembered.[2-7]

■■

Floyd "Dad" Wellington took a running start and shoved with all his might. Scurry County Sheriff Earl Strawn flew backwards out the door of the little house and into the moonlit gloom of the front yard. The sheriff sprang back onto his feet, but "Dad" was already upon him. The two men grappled and pummeled one another into the street. "Dad" grabbed the sheriff's revolver from its holster and backed quickly away.

As "Dad" raised the gun to fire, Sheriff Strawn lunged hard to his left. A single shot rang out through The Flat and echoed among the homes of nearby Snyder. A .38 caliber bullet tore through the soft tissue of the sheriff's right bicep, shattering his humerus bone. Strawn landed hard in the middle of the street, cradling his wounded arm. The moon turned red in a muddy puddle on Avenue M.

Voices pleaded from the nearby windows to call an ambulance for the wounded lawman. *"No!,"* shouted Mr. Wellington. *"Let the bastard die!"*

Anyone who touched a telephone would get the next bullet.

Sheriff Strawn and "Dad" Wellington had known each other for a while. During a routine bust at the home of "Big Anderson" Davis in February of 1946, the sheriff caught Mr. Wellington running a dice game. "Big Anderson", with his virtual monopoly on Snyder's most popular vice, paid the fines and walked away. Unlike the old bootlegger, "Dad" Wellington couldn't afford to simply ignore the two gambling charges that were filed against him.

The night of the shooting in August of 1946 began as a repeat of the February incident. Sheriff Strawn was *"making his usual Saturday night check-up on the colored section in the south* part of Snyder," when he "discovered a very enthusiastic craps game in the home of Wellington." The sheriff "watched the action for some minutes from an open door in the rear of the house, and then went around to make his entrance from the front." When fifty-five-year-old Floyd "Dad" Wellington charged at the door, Sheriff Strawn "pulled out his 'black jack,' but the charge of the negro with both of his hands pushed him into the front yard."

In an interview from the local hospital, Sheriff Strawn couldn't recall exactly how long he was lying in the street.

"After finally permitting other colored people to place a call for an ambulance, Wellington strolled away toward a creek to the south of the colored section, firing another shot some distance away, but Strawn said he did not know in which direction the negro had fired, or for what purpose."[8]

What followed was the largest law enforcement standoff in the county's history up to that time. The Flat was sealed off by the Snyder Police, Scurry County Sheriff's Department and the Texas Highway Patrol. A pair of Texas Rangers eventually approached the house, convinced "Dad" of the hopelessness of the situation, and delivered him to Lubbock pending trial.

Sheriff Earl Strawn circa 1944.
Courtesy Scurry County Sheriff's Department.

Four months later, on the afternoon of December 5, 1946, Floyd "Dad" Wellington was brought back to Snyder where he plead guilty to the shooting of Sheriff Strawn. Wellington was returned to Lubbock to await his transfer to a state penitentiary for twelve years.[8-10]

■■

The end of school segregation in Texas began with Houston postal worker Heman Sweatt. Mr. Sweatt met all of the necessary requirements to attend the University of Texas School of Law in 1946. Except one. When he was rejected by the school on the basis of his race, he made an appeal to the Texas Attorney General's office.

"People of this entire trade area should be intensely interested in the test case Texas faces on the question of whether it is providing adequate higher educational facilities for Negro students," reported the Scurry County Times. "The University of Texas, for example, rejected the application of a Negro, Heman Marion Sweatt of Houston, for admission to its law school, pending an opinion for Attorney General Grover Sellers on the question of 'whether or not a person of Negro ancestry, otherwise qualified for admission into the University of Texas, may legally be admitted as a student.'

"Dr. Painter, acting president of the university, noted in his letter asking the opinion that 'it has never been the policy of this institution to admit negroes as students,' and that it was the first time in the history of the school that a negro has presented himself for admission.' Dr. Painter says further that 'it has been the policy of the Texas Legislature to provide for the separation of races for the purpose of higher education as well as separating the races in the public schools.'[...]

"The present test case is expected to settle the matter of admitting Negroes to higher institutions of learning, with whites, for many years down the line. If we let the bars down now, we might as well prepare to witness another racial and social revolution."[11]

On May 15, 1946, after Texas Attorney General Grover Sellers decided to uphold school segregation in the state, Heman

Sweatt sued the president of UT Law. The judge in the *Sweatt v. Painter* case denied Mr. Sweatt's admission request and ordered the State of Texas to create an institution that was separate from, but equal to, The University of Texas Law School within six months.

The Texas State University for Negroes Law School, known in later years as The Thurgood Marshall School of Law at Texas Southern University, was founded as a result of the initial *Sweatt v. Painter* ruling. For now Mr. Sweatt would study law at TSUN, but in time the case would make its way to the US Supreme Court.[12]

In July of 1946 all African American enlistments and reenlistments into the US armed forces were suspended. The order was described to the press as *"based on a percentage basis in all categories of nationalities (or racial colors) and not on discrimination."*[13]

A few days later, an opinion piece in the Scurry County Times reacted to the army's decision.

"On the same day Selective Service reduces occupational exemptions to practically nil, the Army orders suspension of Negro general enlistments. [...] It invites the question: Why shut off the flow of voluntary recruits, whatever their color? And from one quarter, at least, comes the cry of racial discrimination.

"The Army explains that it is simply following its policy of keeping the ratio of Negro to white soldiers at the same level as that in the United States total population - one in ten. Negroes have been enlisting for some months at twice this rate. [...]

"[L]arge numbers of Negroes, frankly, still present the Army with a serious problem. It is not that they cannot be made into good soldiers, some Negro outfits have been of the best. But whole regiments of Negroes cannot be stationed just anywhere where there is an Army post, without difficulties - perhaps even more in the North than in the South.

"This is not an indictment of the Negro. It is not an indictment of the Army. It does point an accusing finger at all the apathy, intolerance, ignorance, and fear which keeps what America calls its 'Negro Problem' a long way from solution."[14]

■■

On the night of December 6-7, 1946, one day after "Dad" Wellington was sentenced for shooting Sheriff Strawn, the *"biggest crack-down on record"* against bootlegging in Scurry County descended upon The Flat. Twenty-six complaints of possessing liquor in a dry county, an *"all-time record,"* were filed against ten people. Among them were the golden-toothed Night Spot restaurateur Will Clay and the recently-released felon and bootlegger "Little Anderson" Davis Jr. His father, "Big Anderson," plead guilty to four counts, paid $494 in cash, and went home like he always did.[15-17]

Meanwhile, in Austin, Marion Price Daniel Sr. became the youngest Attorney General in the history of Texas at the age of thirty-seven on January 21, 1947. Price Daniel, as he preferred to be called, joined the Texas House of Representatives in 1939 and was unanimously elected Speaker in 1943. After serving in the Pacific as a Judge Advocate General during World War II, Second Lieutenant Daniel returned to Texas and immediately began his campaign for Attorney General.

Over the course of his career, Price Daniel would be elected to more state offices than any other person in the history of Texas. He would also be the state's greatest champion for school segregation.[18]

Back in Snyder the school year was coming to an end in the late spring of 1947. A "Tacky Party" was held at Dunbar on May 8th. The students performed for the public dressed as nursery rhyme characters. Costumes included Old Mother Hubbard, Grandma Gray, and Humpty Dumpty. Dunbar PTA president Bessie Newsome jokingly assured the people of Scurry County that the musical performance would *"be a program of dignity and inspiration."*[19,20]

May 23, 1947 was graduation day at Dunbar. The one-room school was open to the public for an exhibition of the students' work during the 1946-'47 school year. A banquet was served for students, family, and friends of the school by the Dunbar PTA and the Snyder Woman's Club. Two eighth grade students, Willie Faye Clay and James Otis Archie, were the honored graduates.[21]

The most prominent business in The Flat in the summer of 1947 was the Social Hour Cafe (formerly The Nite Spot). Despite the new name and ownership, The Social Hour was just as much of a magnet for lawlessness as its predecessor had been.

George Davis, the restaurant's owner, did not possess the same relaxed demeanor as his golden-toothed predecessor, Will Clay. On October 12, 1947, Mr. Davis murdered his employee, Sam Cole, in a fit of rage.

OPEN PIT
Barbecue

Whether it's a side of a beef, mutton or a young pig, you'll be glad to know Will Clay is ready to barbecue meat to your order.

Barbecuing on Friday, Saturday and Sunday

TELEPHONE 9521
FOR FREE DELIVERY IN THE SNYDER CITY LIMITS

For that week-end picnic or family gathering, have meat barbecued for the event by

WILL CLAY

YOUR   BUSINESS   APPRECIATED !

The Scurry County Times. May 22, 1947.[16]

Sam Cole was sixty-four years old on the night he was killed. Mr. Cole had come to town from Texarkana in 1946 and soon started working at The Social Hour. After an argument between the two men over a gambling debt, Davis shot Cole point-blank in the abdomen with a .38 caliber revolver in front of at least twenty-five witnesses. The bullet *"left a hideous wound"* according to The Scurry County Times. Cole died five hours later at Snyder General Hospital.

After defaulting on a $5,000 bond, George Davis spent the next five months in the Scurry County Jail. After a three-day trial, the jury reached a verdict in one hour and fifteen minutes. On March 24, 1948, George Davis was sentenced to ten years in prison for the murder of Sam Cole.[22]

■■

In the late fall of 1947, after a year of meticulous research, The President's Committee on Civil Rights presented their findings to President Truman. The president now had to present these ideas to Congress despite the anticipated objections of numerous southern senators. On February 2, 1948, the president delivered his Special Message to the Congress on Civil Rights.

"Today, the American people enjoy more freedom and opportunity than ever before. Never in our history has there been better reason to hope for the complete realization of the ideals of liberty and equality.

"We shall not, however, finally achieve the ideals for which this Nation was founded so long as any American suffers discrimination as a result of his race, or religion, or color, or the land of origin of his forefathers.

"Unfortunately, there still are examples—flagrant examples —of discrimination which are utterly contrary to our ideals. Not all groups of our population are free from the fear of violence. Not all groups are free to live and work where they please or to improve their conditions of life by their own efforts. Not all groups enjoy the full privileges of citizenship and participation in the government under which they live.

"We cannot be satisfied until all our people have equal opportunities for jobs, for homes, for education, for health, and for

142

political expression, and until all our people have equal protection under the law. [...]

"I recommend, therefore, that the Congress enact legislation at this session directed toward the following specific objectives:

"1. Establishing a permanent Commission on Civil Rights, a Joint Congressional Committee on Civil Rights, and a Civil Rights Division in the Department of Justice.

"2. Strengthening existing civil rights statutes.

"3. Providing Federal protection against lynching.

"4. Protecting more adequately the right to vote.

"5. Establishing a Fair Employment Practice Commission to prevent unfair discrimination in employment.

"6. Prohibiting discrimination in interstate transportation facilities.

"7. Providing home-rule and suffrage in Presidential elections for the residents of the District of Columbia.

"8. Providing Statehood for Hawaii and Alaska and a greater measure of self-government for our island possessions.

"9. Equalizing the opportunities for residents of the United States to become naturalized citizens.

"10. Settling the evacuation claims of Japanese-Americans [...]

"We know that our democracy is not perfect. But we do know that it offers a fuller, freer, happier life to our people than any totalitarian nation has ever offered.

"If we wish to inspire the peoples of the world whose freedom is in jeopardy, if we wish to restore hope to those who have already lost their civil liberties, if we wish to fulfill the promise that is ours, we must correct the remaining imperfections in our practice of democracy.

"We know the way. We need only the will."[23]

President Truman's civil rights proposals were poorly received by a majority of white conservatives in western Texas. They expressed this disapproval to their representatives. In early February of 1948, as President Truman's civil rights recommendations were being debated in Congress, Texas 19th

Congressional District representative George H. Mahon wrote the following letter to The Scurry County Times.

"The so-called civil rights program includes proposals for the passage of federal anti-poll tax and anti-lynching legislation, plus a so-called FEPC law and legislation which would prohibit the segregation of whites and colored in inter-state travel, and eventually in the schools. In previous years we have been confronted with parts of this program and by voice and vote I have always opposed it and I am continuing my active opposition.

"I maintain that a federal anti-poll tax law would be unconstitutional because Article 1 of the U.S. constitution provides that the states, not the federal government, shall fix the qualifications of voters. The people of Texas, if they desire, can amend the Texas constitution which provides for the poll tax and substitute a system of registration, but the U.S. Congress has no authority to indirectly amend the Texas constitution.

"Lynching is a crime which is local in character and should not be handled by Washington authorities but by local and state officials. As to the FEPC and the proposals to prevent the segregation of the whites and colored on railroad trains and in schools, I take the position of those who say that the federal government has no right to interfere with local laws and customs in this respect, and that our system for segregation of the races is necessary and in the best interest of both races.

"But many of the Northern Democrats and many Republicans are loudly advocating the so-called civil rights program in an effort to get the negro and minority votes In the doubtful states of the North and East.

"The Republicans have a majority in both the House and Senate. Therefore, the only chance to stop this program is through a non partisan fight against it by both Democrats and Republicans such as proved successful in our effort to eliminate the so-called civil rights rider from the appropriation bill."[24]

President Truman's civil rights policies were creating a widening rift between conservatives and progressives in the Democratic Party. The issue threatened to alienate southern states from the New Deal Coalition that the late President Roosevelt had so carefully constructed.

"*Texas, which always manages to keep a lot of fire and color in state and national politics, is likely to bob up this year as a real trouble spot in the stemming Southern Democratic revolt*", wrote Scurry County Times writer Leon Guinn.

"*It is unfortunate that Harry Truman came forth at this time with his civil rights program. Truman badly misjudged Southern reaction when he opened up both barrels to corral the 'nigger' vote. We only have about 10,000,000 Negroes in the U.S. and perhaps 75 per cent of them could not otherwise qualify to vote after poll taxes were eliminated.*"[25]

Mr. Guinn also observed the president's deteriorating chances of winning the 1948 election.

"*President Truman, according to rather reliable sources on Capitol Hill, is resigned somewhat to a defeat next fall and henceforth will conduct himself accordingly. He tells close friends that he 'will do the best for his country' throughout the rest of his term, regardless of where the chips keep falling. [...]*

"*Although Harry Truman got off badly on his civil rights program as far as the South is concerned, he declares he will stand by this part of his strategy until he ends his tenure of office.*

"*Sane, impartial observers have declared for the past decade that the South's problem with the Negro race has been vastly exaggerated and overdrawn, world without end. Had it not been during the past 10 years for a few groups like the Ku Klux Klan, the idea of fomenting strife would have, in the main, been ignored.*

"*The Negroes are a minority race in the South, unworthy of half the propaganda put out by 'pinks' and others about their sad mistreatment, separation in our schools, and illiteracy. If the North keeps on advocating racial equality with the Negroes, the South would indeed be more than willing to have them all shipped to some haven around New York, Brooklyn, and even in Washington, D. C., even if it took another "Father Divine" to provide the fried chicken, watermelons, and the gravy train.*"[26]

Resistance to any new civil rights legislation continued to grow throughout the spring of 1948. On April 22nd, The Scurry County Times reprinted an opinion piece from the Terry County Herald titled "*Negro Propaganda*" as their editorial of the week.

Despite its derisive tone and numerous historical inaccuracies, the article captures the mood of many white Texas conservatives in the late 1940s.

"Is the negro race really being held down as per the oft-repeated assertions of the Association for the Advancement of the Negro Race? The negro began to be brought to America, against his will, and as a slave some 200 years ago. They were brought over in foreign ships and sold to Southern white planters. Some 85 years ago, these slaves were freed by the proclamation of President Lincoln.

"Where this race came from, most of the time for 1,000 years or more, they have had their own tribal government. They are still barely out of a state of savagery.

"On the other hand, the 'held down' race in the U.S.A., and even in the South, are moderately well educated and informed. Many of them own good farms, some have good comfortable homes in towns and cities. Many have good jobs, and are in comfortable circumstances. They have their public supported schools and the churches of their own choice. They have begun to build hospitals and orphanages. To be perfectly clear, they are hundreds of years ahead of their own race In Africa, where they 'are not held down.'

"This comparison makes the wild assertions of the Advancement Association look silly. And, to top it all, there is not a negro in the United States that has the least idea of ever returning to his native shores to live unless as a missionary. So, unless we get some better reasons from this CIO-PAC organization to stir up trouble between whites and blacks in the South that the colored folks are being 'held down,' we shall have to conclude that it is some scheme to feather someone's nest."[27]

The odds of President Truman's reelection in November were growing slimmer by the week. In June, the Snyder paper reported again on the escalating backlash against the proposed civil rights reforms.

"[...] Texas Democrats can look for almost anything to happen before the presidential sweepstakes. The Negroes, as a race, are not such a problem in the South, but the people of the North and East will not let the issue alone. If they keep up certain

tactics, we will one day have civil warfare over America's racial problem.

"Given an ample supply of mesquite clubs, the South can keep the Negro race in line. But, if candidates keep stirring up the 'civil rights program,' the clubs could be put first to mighty good use on the pumpkin heads of some of the candidates.

"If we're going to go all the way on this rights program, we might as well get ready to openly sanction interracial marriage, for open love for people over race or color might as well be carried to its extremity."[28]

■■

Bundled up against the January frost of 1948, dozens of teenagers filed through the south door of Snyder Public School. Among them was high school student Donald Boren. There would be a show-and-tell today and the young Mr. Boren came prepared.

Miss Katherine Northcutt and Mrs. J.P. Nelson, history teachers at the two-story high school wing, called the students' names in turn. When Donald's turn came, he produced what the Scurry County Times called *"an especially interesting historical document"* from his bag.

The all-white classroom was presented with a bill of sale for *"Ned, an eight-year-old negro boy, for $700 in 1859."* The receipt belonged to Donald's great-grandfather who had purchased the enslaved child some eighty-nine years earlier.[29]

A few days later and three quarters of a mile away, "Big Anderson" Davis was arrested again for bootlegging. *"Ho, hum...",* wrote the Times, *"Big Anderson Davis was arrested and fined on charges of possession of intoxicants in a dry territory."* The serial scofflaw and long-time beer baron of Snyder was busted eleven times in 1947, paying a total of $1,225 in fines and $258.50 in court costs. He would be arrested another fifteen times in 1948.[30,31]

The Charity, Social, and Arts Club of Colored Women of Snyder was founded on April 3, 1948. Mary Baker was the organizer and founding president. Their first official act that spring was to create a "Friendship Quilt" to be sold in a raffle. Their efforts would eventually raise fifty-four dollars to buy a new piano for the students at Dunbar.[32,33]

The history of the Freemasons in Snyder began with the founding of Scurry Lodge #706 in 1890. At the time, and throughout most of the 20th century, the Grand Lodge of Texas forbade membership to the descendants of enslaved people. The tradition of Black Freemasonry in Scurry County began sometime in the spring of 1948 when a new lodge was organized by fifty-one year old Mount Olive deacon, John Baker.

The Scurry County Times reported that *"recently organized colored Masons of Hunter Lodge No. 920, A.F. & A.M., will stage formal installations of officers in an elaborate ceremony Sunday, May 9, at the Mount Olive Baptist Church, it was announced this week by John Baker, worshipful master. The rites will be [...] beginning at 2:00 o'clock p.m."*

"Visiting Masons from Sweetwater, Abilene, Loraine, Lamesa, and Rotan are expected to attend the installation services. [...]

Worshipful Master John Baker (front row, right) with Hunter Lodge No. 920 in 1952.
Courtesy Scurry County Museum.

"Following the installation ceremonies, a banquet will be served to the visiting colored folks, prepared by Lilac Court No. 180, auxiliary of the Masonic Lodge."[34,35]

■■

The impact of the oil boom in the summer of 1948 on the economy, demographics, politics, and culture of Snyder is difficult to overstate. It was, at the very least, the most transformative event in Scurry County's history since the destruction of its last buffalo herd seventy years earlier.

"Additional storage facilities at the Sun Oil Company's No. 1 Emil Schattle well, seven miles southwest of Snyder, that blew in for production of 500 barrels per day 10 days ago, had been filled first of the week, and the well was shut in again until the oil could be moved", reported the Scurry County Times on July 15, 1948.

"The new Scurry County discovery in the Canyon lime of the Pennsylvanian flowed naturally 149.1 barrels of 44.2 gravity oil in seven hours ending at 5:45 o'clock Friday morning. This almost filled storage and the well was shut in. Additional storage was brought in over the weekend, and this was filled first of the week.

"Production averaging 21.3 barrels hourly was from an open hole between 6,858 feet, where seven-inch casing was cemented, and 6,891 feet, the total depth. There was no water. Gas-oil ratio was 320-1. [...]

"Oil-cut mud flowed in 15 minutes and clean oil in 30 minutes. Tubing pressure when the well began flowing was 500 pounds; it was 625 pounds when the gauge ended. [...]

"Leases for several miles in every direction from the well continue to bring good prices this week. Several deals involving prices up to $600 per acre are reported to have been made since the strike early last week."[36,37]

Just two weeks earlier that same land had been valued at $18 per acre.[38]

More than two thousand oil wells would be drilled in Scurry County over the next two years and six months. During the same period, Snyder's population exploded from about 4,000 to more than 16,000 before finally stabilizing at about 11,000 near the end of 1951.[39,40]

CHAPTER 10

TO DAM HIGH

Vandalized road sign near Snyder, Texas. LIFE Magazine. December 5, 1949.[1]

"We Don't Want An Oil Boom"

"During the past two months, since interest in the possibilities of increased oil production in Scurry County has cropped out, many people have predicted a real boom for Snyder. We are frank to say that we hope an oil boom does not come.

"We hope Snyder never becomes a Burkburnett, a Desdemona, a Caddo, a Ranger or a Holliday. Sudden, over-grown, lop-sided oil boom towns just do not appeal to us—that will mushroom up for a few months, then the bottom drops out, and the town is left a shell—disheveled, vacant buildings, disrupted services, ruined streets, and what-have-you.

"Rather, we hope the new impetus given to our oil possibilities will mean more leasing of lands at good rates, casual development of our fields without waste and without depletion of the reserves under the surface. Nominal production for years to come will mean more to our county than gushers that soon play out.

"Much of the riff-raff of labor that follows the boom towns are of low moral character; unchaste women follow the boomers; crime breeds on the elements of of the boom.

"No, thank you, we do not care for an oil boom for our little city."

-The Scurry County Times. August 12, 1948.[2]

The Scurry County Rodeo Parade, 1948. Courtesy Scurry County Museum

Change was everywhere but it was hard to see at first. Snyder was, by all appearances, still the same little cow town and cotton hub it had been for 70 years.

The 12th annual Scurry County Rodeo was held on the evenings of July 14-17, 1948. Each night a parade would pass through the Snyder square before leading the crowds out to the rodeo grounds. The chamber of commerce offered cash prizes for the best float decorations.

"*Colored Folks Float Wins Prize in Parade,*" announced the Scurry County Times. "*Float entered by Mrs. Bessie Newsome, colored, and labeled 'Arkansas Travelers' won first prize of $15 in the Scurry County Rodeo parade in judging following the opening day's parade Wednesday evening, according to a report of the Judges to The Times Thursday morning. An early day wagon, drawn by horses, typified an almost-forgotten era of 40 and 50 years ago.*"3

For decades The Scurry County Times, like The Snyder Signal before it, hired correspondents to describe events in the small farming and ranching communities that surrounded the City of Snyder. Subscribers could read *"News from Fluvanna," "News from Dunn,"* or *"News from Ira"* in the back pages of The Times each week. *"News from the Flat"* made its debut on July 22, 1948.

"Editor's note- The Times is this week inaugurating a regular 'News from the Flat' column from the colored section of town. The paper and Mrs. Mary Baker, our correspondent, will appreciate the cooperation of the colored population in reporting items of news to the writer not later than Monday morning."

Prior to the summer of 1948, Snyder's Black community was often ignored in the local paper unless they were committing a crime. Instead of a dangerous area rife with gambling, booze, and armed criminals, Mary Baker's reporting revealed The Flat to be a vibrant community full of virtuous people living happy, normal lives.

"Mount Olive Baptist Church has a new pastor, Rev. A.S. Oliver who came from Abilene. He preached his first sermon as pastor in the church Sunday."

"Mrs. Odessa James was in Colorado City Monday writing insurance for the colored folks."[4]

"Mr. and Mrs. Ralph Johnson have a new baby, born August 5. The little lady, who weighed six pounds, 13 ounces, will be called Mary Elizabeth."[5]

"John Baker and Marshall Miles are at Galveston this week attending the colored A. F. & A. M. State convention. Charlie Hunter and Mrs. Mary Baker motored to Abilene with them from where they rode a special bus to Galveston."

"Howard Hunter, Anderson Davis Jr., and Matthew Davis are vacationing at Houston this week."[6]

Meanwhile, just north of Snyder's city limits, a makeshift trailer park and tent city was beginning to form as oilfield workers and their families poured into a town with limited space.

"Snyder People Urged To Provide Housing", exclaimed The Scurry County Times. *"Recent influx of scores of people attracted by oil activity in Scurry County has overtaxed the available housing supply in Snyder and folks are calling by the score for apartments and houses at The Times and the Chamber of Commerce office.*

"Chamber of Commerce officials this week issued an appeal to Snyder people to help the situation by arranging bedrooms, apartments, and rent houses for newcomers.

"People who have such apartments or rooms are asked to phone 12, the Chamber of Commerce, which is acting as a placement agency."[7]

■■

Frustrated by resistance to his civil rights agenda in Congress, President Truman signed Executive Order 9981 on July 26, 1948.

"It is hereby declared to be the policy of the President that there shall be equality of treatment and opportunity for all persons in the armed services without regard to race, color, religion, or national origin. This policy shall be put into effect as rapidly as possible, having due regard to the time required to effectuate any necessary changes without impairing efficiency or morale."

Presuming Truman's imminent defeat in November, Secretary of the Army Kenneth C. Royall initially refused to comply with the president's order to integrate the military. Further resistance from within the armed forces would continue to impede the process of full desegregation into the 1950s.

On July 29th, three days after Executive Order 9981 was signed, The Scurry County Times reported on the progress of Mr. Truman's other civil rights proposals.

"After seven days of wrangling, a platform pledging the Democratic party more specifically than ever before to work for basic constitutional civil rights was adopted after a floor fight which proved rather tame in view of the anticipated knock-down, drag-out battle. [...]

"The long-heralded southern revolt [...] failed to develop into the Dixie-wide proportions predicted. Only Mississippi's 22 delegates and 13 of Alabama's 26 stalked out of the convention in protest against President Truman's nomination and adoption of the strong civil rights plank.

"However, 263 remaining southern delegates registered that area's protest by voting for the presidential nomination of Sen.

Richard B. Russell of Georgia. Size of the protest vote indicated the Democratic Party still has a problem on its hands in the South."[8]

■■

Pressures were mounting on the administration at Snyder Public School in the late summer of 1948. The main school building would be pushed to its limits in the fall by a wave of new children arriving with the oilfield workers. New educational spaces would be needed, new teachers had to be hired, and new oil taxes would pay for it all. The paper announced the sale of many small rural school buildings in Scurry County, including an *"old negro schoolhouse"*.[9]

The Scurry County Times. October 21, 1948.[14]

After twenty-three years in operation, the Dunbar School of Snyder was sold off and two single-room buildings were constructed a few dozen yards away near the southeast corner of 34th Street and Avenue L. Officially named Snyder Negro School, the simple buildings were still referred to by teachers and students as Dunbar. As Snyder's Black section began to spread eastward across the R.S.&P. Railroad tracks, the colloquial name for the area east of Deep Creek and south of the city limits at 32nd Street was suddenly pluralized from "The Flat" to "The Flats".

Bernhard Bartels celebrated his twenty-ninth birthday in Snyder on August 26, 1948. In his 2016 memoir, *"96 And Going Strong"*, Mr. Bartels recalled the early months of Snyder's oil boom in the fall of 1948.

"A leasing rush got started and pretty soon several more wells came in, scattered over a pretty wide area in the northern and western parts of Scurry County. This really brought in the drilling rigs. [...] Since the rigs operated for 24 hours per day the night scene with all its lights looked like some giant Christmas display.

"There is no accurate record of how many people squeezed into what had been a sleepy little country town of 4,000 people. You could hear building going on in every direction. All the bigger oil companies built oil camps in their lease areas. Lumber sold as fast as it could be brought in by truck and rail car. In the meantime people were living in hundreds of travel trailers, some in hastily constructed trailer parks and one or two in many of the yards around town. Bob Dupree, a friend of ours, operated a bunkhouse and rented the bunks in eight hour shifts. All the bunks got was a change of sheets. Most of the eating places and a lot of other businesses never closed their doors. [...]

"Luckily Snyder did not boom and bust like many of the other oil field towns. We lost a lot of people but we did not collapse. Of course the continued flow of oil field money helped a lot."[10]

In early September of 1948, with the town's population exploding and a new school year fast approaching, Snyder Public School boasted a faculty of forty-two. The school offered three or four teachers each for grades one through six plus another six junior high teachers. The high school wing was staffed by four English teachers, two athletics coaches, and one teacher each for mathematics, social science, agriculture, homemaking, typing, and shorthand. The budget also provided for a librarian, a cook, and a custodian. Another six teachers would be hired before the end of the school year to accommodate the ever-growing flood of new students brought in by the oil boom.[11]

Less than a mile to the south, the entire faculty, staff, and administration of Snyder Negro School existed in the person of Eunice Johnson. The first day of school was October 11, 1948.

"Snyder Negro School opened Monday morning with an enrollment of 30, according to Eunice Johnson, teacher", wrote Scurry County Times correspondent Mary Baker in News from the Flat. *"City School Superintendent M. E. Stanfield and a number of parents and others were present for the opening.*

"Plans were made this week to organize a Parent-Teacher Association and a booster club through the school."[12]

Unlike the Dunbar School that preceded it, Snyder Negro School would soon have no need for a wood-burning stove since *"a 2,800-foot two-inch main was laid to the colored section of Snyder to give service to a section long requesting the use of natural gas for cooking and heating."*[13]

When Election Day finally came on November 2, 1948, the people of Scurry County dutifully cast their ballots. 88.4% of local residents who could afford the poll taxes voted for Harry Truman. While Snyder's support for the party that led them through the Depression remained strong for now, President Truman's civil rights policies had cost him vast swaths of the South. His campaign was successful, but only by a tiny margin.[15]

■■

None of the 1949 Scurry County Times issues survive to the present. At some point in that year, The Times was sold to Harte-Hanks Newspapers, Inc. A new staff was hired to prepare for the paper's relaunch as The Snyder Daily News in 1950. Mary Baker was not on the roster. After less than one year in publication, News from the Flat disappeared from the Snyder paper.[16]

During the same period, Central Elementary School was built just southeast of the main school campus. The building that had been known since 1923 as Snyder Public School became Snyder High School.[17]

In November of 1949, a correspondent from LIFE Magazine arrived in Snyder to report on the town's ongoing oil boom.

"Few of [Scurry County's] farmers imagined that a pool of black gold might lie under their pastures and cotton fields; they expected to go on fighting drought and dust storms the rest of their lives.

"But today Snyder and all of Scurry County are shaking with the excitement of the state's biggest oil boom since the 1930 east Texas strike. Snyder has mushroomed from 4,500 to nearly 15,000 population in less than a year, expects to reach 30,000 next year. The county boasts 200 producing wells, 133 more are being hopefully pushed down by drillers, and new ones are coming in almost every day.

An oilfield worker sleeps north of Snyder, 1949. Courtesy Scurry County Museum

"The oil is pouring from the vast Canyon Reef limestone formation, and geologists who had once written it off say there may be a whopping billion barrels of it down there (a 100-million-barrel field is regarded as a major strike). [...] [T]he big west Texas oil strike, which has choked Snyder with the industry's drillers, riggers, roustabouts, scouts, and promoters [...] has dazed a good many local residents who today find themselves on the exhilarating road to undreamed-of wealth. [...]

"Snyder happens to be dry, and while on Saturday night the jail may be so tightly packed with drunks that they have to stand up, most newcomers are so tired at the end of a shift that they are ready to fall into bed. But the dusty, oily atmosphere of Snyder is intoxicating enough without liquor fumes. The dingy Manhattan Hotel is packed with oil men scanning linen-backed maps of Scurry County (priced at $15 and obsolete every fortnight) and making big deals left and right. [...]

"For all the excitement there was little splurging so far by Scurry County's new rich. The Cadillacs and mansions would come later. 'They just want to jingle that money in their pockets awhile,' observed one oilman. And Farmer [Arthur "Booger Red"] Townsend, confidently waiting for his well to come in, opined grandly, 'A man don't need no million goddam dollars; all he needs is some comfortable circumstances.'"[1]

■■

When 1950 began, 12,010 people were living in Snyder. Two thirds of them had been there for less than two years. The city's public infrastructure was severely inadequate for the number of people it now served and a building spree resulted.[18]

A new church building for Mount Olive Baptist was constructed early in the year to handle a growing membership. A portion of the original building was used to create a foyer for the new sanctuary, preserving a physical and spiritual link to the congregation's origins that remains intact at the time of this writing. Construction cost $7,000.[19,20]

Around the same time, Northwest Elementary was built just outside the city limits to help accommodate the new children from the oilfield camps. Two massive bonds, one for $600,000 &

another for $3.5 million, were approved by the city council to further expand Snyder's overburdened school system.[21]

The first issue of The Snyder Daily News (SDN) was published on May 1, 1950. A far more capable organization than the newspapers that preceded it, SDN's reporting makes it possible to tell Snyder's stories in much greater detail during the second half of the 20th century.[16]

■■

Price Daniel was chosen to represent the University of Texas Law School in the *Sweatt v. Painter* hearings at the US Supreme Court. In the transcripts, the Texas Attorney General frequently refers to his NAACP counterparts Robert Carter and Thurgood Marshall as *"outside agitators."* The phrase would become his favorite pejorative for anyone who challenged traditional Southern customs.

As the case dragged on in Washington, Mr. Daniel wrote to Georgia Attorney General Eugene Cook to warn that segregated states would soon be *"deluged with law suits for entry of Negroes into white colleges, high schools, and grade schools."* Eleven southern attorneys general submitted briefs in support of continued segregation but were unable to sway the court.[22]

The *Sweatt v. Painter* case was decided on June 5, 1950. The Supreme Court unanimously ordered The University of Texas School of Law to admit Heman Sweatt as a student in September.

After four years as the subject of a nationally famous court case, the physical and psychological pressures had taken a toll on the brilliant Mr. Sweatt. As his health deteriorated, he began to miss classes and fail courses. Heman Sweatt would drop out of UT Law in the summer of 1952. But the *Sweatt v. Painter* decision would provide an important legal precedent for the *Brown v. The Board of Education* decision in 1954.

The building where Mr. Sweatt lost his initial court case in 1946 has since been renamed as The Heman Marion Sweatt Travis County Courthouse.

■■

Former Snyder Mayor Howard Garfield Towle suffered a heart attack in early November of 1950. The bright optometrist from Wisconsin who served the people of Snyder through the Great Depression, the Dust Bowl, and World War II died at Snyder General Hospital on November 11th. His wife, Mary Towle, donated about 200 acres to the city to create a park in his honor. As of this writing, Towle Park in Snyder still bears his name.

"For more than 20 years Dr. Towle was mayor of Snyder, a job which then, as now, was largely compensated in the gratitude of fellow citizens rather than monetary gain. During those years many improvements were made in the city, and it was during Dr. Towle's tenure and through his efforts that the Ku Klux Klan was prevented from organizing here. He went out of office in 1946."[23]

With the population of The Flats having almost doubled since the oil boom began, Eunice Daniel was still teaching Scurry County's Black children during the 1950-'51 school year. On the day before Christmas in 1950, The Snyder Daily News mentioned Snyder Negro School for the first time.

"Miss Ivan Perry's fourth grade students at the Northwest elementary school win the season's prize for unselfish giving. They sent the little Negro school south of town funny books, games, puzzles, and some clothing to swell the packages under the tree of less fortunate youngsters. The spirit grew, as all good ideas do, and now this fourth grade group are dead set on saving all magazines, games, and used toys to give to those who don't have them."[24]

As Snyder's oil boom approached its climax, the city's population briefly rose above 16,000 in early 1951. On February 13th, the school board approved plans for a new Snyder High School campus to be built in the southwest part of town near the new Towle Park. *"The board also approved the drafting of plans for a new Negro school. It is to be located on the site of the present building. Negro classes now meet in a two-room frame structure with outdoor toilet facilities."*[25]

Final approval came one month later on March 13, 1951, when the board approved *"a new school system administration building and a new Negro school. [...]*

161

"The Negro school will be built on the location of the present school in the Negro section of Southeast Snyder, which site was recently enlarged by the purchase of adjoining land. The building will include four classrooms, a kitchen, lunch room, an administration office, and rest rooms. The 55 by 126-foot one-story building will be constructed of brick and tile."[26]

About three weeks later "the Keenan Construction Co. of Monahans and Snyder was awarded contracts for constructing a new Negro School and an administration building for the Snyder school system last night [June 12, 1951].

"The school board accepted the Keenan bids, which were the two lowest of 17 bids presented by 8 contracting companies. The two totaled $189,448 [...] $79,671 on the administration building and $109,777 on the school [...] and a time of 245 days was allowed for the completion of both buildings." Another $2 million was set aside for the new high school and $650,000 to construct East Elementary and West Elementary with eighteen classrooms each.[21,27]

As the school year began in September of 1951, the total enrollment in Snyder's five white schools was 3,242. Just southeast of town at Snyder Negro School, two teachers were educating all the students of The Flats. "In the Negro school [...] by grades the enrollment is: seventh, 10; sixth, 6; fifth, 9; fourth, 8; third, 1; second, 15; first, 15."[28]

The school board asked Daniel and Rosetta Johnson, the new teachers at Snyder Negro School, to name to the new building being constructed next door on the former site of the Fuller Cottonseed Oil Mill. They called it The Abraham Lincoln School. Over the next fifteen years, Daniel Johnson's tireless work would make him the most important individual in the history of Black education in Scurry County.[29,30]

In the early months of 1952, after a year of rapid decline, Snyder's population stabilized at about 11,000. With much of its petroleum infrastructure already in place and an abundance of affordable housing for sale, Scurry County's oil boom had come to an end. But the oil still flowed. And the boom years had left a transformed society in their wake.

Scurry County began a 157-mile farm to market road improvement program in May of 1952. Paving work was done on 37th Street and the old wooden bridge across Deep Creek was replaced by a new span of concrete and steel.[31]

When the summer of 1952 began, the new Snyder High School campus was only about two thirds complete. Originally planned to be ready for classes in September, the construction crew was now hoping to finish by late January of 1953.

A significant upgrade from the old Snyder High, the new campus would boast more floor space than all of Snyder's other schools combined. Called *"the most modern in the state"* by The Snyder Daily News, the new school will accommodate 1,000 students. When completed, the building will feature thirty classrooms, a 350-seat cafeteria, a 1,500-seat gymnasium with a separate gym for girls, a 5,700 seat football stadium, a practice field, a library with private study rooms, a separate music library, a nine-room shop, band and choir rooms with elevated platforms, an audio-visual education room, a dark room for photographs, an x-ray machine, and a clinic.

Home economics will have its own section of the building *"including every type of room found in a home."* Eighty-five-foot wide steps will lead to a 1,000 seat auditorium with a forty-eight-foot high fly rail system to accommodate large sets. The main building will have an eighty-five-foot tall cooling tower and, despite being entirely fireproof, an alarm system and fire hose connections throughout.

Lincoln School under construction. Late November, 1951 (damaged microfilm).[32]

The original Lincoln School plaque. Courtesy Scurry County Museum.

The main structure will contain one mile of gas pipes, one mile of steam pipes, two miles each of water and sewer pipes, 135 miles of conduit, and 2,000 miles of electric wiring. Filling out the sprawling campus will be eight tennis courts, four volleyball courts, and three baseball diamonds. Covered walkways will connect all the smaller buildings to the large one.[33]

Thursday, September 4, 1952 was the first day of classes at the new Abraham Lincoln School. Principal Daniel Johnson, who also served as a teacher and the school's athletics coach, bounced from room to room throughout each day. His wife, Rosetta Johnson, prepared meals in the cafeteria. Three more teachers and two custodians rounded out the staff.[34,35]

In those early years, Lincoln School offered no classes beyond the Jr. High level. In his 1990 book *Reflections: An Album of West Texas History*, Scurry County historian Charles Anderson wrote that *"Blacks were not allowed to attend the regular schools in Snyder. [...] High school students were uprooted from their homes and sent away to other places where they lived in a barrack with other students. Most went to a Catholic school in San Antonio and their expenses were paid by Scurry County school funds. One local Black who still remembers being sent away said, 'I resented it like being in prison. It was the poorest boarding school at the least amount of money to the taxpayers in Snyder.'"*[19]

■■

After Democratic presidential candidate Adlai Stevens refused to endorse state control of coastal tidelands for petroleum development in the autumn of 1952, Price Daniel and many other conservative Texas Democrats joined in a revolt against their party. Attorney General Daniel, who was himself campaigning for a seat in the US Senate, urged his fellow conservatives not to sacrifice their principals *"on the altar of party loyalty"* and to resist becoming *"slaves to the name of the Democratic Party."* Their endorsements helped to bolster Republican Dwight Eisenhower's already enormous national appeal.[22]

On November 4, 1952, the voters of Scurry County favored a Republican presidential candidate for the first time in their history. At 51.4%, Eisenhower's margin of victory in the county was slim. Most Snyder residents remained loyal Democrats down-ballot.[15]

Senator Price Daniel (D-TX) was sworn into office on January 3, 1953. President Eisenhower would be inaugurated two weeks later.

■■

The new Snyder High School campus was still under construction in January of 1953. Now over budget and several months behind schedule, the contractors still predicted that the campus would be ready to host classes in the fall.[36]

Meanwhile, Principal Johnson's skills as an athletics coach, administrator, and educator were already being noticed by the local paper. *"After winning their district track meet several days ago, students of the Abraham Lincoln School returned to San Angelo last weekend and won their district interscholastic meet in other events,"* wrote The Snyder Daily News.

Old Snyder High School (formerly Snyder Public School). Winter, 1952-'53.
Courtesy Scurry County Museum.

"Daniel Johnson, principal of the school, said his students won firsts in junior and sub-junior spelling, arithmetic, and story telling at the meet."[37]

The writers at the local paper were not the only ones to notice Mr. Johnson's successes. In May of 1953, the Snyder school board "voted unanimously to remodel one of the system's frame buildings now used for temporary classrooms, converting it into a small but modern dwelling for use by the principal of the Negro school. The principal of Lincoln School is Daniel Johnson.

"The trustees said the matter was entirely their idea in view of the usual handicaps of Negroes in obtaining high-standard quarters in their section of the city. The school is to own the property and lend it to the principal and his family. Johnson is also a teacher and is paid a teacher's regular salary plus only $300 a year for being principal also.

"Cost of remodeling the building and moving it is estimated at $2,600."[38]

At the time of this writing, Daniel and Rosetta Johnson's former home on the southeast corner of 34th Street and Avenue L in Snyder is still standing.

May 26, 1953 was the last graduation day at the old Snyder High School building. The former Snyder Public School campus would reopen in the fall as Snyder Junior High.

Eleven blocks to the south, Principal Johnson distributed diplomas to Lincoln School's first eighth grade graduates. *"The four Students are Johnny Walker, Robert E. Williams, Willie T. Thompson, and Rosie Davis."*[39]

On September 3, 1953, the modern Snyder High School building held classes for the first time. The Snyder Independent School District now boasted 148 teachers, two nurses, and two librarians. Thirty-six of those teachers were now working at the new high school. Lincoln School began the 1953-'54 school year with four teachers and sixty-six students.[40]

The City of Snyder wanted to pave the "Main Drag" of The Flats (Avenue M below 33rd Street) to give their fleet of new busses an easier route to 37th Street. On November 2, 1953, the city council voted to extend the southeastern city limits five blocks to the south. *"Included in the annexations are: the area including Lincoln School in Southeast Snyder, the colored section of town, [...] from the present city limits south to 37th Street."*[41]

The people of The Flats went to sleep in an appendix of Snyder and woke up in a neighborhood. Thirty-eight years and four months after the bombing at Jim Percy's hotel, Black families were residing within the city limits again.

Lincoln School's state-wide reputation for athletics was cemented in late February of 1954. *"When the boys' and girls' basketball teams from Abraham Lincoln School go to the state Negro Interscholastic League cage tournament next year, both of them will be defending state championships."*, reported The Snyder Daily News.

"Teams of both sexes went to McCamey last week to the state meet, but when they got there they found that no other Class C schools sent teams, so they brought back trophies for winning the championship by default.

"Since the teams were there, however, they saw no reason to waste their trip, so they matched games with Class B schools. The teams they played were those from high schools. Those from here were from students up to the eighth grade.

"Even though they were matched with high school teams, the Snyder teams did all right. The boys' team, coached by Daniel Johnson, lost to the McCamey team 20-10. The girls' team,

coached by Mrs. Cleopatra Stapleton, played two games, losing to McCamey 28-8 and to Crane 25-5."[42]

The Abraham Lincoln School of Snyder now had two state championship basketball trophies despite having no gymnasium in which to practice. About two weeks after the victorious defeats at McCamey, the Snyder School Board invited Principal Johnson to speak at their regular meeting.

"Johnson presented a written resume of the twenty-fifth annual education conference for Negroes, held recently at Prairie View Agricultural & Mechanical College, then gave an oral report of his attendance of the conference.

"Johnson said that at the conference held Friday, emphasis was placed on the importance of Negro schools endeavoring to broaden their programs to cover and influence their entire communities rather than being restricted, more or less, to classroom activities.

"'While academic training rightfully remains the major necessity, it is still important that schools realize the great necessity of relating their work to their communities, leaving the strict traditional mode of operation and adopting a concept-of-service for the public-at-large', Johnson said.

"'This is particularly important in Negro schools', he said, 'and must be done before entire Negro communities can be expected to become genuinely interested in public education.'

"He said he had given much study to the problem of increasing community interest in the Negro school in Snyder. 'Such a problem must be solved by patient, continued, faithful and unfailing work of all those interested' he said. 'It cannot be solved over night.'

"School board members discussed the progress of Negro education in Snyder with Johnson in view of its affect here on the general standard of living in the community. Johnson said that increased interest in public education among the Negroes was indisputably the answer to needed increases in living standards.

"The Snyder school system has no facilities for Negro students who wish to attend school after they complete the eighth grade.

"'The gradual progress in this respect is reflected by the steady increase in enrollment,' Johnson said, adding that the Negro school here had a present enrollment of 72. This time last year there were 68, and a year earlier there were 66. This, in view of the fact that the Negro population here is not increasing proportionately as fast as the white population, is considered significant."[43]

As Lincoln School was wrapping up its second school year and Snyder High School its first, the US Supreme Court reached a decision in the case of *Brown v. The Board of Education*. The old 1896 *Plessy v. Ferguson* ruling, with its prescriptions of separate but equal facilities, was nullified and public school segregation based on race declared unconstitutional.

The eyes of Snyder fell on Daniel Johnson.

CHAPTER 11

KEEP THE PEACE

"The reason for segregation is to keep the peace. In some areas where we have hot-headed individuals of both races, we may have some intimidation. [...]

"[Brown v. The Board] will have a serious adverse effect upon education in some southern areas. In many areas, there will be segregation by choice. The majority of our Negro citizens, I feel sure, by choice will continue to go to their own Negro schools.

"Texas is so proud of its public school system that it will keep it despite the Supreme Court ruling."

-Senator Price Daniel. May 18, 1954.[1]

1954 school yearbook. Courtesy Scurry County Museum

Daniel Johnson paused for a few seconds in the calm coolness of the Snyder Independent School District administration building parking lot. It was about 7 a.m. on Tuesday, May 18, 1954. The *Brown v. The Board of Education* ruling had been announced less than twenty-four hours earlier and Mr. Johnson had been called in to answer a few questions. The schools would open soon. Time was short.

The whole building fell silent when the Lincoln School principal walked in the door. Staring back at him were Snyder ISD superintendent Dr. Cecil Yarbrough, school board president Lee Stinson, and reporters from The Snyder Daily News. The conversation immediately turned to integration.

"At least a few problems will probably arise in some of your larger cities such as Dallas, Houston, and San Antonio," said Superintendent Yarbrough, *"but I doubt any will arise in West Texas, particularly in cities the size of ours."*

When asked for an opinion about ending school segregation in Snyder, Mr. Stinson said *"I'm somewhat like Governor [Herman Eugene] Talmadge of Georgia—as long as I have anything to do with schools, I'm not going to favor it."* Mr. Stinson *"further clarified his viewpoint by saying, however, he favored provision for equal educational opportunities for Negroes. 'We have facilities here for Negroes for a long time to come.' Stinson said. 'I don't look for any changes or any problems in the near future.'*

"Asked whether the lack of a Negro high school in Snyder would likely cause any problem in the near future, however slight, Stinson said, 'Most Negroes in Snyder have not advanced in this respect far enough yet to want to attend high school.' He added that arrangements were made to meet exceptions to this fact.

"At present, the school system here is paying expenses of one Negro student who is attending a boarding high school in San Antonio. She is the only Negro of Snyder eligible to attend high school who currently shows a sincere desire to obtain this education, Yarborough said. The school system assists her by paying much of the expense incurred, and this is paid in the form of tuition.

WHERE YOUR CHILDREN GO TO SCHOOL . . . .

North Elementary
Grades 1-6

Central Primary
Grades 1-3

West Elementary
Grades 1-6

East Elementary
Grades 1-6

Senior High School
Grades 9-12

Central Elementary and Junior High School
Grades 4-6 and 7-8

Lincoln School

1954 school yearbook. Courtesy Scurry County Museum

"The Negro school here, Abraham Lincoln School, is equipped for eight grades, but ninth-grade work is also being done by some because of extra facilities available in the school.

"The principal of the Abraham Lincoln School, Daniel L. Johnson, said he did not believe the high court's ruling would cause any problem here. 'I look for no immediate change,' he said. 'Any attempts for immediate changes would certainly cause many *problems. I do believe, however, there will be a gradual change over the years to come.'*

"Asked whether he could determine the general attitude of the Negro people of Snyder concerning the supreme court's ruling, Johnson said: 'I don't believe there is any more comment among our people on this matter now as there was before the court's ruling. I have heard many say before the court decided the issue that if it were decided against segregation, the people should continue to live and act as usual here.'

"Yarbrough said he believed that would-be problems which would necessarily arise from any attempts to change practices in such places as Snyder would be delayed by the actual application of the court's ruling, thereby minimizing such problems.

"Much will depend, he said, on how soon the laws arising from the supreme court ruling become effective. Even should there be some small problems here, the matter will not become near the problem here as elsewhere, the superintendent added.

"Asking whether the ruling would possibly lead to any action requiring white students who live closer to Negro schools than to white schools to attend the Negro schools, Yarborough said he did not believe such would ever be the case. 'There is nothing now to force us to send any student to a school that the school board does not want to send him to,' he said."[2]

■■

May 25, 1954 was graduation day at Lincoln School. Nine days had passed since the Supreme Court's *Brown v. The Board* decision. Ceremonies were held at 8 p.m. in the cafeteria for three eighth grade graduates. Reverend O. L. Holiday of Mother Zion Baptist Church in Henderson, Texas was introduced as speaker by Principal Johnson. After the commencement speech, it was announced that all three graduates would be attending high school at St. Peter Claver's School in San Antonio in the fall.[3]

"The largest 'Juneteenth' celebration ever held here is being planned by the Negro population," announced The Snyder Daily News on May 30, 1954. After their annexation last November, this was the first time that the residents of The Flats celebrated their freedom as citizens of Snyder.

The whole city was invited. The biggest challenge was securing the meat for the free barbecue but some white locals helped to make up the deficit. The first such contribution was a live goat donated by rancher Wilson Connell.

A parade was held. A double-header baseball game was played at Winston Park. The dancing began around sunset, and the night culminated in a jitterbug contest. There was plenty of barbecue for everyone.[4]

Meanwhile, the San Antonio city council passed the "Juneteenth Ordinance," becoming the first large city in Texas to fully integrate all public facilities except swimming pools. The presence of large military bases nearby, racially integrated since 1948, brought a sense of urgency to the city's desegregation.

As the summer of 1954 drew toward an end, the pressures of the post-war baby boom were beginning to mount at Snyder ISD. The first day of school was fast approaching and the annual scramble to prepare was on.

The Snyder Junior High campus, formerly Snyder Public School, felt relatively empty compared to the bustling elementary schools. In 1951 there had been talk of abandoning or demolishing some of the temporary buildings for lack of need. But now Snyder's white elementary schools were overflowing and temporary expansions supplemented each one.[5-8]

The pressure was particularly high for medical staff. There were two more suspected polio cases in Snyder in the first half of August. Ages five and thirty. Although a new polio vaccine had been invented the previous year, a ready supply was not yet available in Scurry County.

Mrs. Eula Williams, Snyder ISD senior nurse, and her junior counterpart Mrs. Nell Spence were tasked with screening the health of more than 3,400 students for communicable diseases, malnutrition, and deficiencies in sight or hearing before classes began in September. When Mrs. Spence finally arrived at Lincoln School on August 15th, she found the atmosphere to be less hectic but the physical symptoms of poverty more acute.

September 3, 1954 was the first day of school in Scurry County. Less than four months after *Brown v. The Board,* Snyder's schools remained segregated. For many Lincoln School students, the most notable change of 1954 would be remembering where to add *"under God"* to the Pledge of Allegiance each morning.[9]

■■

The former Snyder Negro School's two buildings were now functioning as annexes to Lincoln School. In 1954 one of the structures was converted into a wood shop. Principal Johnson began teaching woodworking there to an initial class of seven. Students were taught to use a surfacer, a sander, a lathe, a saw, a welding machine, and a few dozen hand tools. W.A. Mayfield, shop instructor at Snyder High School, stopped in occasionally throughout the year to drop off equipment and assist with instruction.[10]

On October 30th, a vote was held in Snyder on a $2,000,000 bond to further expand the schools. Turnout was higher than any other bond election in the city's history. In order to participate, voters must have resided in Texas for one year and in Snyder for thirty days, must own tax-rendering property in the school district, and must have paid last year's poll taxes in full.

If passed, the bond would create fifty-five more classrooms in Snyder. Of those rooms, twenty-two would be at a new Northeast Elementary School. North and East Elementary Schools would both expand from eighteen rooms to twenty-seven. At the eighteen-room West Elementary, by far the most crowded in the system, a new wing would add another thirteen rooms. Limited space at Central Primary would only allow two more rooms to be added to the current fifteen.

Snyder's state basketball champions at Lincoln School would get a gymnasium and a new wooden annex to house the wood shop equipment. The total cost of the Lincoln School improvements would be $36,000, roughly 1.8% of the total bond. If the bond failed to pass, Snyder ISD would be over capacity by more than 1,000 students within the next five years. The measure passed by a vote of 845-302.[11-15]

"A few years ago there were no Negro children in Snyder completing high school", noted The Snyder Daily News in February of 1955.

"Now, although none has finished school, there are six Negro students who are attending out-of-town high schools under sponsorship of the local school district."

"That number of high school students from the comparatively small Negro population in Snyder points to progress in the educational processes here. Even now, there are three local students who will finish at Lincoln School this year and plan to attend high school next year.

Snyder's two Cub Scout packs. Snyder Daily News. February 6, 1955.

"The progress in further education of the local Negro children stems from several factors. Among them is the school administration's encouragement to the children here in furthering their education, the constant counseling done by Lincoln principal Daniel Johnson, and the encouragement of the present high school students give local Negro children unconsciously when telling them of their studies and experiences in high school.

"Five of the six children are attending school at St. Peter Claver Academy, San Antonio. The other one is attending the Negro high school at Temple and living with relatives there. The Snyder school district pays the tuition of these children. Dr. Cecil Yarbrough, superintendent of schools here, said that the San Antonio school is the only one the local district can find in the state which makes special provisions to accept scholastics from other districts."[16]

The Interscholastic League of Negro Schools district contests were held in Midland on March 26, 1955. The students from Snyder competed against Andrews, Santa Anna, Stanton, Ft. Stockton, and Kermit. Lincoln School won first place in declamation, arithmetic, solo singing, and one award to the entire school for their hobbycraft exhibits.[17]

30th wedding anniversary of John and Mary Baker, 1955. Courtesy Scurry County Museum

■■

The US Supreme Court issued a clarification on its *Brown v. The Board* decision on May 31, 1955. In a statement later known as *"Brown II,"* the court ruled that nationwide school desegregation must occur *"with all deliberate speed."* This vague language provided a legal footing for individual states to delay school integration.

One of the first such delays happened just a few dozen miles from Snyder in August of 1955. *"Desegregation May Be Postposed,"* announced the Associated Press in The Snyder Daily News.

"A week ago it looked like one of the South's oldest traditions—the separation of Negro and white children into their own schools—was crumbling fast in Texas.

"Some 64 school boards, all located in the western two-thirds of the state, had announced the two races could sit in the same classrooms this fall.

"Then a radical change in the segregation outlook occurred overnight. There is a slight possibility now that there will be no desegregation in Texas this fall. [...]

"What caused this turnabout? It was a court suit filed at Big Spring and scheduled to be heard in district court next Friday.

"A group of Dallas and Big Spring men, leaders of the Texas Citizens Council, filed the suit. The Citizens Council was organized to fight integration.

"There are citizens councils active in at least Dallas, Fort Worth, Gilmer, Kilgore, and Big Spring.

"The suit seeks two things:

"1. An injunction to prevent integration of Big Spring public schools.

"2. To prevent state funds from going to any school in Texas which permits integration. [...]

"It's doubtful if Texas schools can operate without state funds. These funds are the meat and bread of the local school systems. [...]

"Most of the integration orders have been issued in West Texas where the Negro population is small. [...]

"Does that mean that all of West Texas has ordered integration? By no means. Many West Texas school boards have voted to continue segregation. [...]

"Many other school districts have so few Negroes that their appearance in the classroom would be no problem and will be welcomed by some officials who must struggle with finances. For education of Negroes in areas of small Negro population can be expensive under current programs of sending them to other cities in school busses. [...]

"Integration has been approved at some schools for many reasons, but it remains for Jimmy Barber, a Kingsville Junior High School teacher, to cut through abstract reasoning and get down to plain facts about the reason Kingsville, he thinks, will accept integration:

"'There are too many good colored athletes of high school age for it (integration) not to be accepted.'"[18]

∎∎

Nobody understood what an important moment the murder of Emmett Till would become. Not yet.

The fourteen-year-old Chicago native was visiting family in Money, Mississippi in the late summer of 1955. While shopping at Bryant's Grocery and Meat Market, Emmett allegedly whistled at the shop owner's wife, twenty-one-year-old Carolyn Bryant.

As punishment for his breach of the social code, the young Mr. Till was abducted at gunpoint, tortured for hours, and finally shot by Mrs. Bryant's husband and brother in law. Emmett's remains were tied to a seventy pound cotton gin fan and thrown into the nearby Tallahatchie River.

The body was discovered three days later by fishermen. When the remains of Emmett Till returned to Chicago, the boy's mother insisted on an open casket funeral. More than 50,000 people attended. The service was filmed.

The Snyder Daily News reported that *"two white prisoners were under guard against threatened mob violence today as a grand jury prepared to study their connection with the fatal shooting of a Negro youth from Chicago. [...]*

"They are charged with kidnapping Emmett Till, a 14-year-old Negro boy from Chicago, after Till whistled at Mrs. Bryant in her husband's country store. They claimed they freed the boy later." [19]

The killers were acquitted. Once safe behind Mississippi's double jeopardy laws, they confessed to the murder and sold the details of the story to a magazine for $4,000.

The sad story arrived at Daniel Johnson's desk on September 5, 1955. It was the third day of school at Lincoln. Emmett Till was the same age as some of Mr. Johnson's eighth graders down the hall.

There were seventy-eight students at Lincoln School this year. Up from sixty-nine the previous year. Across town, about 700 white students were enrolled at Snyder High School. The junior high had roughly 400 and the ongoing Baby Boom had flooded the elementary schools with a combined 2,107 children. [20,21]

Principal Johnson finished his coffee, placed the newspaper on his desk, and left the quiet solitude of his office to begin his first class of the day. The sound of children's voices echoing through the halls competed with the racket of construction workers building the new gymnasium outside. [22,23]

Three months later, on December 5th, Mr. Johnson was preparing for the school's annual Silver Tea to raise money for the high school students in San Antonio. He needed a new suit. John Baker would be there again, showing off his latest three-piece, and the principal of Lincoln School needed to look like he belonged. [24,25]

Then the paper arrived.

"Montgomery Ala. (AP)- City policemen were alerted for duty today in the event violence develops in the scheduled boycott of city buses by Negroes protesting a segregation arrest.

"Rosa Parks, Negro seamstress whose arrest last Thursday brought on the boycott threat, was to be given a hearing in Recorder's Court today on a charge of violating city segregation laws. [...]

"A mass meeting of Negroes has also been scheduled tonight to discuss 'further instructions' in the 'economic reprisal' campaign against the bus lines." [26]

That mass meeting featured twenty-six-year-old Baptist preacher Martin Luther King Jr. as speaker. The Montgomery Bus Boycott would continue for the next 381 days. In later interviews discussing her refusal to give up her seat, the already seasoned civil rights activist Rosa Parks would recall: *"I thought of Emmett Till and I just couldn't go back."*

On March 11, 1956, The Snyder Daily News sent reporters to survey the facilities and faculty at the Abraham Lincoln School.

"Increased interest in education has been indicated among Negro students here, according to records of the Abraham Lincoln School.

ABRAHAM LINCOLN Elementary School's principal here is Daniel Johnson, shown here in the school's new gymnasium. Johnson also works with boys of his school as physical education teacher. (Lee Watson photograph)

The Snyder Daily News. March 11, 1956.

"While the Negro population of Snyder has not increased in any noticeable amount, enrollment in the Lincoln School has increased during the past year by 12, which represents more than 13 per cent of the present total enrollment of the school.

"In addition, interest has picked up among those students in attending high school. While there were some two Negro students here who were attending high school about three or four years ago, there are now nine Snyder Negro students attending high school in other towns and four students who are taking ninth and tenth grade work here. The Lincoln school's regular grades go only as high as eighth. The principal, Daniel Johnson, however, works with the four students on the high school level because those students cannot leave Snyder to attend school for various reasons.

"The students who are attending high school out of town either attend a boarding high school in San Antonio or a high school in another town if they can make their own boarding arrangements, such as living with relatives. The San Antonio school is St. Peter Claver Academy. [...]

"Many of those students who are in high school are making plans to attend college. In this connection, scholarship funds are being collected through activities which have been held at the Lincoln School."[27]

■■

Price Daniel and eighteen other senators signed a Declaration of Constitutional Principles on March 12, 1956. The document soon became popularly known as The Southern Manifesto.

"The unwarranted decision of the Supreme Court in the public school cases is now bearing the fruit always produced when men substitute naked power for established law. [...]

"We regard the decisions of the Supreme Court in the school cases as a clear abuse of judicial power. It climaxes a trend in the Federal Judiciary undertaking to legislate, in derogation of the authority of Congress, and to encroach upon the reserved rights of the States and the people.

"The original Constitution does not mention education. Neither does the 14th Amendment nor any other amendment. The debates preceding the submission of the 14th Amendment clearly

show that there was no intent that it should affect the system of education maintained by the States. [...]

"In the case of Plessy v. Ferguson *in 1896 the Supreme Court expressly declared that under the 14th Amendment no person was denied any of his rights if the States provided separate but equal facilities. This decision has been followed in many other cases. [...]*

"This interpretation, restated time and again, became a part of the life of the people of many of the States and confirmed their habits, traditions, and way of life. It is founded on elemental humanity and common sense, for parents should not be deprived by Government of the right to direct the lives and education of their own children.

"Though there has been no constitutional amendment or act of Congress changing this established legal principle almost a century old, the Supreme Court of the United States, with no legal basis for such action, undertook to exercise their naked judicial power and substituted their personal political and social ideas for the established law of the land.

"This unwarranted exercise of power by the Court, contrary to the Constitution, is creating chaos and confusion in the States principally affected. It is destroying the amicable relations between the white and Negro races that have been created through 90 years of patient effort by the good people of both races. It has planted hatred and suspicion where there has been heretofore friendship and understanding.

"Without regard to the consent of the governed, outside mediators are threatening immediate and revolutionary changes in our public schools systems. If done, this is certain to destroy the system of public education in some of the States.

"With the gravest concern for the explosive and dangerous condition created by this decision and inflamed by outside meddlers:

"We reaffirm our reliance on the Constitution as the fundamental law of the land.

"We decry the Supreme Court's encroachment on the rights reserved to the States and to the people, contrary to established law, and to the Constitution.

Children in The Flats of Snyder, 1956. Courtesy Rose Nell Walker

"We commend the motives of those States which have declared the intention to resist forced integration by any lawful means.

"We appeal to the States and people who are not directly affected by these decisions to consider the constitutional principles involved against the time when they too, on issues vital to them may be the victims of judicial encroachment. [...]

"We pledge ourselves to use all lawful means to bring about a reversal of this decision which is contrary to the Constitution and to prevent the use of force in its implementation.

"In this trying period, as we all seek to right this wrong, we appeal to our people not to be provoked by the agitators and troublemakers invading our States and to scrupulously refrain from disorder and lawless acts."[28]

Texas' other senator, Lyndon Johnson, refused to join Senator Daniel in signing The Southern Manifesto.

Senator Daniel hated being in Washington. Although the two U.S. Senate seats are usually regarded as Texas' highest political offices, Mr. Daniel's real ambition had always been the Governor's Mansion. When Governor Robert Allan Shivers announced his imminent retirement in 1956, the opportunity that Price Daniel had craved for almost a decade was finally within reach.

CHAPTER 12

A FORGOTTEN ERA

"Lincoln School, located in the 'Flats' near Avenue M, is probably a forgotten era in Snyder's history. Few people in Snyder know about the history of that school. [...]

"When integration forced equal and fair treatment for minorities, the taxpayers built Lincoln School and hired faculty for the school. High school students returned home in 1957, and the school remained open for high school."

-Historian Charles Glenn Anderson, 1990.[1]

The Snyder Daily News. September 10, 1956.

There was no time to waste. Principal Johnson urgently hustled his students off the bus for the Interscholastic League competitions in Littlefield on April 6, 1956. The Lincoln School team would dominate their Class C competition, bringing home first place certificates in 200-yard relay, 440-yard relay, 50-yard dash, broad jump, discus throw, spelling, arithmetic, declamation, quartette, vocal solo, and story telling. The children from Snyder won a total of twenty-eight certificates in a single day, putting them on par with Class B schools twice their size.

The majority of the day's plaques and trophies had been for athletics. But when interviewed by The Snyder Daily News, Mr. Johnson expressed the most pride for the academic and literary awards.[2]

About two weeks later, on April 21st, the people of Scurry County voted for a $205,000 local infrastructure bond. The bond included $90,000 to establish the Scurry County Library and provide bookmobile services to rural areas, $50,000 for an east-west runway at Winston Field airport, and $65,000 to provide new park facilities. Winston Park near The Flats was to be given playground equipment, shaded picnic tables, and a segregated swimming pool at the park's southernmost corner. The old baseball diamond was upgraded with shaded dugouts, covered bleachers, and fencing.[3]

Athletics coach Calvin J. Edwards joined principal Johnson, Elizabeth Norton Grandison, Lois Powell, and Anniece Hawkins at Lincoln School in the late summer of 1956. Edwards held a bachelor's degree from Prairie View A&M University near Houston. The Snyder Daily News reported that sixty-five students would be enrolled at Lincoln during the 1956-'57 school year. Another fifteen were attending high school elsewhere.[4]

■■

With school integration being the hottest political issue of the day, the 1956 Texas Democratic Party primaries became a series of debates on how the state should respond to *Brown v. The Board*. Only four of the six candidates for governor stood a real chance of being elected.

W. Lee "Pappy" O'Daniel was a veteran Texas politician, an old-time showman, and a pioneer of radio electioneering. In addition to criss-crossing the state to give stump speeches, his successful 1938 campaign for Texas governor involved hosting a radio show sponsored by his own Ft. Worth-based flour company. During many of these broadcasts, he would perform as the lead singer and songwriter of *Pat O'Daniel and His Hillbilly Boys*.

In 1956, Mr. O'Daniel sought to win back his old job with a segregationist platform. During the debates "Pappy" called school integration a *"screwy idea"* and said that it would lead to *"the red blood of both whites and Negroes"* running in the streets. He referred to the Supreme Court as *"cowards"* who pick on *"little urchins toddling off to kindergarten."*

Author, historian, and West Texas rancher J. Evetts Haley represented the state's most extreme segregationist faction. His campaign distributed pamphlets calling for *"continued separation of the races without compromise."* Playing on the worst fears of many white conservatives of the time, Mr. Haley promised to deploy the Texas Rangers to stop federal marshals from enforcing desegregation orders if necessary. He also called on Congress to impeach the entire Supreme Court for its *"illegal and immoral"* decision and even suggested reviving the 19th century Doctrine of Nullification to declare *Brown v. The Board* null and void.

Ralph Yarborough represented the liberal wing of the Texas Democratic Party. Yarborough had nearly won the Texas governorship four years earlier in 1952. His widespread popularity made him one of the last serious threats to Texas conservatives from Roosevelt's New Deal Coalition. Throughout the 1956 campaign, Yarborough tried to steer the conversation away from his progressive views about integration. The electorate noticed. Although he would ultimately lose the 1956 race for governor, Ralph Yarborough's enduring favor among Texas liberals would soon lead him to the US Senate.

Price Daniel's position on integration in 1956 was no secret. Although a more reserved and deliberate speaker than firebrands like O'Daniel and Haley, Senator Daniel's speeches were peppered with his favorite phrases like *"forced integration"* and *"outside agitation."* He referred to the recently proposed Powell

Amendments to deny federal aid to segregated schools as *"the most vicious effort since Reconstruction days to force upon Texas and the South total federal control of our local affairs."* During the debates, Mr. Daniel promised to preserve segregation in any Texas municipality where the majority is opposed to integration.[5]

The candidates' bluster blew across the pages of The Snyder Daily News throughout the spring and summer of 1956. On May 30th, just after Snyder ISD closed for the summer, the following Associated Press article appeared in The Snyder Daily News.

"The more evenly divided the races, the more difficult the problem of integration. That is axiomatic, a situation exemplified throughout the deep South.

"For the Catholic Digest, George Peabody ran a survey of the integration sentiment of the country for its June Clip Sheet and established as nearly as such surveys can establish that 48 per cent of whites and 90 percent of Negroes felt the races should be integrated.

"In the South, the whites opposed registered 74 percent, those in favor 17 percent. Among Southern Negroes, 8 percent opposed and 87 percent favored. Nine percent of whites and 5 percent of Negroes had no opinion. [...]

"The question that evoked these results was rather loosely put, or generalized. It read as follows:

"Most suggestions for solving the Negro - White problem seem to be of two general kinds. One is to keep the two races far apart, the other is to bring them closer together. Which do you think is the better idea— to keep them apart or bring them together?"[6]

■■

On the hot summer morning of August 30, 1956, a tattered effigy of a Black teenager swayed ominously in the breeze atop a flag pole in Mansfield, Texas. It was the first day of school.

At the time, African American children in Mansfield attended a segregated local primary school while the teenagers were bussed seventeen miles to Ft. Worth for high school.

On August 12, 1956, two weeks before classes were to begin, the NAACP filed its first lawsuit against a school in Texas. The suit was on behalf of three Black students who wished to attend Mansfield High School. A federal court order was granted and the Mansfield school board immediately announced its compliance.

About 400 white citizens, including Mansfield's mayor and chief of police, formed a ring around the school to prevent any Black students from entering while classes commenced inside. Three reporters were driven off. The Tarrant County Sheriff was threatened with violence if he attempted to disperse the crowd. Vigilantes stood guard on the roads entering Mansfield to deny access to counterprotestors. Downtown shops closed their doors in solidarity with the crowd at Mansfield High. Texas gubernatorial candidate "Pappy" O'Daniel rushed to the scene to give a speech in praise of the protestors.

President Eisenhower, busy with his own 1956 reelection campaign and wary of alienating southern conservatives, did not intervene. Texas Governor Allan Shivers didn't have the luxury of ignoring the Mansfield Crisis. With less than four months left in office and an even bigger protest planned for the following day, the governor was forced to take action.

"Gov. Shivers ordered Texas Rangers to Mansfield today 'to cooperate with local authorities in preserving the peace'", reported the Associated Press in The Snyder Daily News.

The governor urged *"that the board go ahead and transfer out of the district any scholastics, white or colored, whose attendance or attempts to attend Mansfield High School would reasonably be calculated to incite violence."*

Meanwhile, *"an assistant district attorney was mobbed, shoved, and cursed today when he appeared in the middle of the angry crowd of white men who for two days have dared Negroes to enter Mansfield High School.*

"Grady Haight, the Tarrant County Assistant D.A., is white. He was shaken when the mob finally released him.

"One unidentified person in the mob claimed Haight was 'looking around so he would know who to prosecute.'

"At least 150 men raced around Haight, and those centered around Haight shoved and pushed him. [...]

"Two sheriff's officers fought their way through the crowd and rescued him. As they led Haight away, he was pale and shaken and had difficulty talking. [...]

"Dangling over the entrance to the school this morning was a new effigy of a Negro. It was so placed that no one entering the school could fail to see it. An effigy hung from the school flagpole yesterday was still there today. A similar figure in downtown Mansfield was cut down Wednesday."[7,8]

After being driven from the grounds of Mansfield High School, one reporter from LIFE Magazine noted that *"I've never seen a meaner mob in my life."* Fearing for his safety at the school, the reporter relocated to the city's Black section.[9]

"Floyd Moody, 17, a rawboned, intelligent looking Negro who is a key figure in the Mansfield High School racial trouble says:

"'Mister, I don't want to go to school in Mansfield. I'd rather go to school with my own people in Fort Worth. But I'll go to the Mansfield school if the NAACP makes me.' [...] 'I'm worried. Those dummies they're hanging up- those signs along the road- they got me worried.' [...]

"Near the corn field where Moody worked sat his mother, Mrs. Estella Moody, 36, mother of four.

"'We don't want any trouble, but I want my boy to go to school. It would be better if Floyd could go to school in Mansfield because he would be near home. When he went to school in Fort Worth last year, he sometimes didn't get home until 8 or 9 at night. We need him here at home to do the chores."[10]

The eventual arrival of the Texas Rangers calmed the mood at Mansfield High. The Rangers had not come to integrate the school, but merely to keep the peace.

Sgt. E.J. "Jay" Banks, leader of the Rangers at Mansfield, did not disperse the crowd or take down the effigies. Banks would later write of his time among the Mansfield demonstrators, saying *"they were just 'salt of the earth' citizens. They were concerned because they were convinced that someone was trying to interfere with their way of life."[11]*

No African-American students would enter Mansfield High School in 1956. It was the first time a federal court order had failed to integrate a public school in the USA.[12]

*Texas Ranger Sergeant E.J. Banks poses with the effigy at Mansfield High School.
August 31, 1956. Courtesy Texas State Library and Archives Commission.*

A few days later, on September 4th, about 300 protesters gathered to prevent three Black students from attending Texarkana College. The Texas Rangers were dispatched from Mansfield, led once again by "Jay" Banks. Sgt. Banks told his fellow Rangers, *"Our orders are to maintain order and keep down violence. We are to take no part in the integration dispute and we are not going to escort anyone in or out of the college."*[11]

When the Black students approached the campus, the crowd drove them back across the street. Steve Poston, age seventeen, was kicked and pelted with gravel under the observation of two police officers and four Texas Rangers. Ranger Sargent Banks threatened the young Mr. Poston with arrest if he attempted to cross the street again. Fifteen minutes after their arrival, the three prospective students decided to leave.

The Snyder Daily News covered the resistance in Texarkana for six days. *"3 Negroes Stopped By Texarkana Picket Line." "Shots Fired Over Church." "Cross Burns In Texarkana."*[13-15]

No African-American students would enter Texarkana College in 1956.

"Jay" Banks retired from the Rangers to become the Big Spring Chief of Police in 1960. In 1961, a twelve-foot bronze statue of Captain Banks titled *"One Riot, One Ranger"* was placed at Love Field Airport in Dallas. The enormous sculpture would be removed fifty-nine years later during the Dallas Black Lives Matter protests of 2020.[9,11]

■■

The Mansfield Crisis and Texarkana unrest dominated the front pages in Snyder during the days before and after the first day of school. When the morning of September 4, 1956 finally came, sixty-five children rushed through the glass and steel doors of Lincoln School in search of their new classrooms.[16]

Two weeks later, school board members Max West and E.H. Williamson each gave speeches at the Optimist Club luncheon. *"The two school board officials discussed a problem currently facing the board- that of integration in the Snyder schools.*

"West and Williams pointed out that the board is considering two proposals: (1) to build a second high school in south Snyder adjacent to Lincoln School, and (2) to open the doors of Snyder High School to Negro students. [...] At a meeting already held with residents of the Negro section of Snyder, parents there strongly favored the second high school.

"A bond election would have to be held to build another high school, the school board men said."[17]

The fate of segregation in the Snyder Independent School District was decided on September 25, 1956. Less than three weeks after the Mansfield Crisis, a meeting was held at Snyder High School.

"A meeting scheduled for 7:30 o'clock tonight by the school board to discuss problems dealing with integration here will be held in the high school cafeteria, not the auditorium as previously reported.

"At the meeting, to which any persons interested are invited, the board will discuss alternatives which could be taken here. [...] The school board does not advocate for either alternative. It has urged community discussion of those who have opinions on either side or suggestions to attend tonight's meeting and help discuss the problem.

"'We want clear, free, and full expression of opinion from both sides', the board said."[18]

It was decided that Lincoln School would be given the new high school wing. Snyder High School would remain segregated.

About two weeks later, on October 10th, The Snyder Daily News announced that *"Tentative School Plans Are Okayed."*

"The Snyder school board last night approved tentative plans for the proposed high school addition at Lincoln Elementary School.

"The tentative plans were submitted by Fred Buford of Dallas, architect, who said they included some 9,000 square feet of floor space and include facilities for all high school courses, such as home making, science, shop, commercial subjects, and others, as well as space for a library, office, and restrooms.

Artist's conception of Lincoln School with the proposed high school wing on the left.
Snyder Daily News. January 3, 1957.

"*The plan also called for slight remodeling of the school's cafeteria-auditorium, providing additional seating space. The addition would be a north-south wing adjoining the east end of the present Lincoln School.*

"*The board is now working on a bond proposal of $160,000 for the addition.*"[19]

■■

Dear Santa:
    "*I am a little girl eight years old and in the third grade. I attend Lincoln School. I try to be good and go to church each Sunday. For Christmas, I want you to bring me a doll with a suitcase and a white bible and some glass dishes. My little brother, Sammie, wants a gun set and a black leather jacket. I have two big brothers and a big sister, so be good to them and all the other girls and boys in Snyder and all over the world. Love to Mrs. Santa.*
                    "*-Frances Davis. December 20, 1956.*"[20]

Three days after Frances Davis' letter appeared in The Snyder Daily News "*about 150 bags of fruit and nuts were distributed to present and future students of the Abraham Lincoln School. [...] The project was sponsored by the school, with the Parent-Teacher Association taking care of distribution.*

"*A Christmas program was presented by students of the school, under direction of Miss Anniece Hawkins.*"[21]

Work began on the Lincoln High School wing on the cold, cloudy morning of January 3, 1957. The campus now sprawled across the entire footprint of the old Fuller Cottonseed Oil Mill between Avenues J and L, south of 34th Street.[22]

In the early spring of 1957, as the teaching staff at Lincoln battled the racket of construction for their students' attention, "*Daniel Johnson, principal of the Abraham Lincoln School here, was installed as second vice-president of the West Texas District Teachers Association at its convention in Abilene during the weekend.*

"*Johnson, his entire teaching staff, and Frederick Sanford, president of the Lincoln Parent-Teacher Association, attended the convention.*

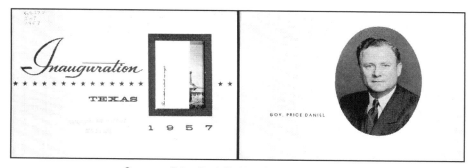

Governor Price Daniel's 1957 inaugural program.
Courtesy Legislative Reference Library of Texas.

"*Johnson was leader during the convention of a discussion group of elementary and secondary principals. He has served the past year on the association's executive committee and as a member of the constitution committee.*"[23]

■■

Price Daniel's success in the primaries practically guaranteed a victory in the general election. The Republican Party of Texas offered only a token resistance to single-party rule in 1956. After sailing into office, Governor Daniel championed new legislation to slow the advance of school integration in Texas.

House Bill #65 would require "*local option elections before abandoning dual school systems,*" taking the choice of integration away from Texas school boards. Schools found to be in violation would immediately forfeit all state funding. House Bill #231 would allow "*standards other than race*" such as health, intelligence, psychological, or moral factors to effect pupil assignment. This provided local authorities in Texas with new legal excuses to avoid enrolling Black students in all-white schools. Governor Daniel signed both bills on May 23, 1957.[5,24]

■■

The chalkboard said "*Mr. Anderson.*" After leading the Pledge of Allegiance, the new teacher, less than three weeks from his 27th birthday, returned to the board and added the words "*Language Arts*" below his name. It was Tuesday morning,

September 3, 1957 and Charles Anderson was teaching his first class at Snyder Junior High.

Educator, tutor, Korean War veteran, newlywed, and recent graduate of Abilene Christian College, Charles Anderson would work for Snyder ISD for the next thirty-two years. In addition to teaching, Mr. Anderson served as principal of Northeast Elementary, Central Elementary, and Snyder Junior High.[25-27]

Over the coming decades, Mr. Anderson would dedicate his spare time to chronicling the history of Scurry County. He published four indispensable books on the subject. In those books, Mr. Anderson would write less than two pages about the history of Snyder's Black community. During his time as chairperson of the Scurry County Historic Commission and the Scurry County Museum Board of Directors, Mr. Anderson shaped the way Snyder's history is remembered and taught.[1]

The efforts of Charles Glenn Anderson made this book possible. His omissions made it necessary.

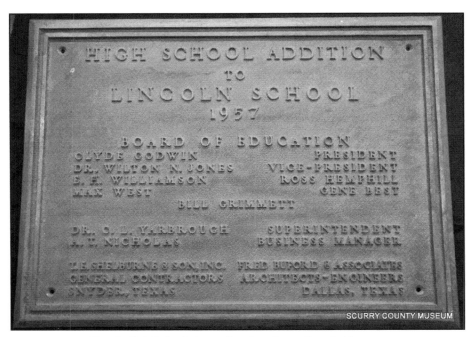

Lincoln High School plaque. Courtesy Scurry County Museum.

Meanwhile, three quarters of a mile to the south, Principal Johnson was settling into his new office at the Lincoln School high school wing. It was a chaotic time. After a summer full of delays, construction was still ongoing. The principal's office, library and two classrooms were already complete and in use despite the noise.[28]

On September 4th, the second day of the 1957-'58 school year at Lincoln, a desperate headline leapt out of The Snyder Daily News: *"Guard Holds Back Negroes"*.

"Little Rock, Ark. (AP) - National Guardsmen called out by Gov. Orval Faubus today forcibly prevented integration of Central High School and Faubus insisted at a news conference later that he is not defying a federal court order.

"The soldiers turned back nine Negro students who tried to enroll at the 2,000-pupil all-white school.

"The troops controlled a disorderly crowd which jeered the Negroes, who were led by a well-dressed unidentified white man. [Presbyterian minister Dunbar H. Ogden Jr.] [...]

"Asked why local and state police could not deal with violence, if it occurred, Faubus said that 'it is better to preserve peace than to quell disorders.' [...]

"A crowd of some 300 whites milled about in front of the school shouting such phrases as 'Nigger go back where you belong' but the whites made no attempt to harm the Negroes. [...]

"An unaccompanied 15-year-old Negro girl made the first attempt to cross a line of about 200 soldiers standing shoulder to shoulder. As she repeatedly attempted to pass through the formation, an armed guardsman stepped forward and silently turned her back. [...]

"The crowd of whites, which doubled in size almost at the instant the Negro girl appeared, was noisy and abusive in its language compared to the quiet, orderly crowd of 500 which gathered in front of the high school yesterday. [...]

"The Negro girl, who identified herself as Elizabeth Echford, was engulfed by whites as she attempted to pass through the guardsmen. They shouted "Nigger go back where you belong" and "Nigger go back to Africa.' One muttered, 'let her go, she's being paid for it.'"[29]

In late September of 1957, as the Little Rock Crisis approached its third week, the Lincoln Trojans football team was in training for their first season.

"The team is composed of boys from both high school and junior high grades. Since this is the team's first year at football, it will play junior high teams this fall. [...]

"A total of 21 boys have been working out with the squad. [...] Only two of the youths have had any football experience. The only one with high school experience is Terry McClain who played at Carlsbad.

"[Coach Calvin] Edwards, now in his second year at Lincoln, has previously had basketball and track teams but no football here. Prior to Edwards' coming, Daniel Johnson, principal, coached both basketball and track, which have been carried on at the school four years.

"Edwards is a graduate of Prairie View College where he played four years and lettered three years as a guard."[30]

The Flats of Snyder. September, 1957. Courtesy Snyder Chamber of Commerce.

■■

President Eisenhower's patience had run out. Appalling footage and stories from Little Rock had dominated every newspaper, radio station, and television channel in the country for more than three weeks. The president had met with Governor Faubus. He had waited patiently for a resolution that never came.

But 1957 was not 1956. Dwight Eisenhower had no more elections to win. He would make an example of Governor Faubus' insubordination. Little Rock would not be allowed to become another Mansfield.

"Stunned by the rioting and strife of the past 24 hours, people in Little Rock reacted with surprise and relief today to the announcement that President Eisenhower has ordered government-commanded troops to take over in the city.

"It was electrifying news here.

"It apparently came as a complete surprise to officials at the Capitol and officers of the Arkansas National Guard—which, under the President's order, will be federalized now and directed by Washington.

"'My God, has he done that?', erupted Claude Carpenter, one of Gov. Orval Faubus' key aides, when informed by the Associated Press today.

"Lieut. Gov. Nathan Gordon, also caught by surprise, said 'I can't conceive of anything I can do if the President has taken that action.'

"He offered no other comment. [...]

"The news came while hard-pressed Little Rock police were cracking down with a genuine get-tough policy today.

"At Central High School, focal point of the 22-day-old racial controversy, they collared 11 persons, including two youths who appeared to be of high school age. All were white.

"That brought the total of arrests for two days to 44, including both whites and Negroes.

"All but one were booked on charges of inciting to riot, carrying a weapon, or disturbing the peace.

"Motorcycle police and police squad cars raced all over the city today. They were stopping and searching automobiles and frisking people for weapons. [...]

"At Central High School, no Negro students showed up today."[31]

President Eisenhower had invoked the Insurrection Act of 1807, allowing soldiers to perform domestic law enforcement duties. The 101st Airborne Division was dispatched to escort nine Black students into and out of Little Rock Central High School each day. Only white soldiers were selected to participate in the Little Rock operation. The president wanted to avoid any images of Black soldiers pointing bayonets at white teenagers.

On September 24th, as the first soldiers were arriving in Little Rock, Price Daniel rushed to the press in Austin to voice his support for Governor Faubus, who *"has done as much to strengthen the cause of the South as all of the others put together."* The Texas governor accused President Eisenhower of adopting *"the tactics of Reconstruction days"* and wondered aloud if the federal government would now *"occupy with troops every non-integrated school in the South?"* Mr. Daniel then concluded by asking the president to withdraw the soldiers as a token of *"good will among the races."* Eisenhower replied within hours that removing the troops too early *"would be to acquiesce in anarchy and, ultimately, the dissolution of the Federal Union."*

Four days later, on September 29th, Price Daniel gave a speech in El Paso placing equal blame on his Arkansas counterpart and President Eisenhower for the Little Rock Crisis. Governor Daniel noted that El Paso ISD had already chosen to desegregate but promised *"no troops, machine guns, and bayonets"* in any Texas school. The governor told the crowd that Texas cities would be able to solve their own problems if not for *"outside agitators"* and urged the Texas Legislature to plan for the closure of all schools in an emergency *"until such time as peace and order can be restored or maintained without the use or occupation of military troops."*[5]

Price Daniel would never publicly admit that it was Governor Faubus, not President Eisenhower, who had provoked the Little Rock Crisis. Two months later, on November 24, 1957, the Texas Legislature voted to immediately close any public school "occupied" by federal troops.

■■

Ticking clocks echoed down the hallways of Lincoln School over the muffled sounds of early morning lessons. Principal Johnson stood in the doorway of his new office admiring the peaceful absence of construction workers. From this vantage point he could see down the length of both hallways. The beautiful new library was only a few paces away.

Everyone was excited for the imminent summer break. Some 3,908 students attended classes in Snyder during the 1957-'58 school year. One hundred and five of them went to Lincoln School.[32]

ABRAHAM LINCOLN high school's first graduating class in history will receive diplomas in commencement exercises set for May 28 in the Lincoln school auditorium. Members of the class, left to right, are Hubert Gift, and Ruby Spells White, seated, and W. C. Stilwell and Terry McClain, standing.

Snyder Daily News. May 25, 1958.

203

The previous six years had been one long march toward this day. Principal Johnson's plan to quietly pack St. Peter Claver's Academy with high school students from Snyder until calls for their return became impossible to ignore had worked. Apart from the tardy construction in the fall, the first year at Lincoln High had gone smoothly.

"The first high school graduation class of the Abraham Lincoln School will have commencement exercises here Wednesday.

"The program is set for 8 p.m. that day in the Lincoln auditorium, with the Rev. Cecil Williams, public relations director for Houston-Tillotson College at Austin, as main speaker.

"This is the first school year Lincoln has had a high school, and it will have four graduates. They are Hubert Gift, valedictorian, W. C. Stillwell, salutatorian, Ruby Spells White, and Terry McClain."[33]

On May 28, 1958, by virtue of alphabetical order, Hubert Gift became the first Black person to receive a high school diploma in Scurry County. Principal Johnson's face beamed with pride as Snyder ISD Superintendent M.E. Stanfield bestowed the certificates.

CHAPTER 13
WHERE PARENTS READ

"There will be several hundred thousand freshmen entering our colleges and universities this month. Many of them will be from homes and schools where books and magazines are plentiful, and where parents read.

"These children will learn a great deal from their parents as they discuss the issues of the day at meals. A student reared in an environment like this has the advantage over a student who came from a home or school where books and magazines are non-existent."

-Principal Daniel Johnson. September 8, 1958.[1]

Lincoln School gymnasium. Early 1960s.
Courtesy Scurry County Museum.

On the first day of school in September of 1958, an article from The Dallas Morning News appeared in the Snyder paper.

"The idea of a pepper-and-salt school, to accommodate the children of whites and blacks who believe in racially mixed schools, with other schools separately maintained for the races, is not new. The heaviest objection has been that it offers no solution for the one-school town.

"A sleeper in the group of bills passed by the special session of the Arkansas Legislature presents a new version of the pepper-and-salt idea. The bill merely says that no student shall be denied the right of attending public school merely because the student refuses to attend a racially mixed class. The implication is that in the integrated school, there will be segregated classes. Or, to turn the thing around, in otherwise segregated schools, there will be pepper-and-salt classes.

"The pepper-and-salt class plan appears to present many difficulties from an operational and administrative standpoint. But proponents of it in Little Rock argue that it may turn out to be the best solution to the integration problem of the South.

"The legal theory of it is that, if the black child has the right to choose a partly-white school for the proper psychological evolution of his character, the white child has the right to choose an all-white class in a partly-white school for the proper psychological development of his character. It does not overlook that some colored parents undoubtedly prefer at this time that their children be spared the unpleasantness of the sort of uproar that prevailed at Central High School, Little Rock."[2]

That was enough of the paper for today. There was much to be done. Almost 3,800 students went to class in Snyder this morning. Ninety-eight of them were now scrambling through the halls of Lincoln School.

Perched in the usual spot outside his office door, Principal Johnson observed the entire symphony of laughter and shuffling shoes at once. He greeted twenty-two high school students as they turned the corner into the new wing. In the main hallway, fourteen junior high students carefully waded through a chaos of sixty-eight excited elementary school children.[3]

The Snyder Daily News reported that *"a branch of the Scurry County Library has been opened at the Abraham Lincoln School here for students and adults living in that area.*

Lincoln School library, 1958. Courtesy Scurry County Museum.

"Daniel Johnson, principal of the school, said the branch library is open three nights weekly, Monday, Tuesday, and Thursday from 6 to 9 p.m. [...]

"The library is located across the hall from the principal's office at the school, near the main entrance.

"A number of volumes are now available to both children and adults, and the number will increase with demand.

"Open a week, the branch library has a participation of children mostly, Johnson said."[4]

The library wouldn't be open tonight. There was a Parent-Teacher Association meeting scheduled in the space. The ambitious Lincoln School PTA would be proposing a joint musical production featuring several schools from surrounding towns, creating official Lincoln School tee shirts as a fundraiser, and sending thirty dollars as a scholarship to a recent graduate attending college in Austin.[1]

A few months later, on November 4, 1958, Governor Price Daniel was reelected with an overwhelming 88.1% of the vote. His petroleum-friendly campaign was awash in industry donations and his bevy of new laws to halt school integration remained wildly popular with Texas conservatives.[5]

By the late summer of 1959, those laws had achieved the desired effect. The Associated Press announced that *"Texas' public schools plan no new racial integration this fall except for a new school on federal property at Burkburnett [...]*

"Of the 1,646 school districts, 101 are listed by the Texas Education Agency and other sources as integrated. But 'integration' does not mean mass integration, the survey by Associated Press member newspapers demonstrates.

"School districts which contain only a few Negroes and which have integrated have integrated totally. But the big-city school systems, in general, go no further than token integration, with a scattering of Negroes in formerly all-white schools.

"And as the 1959 school term approaches, fresh evidence arises that the 1957 Legislature slowed and almost stopped desegregation with its anti-integration laws. [...]

"The 1957 Legislature halted a major trend toward integration with a measure providing punitive measures for districts which integrate without approval of voters.

"Since then, only two schools have desegregated, both after favorable referendums. [...]

"The 1957 law withdraws state aid and accreditation from any district which integrates without approval of voters. It provides fines up to $1,000 for school board members who permit integration without a favorable vote of citizens. [...]

"The 100 or so districts which integrated before the 1957 laws are not subject to the state segregation law. Even in these districts, integration mainly is token. [...]

"Texas has a pupil placement law frankly aimed at limiting mass integration. Similar laws have been upheld by the U.S. Supreme Court. But even before Southern states rushed to pass placement laws, Texas districts sharply curbed the number of Negroes entering formerly all-white schools. [...]

"Odessa technically is integrated - the school doors are open to Negroes. But they live in a compact area and do not cross the school residence lines to attend elementary school. Negroes also say they feel

they would be lost in the 1,200 to 1,500-pupil white high schools and continue to attend their own school.

"Pecos had other reasons for integrating several years ago. The small Negro school had three all-state basketball players.

"At McCamey, Negro students attend their own school but go in a body to the white high school for courses not available at the Negro school. San Angelo has 700 Negroes in the district, and 32 attend school with the 10,099 whites. [...]

"The Texas Education Agency does not compile any records of integrated districts other than what it obtains from newspapers."[6]

Snyder ISD topped 4,000 students for the first time in 1959. One hundred and thirty-one of them went to Lincoln School. Lamar Junior High (later Snyder Junior High, Snyder Intermediate School) was under construction on the west side of town to accommodate the Baby Boomers' continuing march through Snyder ISD. The 1923 Snyder Public School campus was renamed as Travis Junior High.[7]

In a single decade the Snyder Independent School District had grown from one building to six elementary schools, two junior highs, a high school, and an administration building. During the same period, educational facilities in The Flats had been upgraded from the tiny and chronically underfunded Dunbar School to the spacious and fully modern Lincoln School.[8]

As the 1960's began, Snyder's total population was 13,850.[9]

■■

The Texas Civil War Centennial Commission began official operations in January of 1960. After personally selecting participants from among the Texas State Historical Survey Committee, Price Daniel laid out his plan to commemorate a glamorized version of Texas' role in the conflict. In a letter to the committee, Governor Daniel insisted that *"the centennial will stress the bravery and noble deeds of all men and women who fought for their cause and then after the war rebuilt their homes, communities, and nation, rather than reviewing and re-enacting the bloodshed, strife, and discord of the period."*

The governor charged the committee with an ambitious project. Over the next four years they would erect new Confederate markers at historic sites, designate the Texas

Supreme Court building as a Confederate memorial, provide support for the activities of the Sons of Confederate Veterans and the United Daughters of the Confederacy, and plan a series of Civil War Centennial events. The tax-paying people of Texas, regardless of race or opinion, would pay for all of it.[10]

■■

On the first day of February in 1960, four Black college students in Greensboro North Carolina purchased school supplies from the local Woolworth's store. They sat at the store's white-only lunch counter, receipts in hand, and waited to be served. Local police quickly arrived at the scene, but the segregated lunch counter was merely a store policy and not local law. An hours-long standoff played out until the Woolworth's eventually closed. More students came on the following day.

As they began to encounter resistance, the students also attracted the press. Newspaper stories and dramatic television footage of the North Carolina demonstrations began to inspire activists in other states.[11]

Two weeks into the Greensboro Sit-Ins, a series of observances began in Snyder.

"A special program titled 'The Negro In Music And Poetry' was presented at the Lincoln High School on Friday by the school's music class. The event was scheduled in observance of National Negro History Week.

"The program included group singing of the Negro National Anthem; prayer by Johnny Garcia; the spiritual 'Swing Low Sweet Chariot'; 'Carry On' by Pearlie Scott; a creative dance titled 'Nobody Knows De Trouble I've Seen', by Louise Archie; 'The Black Man's Plea For Justice' by Jessie McClain; 'Ride The Chariot' by the choir; 'What Time Is It' by Louise Archie; 'An Ode To Booker T' by Gwendolyn Newsome; 'I Come' by Mary H. Goosby; 'Listen To The Lambs' by the choir; 'A Tribute To George Washington Carver by Emma Garrett; 'Build Me A Race' by Johnny Garcia; 'In Dat Great Gettin' Up Mornin'' by the choir and "You'll Never Walk Alone" by the choir.

"The program was presented under direction of Mrs. Anniece Camille Johnson, instructor.

211

Lincoln School boys choir, early 1960s. Courtesy Scurry County Museum

"Principal Dan Johnson of the Lincoln School announced that enrollment in the school now totals 122. The school expects to graduate four or five seniors this year, and some 23 new students are expected to enroll next fall."[12]

■■

A solemn prayer rose up from the flagpole at Texas Southern University in Houston on the morning of March 4, 1960. Fourteen voices called out *"amen."* Leading the open-air prayer service that morning was Reverend William Lawson, founder of Houston's Wheeler Avenue Baptist Church. The preacher led thirteen TSU students in a recitation of the Pledge of Allegiance and embraced each in turn. This was as far as he could go. For now.

The students then passed beneath the heavy rumble of Houston's South Freeway, walked to the nearby Weingartens store, and took seats at the segregated lunch counter.

In the four weeks since the Greensboro Sit-Ins began, hundreds of demonstrators throughout the South had already been arrested. Television news was saturated with footage of protesters being assaulted with insults, sugar, water, mustard, ice, fists, plates, chairs, fire hoses, and German Shepherds. Today, a small group of teenagers and young adults from TSU brought the Sit-In Movement to Texas.

On March 11th, one week into the Houston demonstrations, the Austin and Galveston Sit-Ins began within hours of each other. The movement came to San Antonio two days later.

"Approximately 1,500 Negroes made plans Sunday for sit-in demonstrations if San Antonio merchants ignore a National Association for the Advancement of Colored People ultimatum to end segregation at lunch counters by Thursday", said the Associated Press in the Snyder Daily News.

"At Dallas, 150 Negroes attending an NAACP meeting were told that every legal means will be used to gain equal rights but no plans for sit-ins at segregated lunch counters were announced for that city.

"The San Antonio action followed protests last week by Negroes at Austin, Houston, and Galveston.

"Picketing of the University of Texas campus ended at least temporarily Saturday after the regents announced expanded housing facilities for Negroes at the state's largest school.

"White and Negro students had carried signs protesting the limited number of dormitories available to Negroes at the integrated school. The demonstration, which was peaceful, also complained that Negroes were not allowed on athletic teams nor in dramatic productions open to the public.

"At Galveston extra police were railed out Saturday as Negroes continued their protest against segregated eating places. A number of downtown stores closed their lunch counters when the Negro youths appeared."[13]

At 10 a.m. on March 26th, thirteen Black students from Bishop and Wiley Colleges sat at the lunch counter at Woolworth's in downtown Marshall, Texas. The population of Marshall in 1960 was 23,846.

After a month of constant news coverage about the nationwide Sit-In Movement, including the previous week's demonstrations at

Corpus Christi, the store manager at the Marshall Woolworth's had a plan. The store immediately closed and all patrons were ordered onto the sidewalk. When the Woolworth's reopened at 12:30 that afternoon, the lunch counter remained closed.

Four days later, on March 30th, twenty students occupied stools at three lunch counters in Marshall simultaneously. All twenty were arrested on charges of *"unlawful assembly to deprive a man of the right to do business."* Within hours, more than 300 students had gathered on the courthouse square to demand the release of the Marshall Twenty. After multiple orders to disperse, an attempt was made to clear the crowd with fire hoses. When that failed, thirty-seven more arrests were made.

The Marshall Sit-ins ended after seven days when the city ordered its lunch counters to close indefinitely. Local judges initially found the protestors guilty and imposed fines. But in December of 1960, nine months after the Marshall Sit-Ins, the Texas Criminal Court of Appeals ruled in favor of the protesters. All charges were dismissed.

Other Sit-In campaigns in Killeen and Dallas during the spring of 1960 ultimately resulted in integration. But Marshall's three lunch counters would never reopen. Rather than being forced to desegregate, the city ordered them removed.[14]

■■

When the school bells rang in Scurry County on September 1, 1960, the faculty of Snyder ISD included 189 classroom teachers, thirteen music instructors, twelve physical education coaches, ten librarians, ten principals, and three councilors. Science classes would be taught at all of Snyder's schools for the first time this year. One of the classrooms in Lincoln's high school wing was modified to create a dedicated science room.[15]

Senator John Kennedy's 1960 *"Kennedy For Me"* campaign opened to a lukewarm reception in Scurry County. After eight years of Dwight Eisenhower, many conservative Democrats in Texas were eager to see one of their own in the White House. But Kennedy's stellar performance in the presidential debates in September and October greatly improved his appeal. When election day came on November 8th, 57.1% of voters in Scurry County cast their ballot for John Kennedy.[16]

Student Raymond Johnson trains with Coach Calvin Edwards at Lincoln School.
Original photo: Snyder Daily News. March 5, 1961. Courtesy Scurry County Museum.

In early February of 1961, three weeks after President Kennedy delivered his inaugural address, the annual National Negro History Week observations were held at Lincoln School. Principal Johnson asked the presenters to respond to the president's speech by examining what they could do for their country and what others had done before.

"Members of the Abraham Lincoln High School choral group, under direction of Mrs. Anniece Johnson, along with the junior and senior classes, presented a special assembly program Thursday calling special attention to achievements of the American Negro. A program of this type is presented each year during the week of Lincoln's birthday.

"The choral group presented several selections, beginning the program with the Negro National Hymn. Randolph Williams led a prayer, and Bonnie McLaughlin repeated the Emancipation Proclamation.

"Johnnie Garcia spoke on 'The Negro after World War II.' Karen Sue Gift cited achievements of the Negro in music and entertainment.

215

Louise Archie reported on Negro scholars and scientists and on integration. Louise Archie also presented an interpretation of 'Nobody Knows De Trouble I've Seen.'

"Daniel Johnson, principal of the Lincoln School, spoke briefly at the close of the assembly. Anniece Johnson directed the choral group and Lois Powell, class sponsor, supervised the junior and senior student activities on the program. Several parents attended the assembly."[17]

The effectiveness of the Lincoln School teaching staff was on full display at the district meet in May of 1961.

"A complete summary of points from the district literary competition received here this week by Dan Johnson, Lincoln School principal, shows that Lincoln swept the field with 86 points." After eight consecutive years of powerful showings at the district and state levels, Lincoln School had developed an intimidating reputation for academics and athletics within the Interscholastic League.[18]

■■

O n the last day of August, mere days before the 1961-'62 school year began, a long-dreaded headline fell across the front page of The Snyder Daily News: *"Texans Start Paying Sales Tax Tomorrow."*

"Texans start reaching in their pockets Friday for something new — a state sales tax.

"Whether you like the tax or not: whether you understand what it is all about, or whether you have the correct forms and regulations, the answer is the same. Friday you start paying and collecting the tax.

"'On Sept. 1 the sales tax will be the the law of our state and as long as the law is in effect it behooves all of us, whether we like it or not, to cooperate in its enforcement,' said Gov. Price Daniel, a long-time battler of the general sales tax. [...]

"Shortly before the midnight deadline of the first special session on Aug. 8 the sales tax bill (HB 20) went to final approval of legislators. On Aug 16 Daniel agreed to let it become law but without his signature.

"As a result of this action, the average Texas family will chip in somewhere around $24 a year in new state taxes. That's figuring a man who makes $5,000 annually will spend about $1,200 for taxable goods."[19]

The people of Texas are not famous for their love of taxation. Governor Daniel was keenly aware of this truism, but the state's solvency would be in jeopardy without more revenue. Price Daniel's signature never appeared on HB 20. But in the minds of many tax-paying Texans, his name was all over it.[20]

Meanwhile, on November 4, 1961, Governor Daniel's Civil War Centennial Commission erected its first Confederate monument at the Vicksburg National Military Park in Mississippi. Its pink granite construction and conspicuous silence about the causes of the conflict would set the style and tone for all future monuments in the Price Daniel Confederate Centennial Set.

Unlike many earlier examples, most of the inscriptions on Price Daniel-era Confederate monuments are historically accurate. They are also carefully worded to portray Texas' involvement in the war from an exclusively positive point of view. The experiences of enslaved Africans in Texas could have no place in such a history.

The Texas Vicksburg Memorial stands atop the Railroad Redoubt, a defensive earthwork built by enslaved people to shield the trains that supplied their owners in Vicksburg from Union Army artillery. The Redoubt contains the bones of many soldiers from the 22nd Iowa Volunteer Infantry Regiment, hastily interred in the artificial mound by their Confederate enemies. At the time of this writing, the names of the Iowa Volunteers are not commemorated anywhere in the park.

The monument has subsided significantly since its construction. The site remains a frequent target for vandals and grave robbers.[21-25]

■■

Good things rarely happen in Snyder after ten o'clock. The school board meeting had begun at 7:30 p.m. on June 19, 1962. It was after midnight now.

According to The Snyder Daily News, *"there were actually two meetings. The first being held in the high school cafeteria with seven representatives of the oil companies in Scurry County.*

"The purpose of this meeting was to discuss the proposed budget for the coming year. The budget under consideration showed an increase over last year from $2,219,756 to $2,285,468, or an increase of $65,712. Salary increases accounted for an increase in the new budget of $104,339.

"R.E. McBride, representing Standard Oil Co. of Texas and the SACROC unit, told the board that Standard was proud to be a part of the Snyder school system, and were glad that the children of their many employees were able to go to such a school. McBride continued that he hoped the board would continue to provide a good, firm education to the students. However, he said, he hoped the board would continue to study the program of the schools, and to eliminate any unnecessary 'frills' which only added expense and did not contribute to the students' education.

"McBride urged the board to provide an 'efficient, effective school system just as economically as possible.' [...] He noted that this year's surplus was approximately the amount of the increase in the budget.

"Superintendent of Schools T.E. McCullom answered that the surplus came mainly from the building program allocations, and that the program is now complete, and the funds which produced the surpluses in the system have been declining for several years.

The Abraham Lincoln School of Snyder, 1962. Courtesy Scurry County Museum.

"Carlton Meredith, representing a number of private operators, asked the board to remember that the money spent on the schools at one time belonged to somebody else, and had been taken away from them to operate the schools. [...]

"Claude Gallamore, speaking for Tidewater Oil, noted that all school budgets seem to continue to rise. He wondered if the schools weren't providing more than is necessary. Many of the courses, he feared, were not offered to educate the children, but rather to satisfy the whims of the parents.

"The school board members thanked the visitors for expressing their views, and said they would all be given consideration. The members then adjourned to the school administration building for their regular meeting.

"In the regular meeting, plans were accepted from the architect for the locker room addition to the Lincoln School."[26]

On September 7, 1962, eight years and four months after the *Brown v. The Board* decision, another academic year began at the Abraham Lincoln School. The postwar baby boom continued to swell the numbers at Snyder ISD. *"Heaviest gains were noted in the senior high school and at the Lincoln School,"* noted The Snyder Daily News. *"The senior high school had 623 students enrolled, compared to 565 a year ago. Lincoln was up from 133 to 177."*[27]

In the last week before Christmas 1962, The Snyder Daily News wrote about the history and future of the Abraham Lincoln School.

"Back in 1950 when Daniel Johnson took over as principal of Snyder's Lincoln School, there were 35 students enrolled. The campus consisted of two white frame buildings.

"Building on that foundation, the Lincoln School has grown steadily throughout the past dozen years until now it is a completely modern plant with a present enrollment of 178 students.

"The first major improvement at Lincoln came in 1952 with the construction of the first brick school building.

"It was decided that with the limited number of students in the upper grades, they would receive better instruction if they

could go away to school. The school board authorized the payment of tuition and expenses to schools in Ft. Worth and San Antonio.

"This policy soon came under the attack of a local minister who contended that it was illegal since one of the schools was a parochial school.

"An election was called, and the citizens of Snyder authorized the bonds to build the high school wing on the existing building.

"The new addition was completed in 1957, and along with the gymnasium, which had been completed in 1956, formed the school as it now stands. The only addition since 1957 is the field house which was completed this year.

"With the new wing came the offering of new courses which were designed to help lower the 'dropout' rate in the upper grades. In the new wing was a homemaking department, a new shop, a science laboratory, a library, and a typing room.

"The success of this effort to keep students in school is evidenced by the fact that the enrollment today of 178 is down only 10 from the high of 188 earlier in the year. [...]

"Success in this area too, is indicated by the fact that in the past few years no less than five Lincoln graduates have gone on to college. As a matter of fact, one Lincoln graduate plans to graduate from Houston - Tillotson College next month. [...]

Lincoln High School athletics. Early 1960s. Courtesy Scurry County Museum.

"The teaching staff also has grown over the years and now includes 10 classroom teachers, a librarian, and the principal. The school also has a custodian and cafeteria personnel.

"In every area, Lincoln School has a record of growth. The growth has been gradual and steady - the same kind of evolutionary development that has characterized all of the Snyder schools. The Lincoln School is another good example of dedicated people doing their best to provide for the needs of Snyder's youth." [28]

The writers at the local paper were not the only ones to recognize Lincoln School's positive impact on the community that it served.

"Daniel Johnson, principal of Lincoln School was notified today [January 11, 1963] of his election to the legislative council of the Texas Interscholastic League of Colored Schools by O.J. Thomas, director of the council.

"The council will meet this month at Prairie View A&M. The council's purpose is to formulate programs for the improvement of the interscholastic program of Texas schools. The programs include scholastic as well as athletic participation." [29]

■■

January 14, 1963 was Price Daniel's last full day as governor of Texas. The '62 primaries had been a disaster. His constituents never forgave him for introducing the sales tax. Governor Daniel would be succeeded by John Connolly, another conservative Democrat, who enjoyed the support of Vice President Lyndon Johnson throughout the primaries.

In 1967, after a short break from public life, Price Daniel would be appointed Director of the Office of Emergency Preparedness by President Lyndon Johnson. He then served as an Associate Justice of the Texas Supreme Court from 1971 until his retirement in 1978.

Price Daniel died of a stroke on August 25, 1988. One year later, Scurry County's new Price Daniel Unit state prison for men was named in his honor. As of this writing, the prisoners at the Price Daniel Unit have never had air conditioning. [30-32]

CHAPTER 14
A GREAT CHANGE

"It is not enough to pin the blame on others, to say this is a problem of one section of the country or another, or deplore the facts that we face. A great change is at hand, and our task, our obligation, is to make that revolution, that change, peaceful and constructive for all.

"Those who do nothing are inviting shame, as well as violence. Those who act boldly are recognizing right, as well as reality."

-President John Kennedy. June 11, 1963.[1]

The Abraham Lincoln School of Snyder. March, 1963.

Dr. Martin Luther King Jr. was released from his jail cell in Birmingham, Alabama on the morning of April 20, 1963. His crime had been parading without a permit for the integration of Birmingham's public spaces and businesses. During his 7 days of solitary confinement, Dr. King wrote a letter to his fellow Alabama clergymen in the margins of a smuggled newspaper.

This letter asserted that *"injustice anywhere is a threat to justice everywhere. [...] The answer lies in the fact that there are two types of laws: just and unjust. I would be the first to advocate obeying just laws. One has not only a legal but a moral responsibility to obey just laws. Conversely, one has a moral responsibility to disobey unjust laws. [...] We know through painful experience that freedom is never voluntarily given by the oppressor; it must be demanded by the oppressed."*

A series of protests, inspired by The Letter From Birmingham Jail, would soon test the resolve of segregated communities across the nation.

■■

In the late morning of April 20, 1963, within hours of Dr. King's release from Birmingham Jail, the students from the Abraham Lincoln School of Snyder scrambled out of their yellow school bus. Eager to finally stand, the children formed a little line in the damp East Texas air that hung lazily over the parking lot. Principal Johnson emerged from the bus and offered a few words of encouragement. Lincoln School's reputation for competitive academics had made it a familiar name at Prairie View A&M University.

"Lincoln High School of Snyder captured a first place and a second place in literary events at the 43rd annual state meet of the Texas Interscholastic League of Colored Schools," announced The Snyder Daily News.

"The debate team composed of Mary Helen Goosby and Woodruff Powell took first place in its division, while Curtis Clay took second place in declamation.

"Daniel Johnson, principal of Lincoln School, is a member of the Legislative Advisory Council of the Texas Interscholastic League of Colored Schools."[2]

Lincoln Trojans basketball team. Early 1960s. Courtesy Scurry County Museum.

The little yellow school bus left Prairie View on the following morning with three more awards for the Lincoln School trophy case. Upon their return, the students could read stories of their recent victories on page 2 of the Snyder Daily News.

But the front pages in the late spring of 1963 were riveted to the news coming out of Birmingham, Alabama.

"Juvenile Court Judge Talbot Ellis said today he will hold in jail an undetermined number of school children whose arrest in a mass anti-segregation drive marked their second commitment to Juvenile Court.

"'If we've had them before, I'm not setting any bond,' said Ellis. 'For first offenders, bond is $500.'

"Several hundred Negro school children were among 600-700 persons, mostly teenagers, arrested Thursday in what integration leaders described as the initial thrust of a renewal of demonstrations against segregation.

"'I wish I could get my hands on the ones responsible for those who misled these kids,' Ellis said. 'They ought to be put under the jail.' [...]

"'The youngest, I understand, was eight,' he said. 'That's what makes my blood boil.' [...]

"'We are definitely starting a stepped-up campaign to lay our grievances before the conscience of the community,' said Dr.

Martin Luther King Jr., symbolic leader of the Southern integration fight. [...]

"The obviously well-planned waves of marches and picketing, mostly by children who skipped school classes, erupted without warning. Ten groups converged on City Hall from all directions. [...]

"Teachers shouted encouragement as pupils, some only first-graders, marched in an eight-block radius of City Hall. One group of about 20 pupils got by police lines and knelt near the City Hall steps to pray.

"School busses were used to haul the Negroes to jail after the first three waves were arrested.

"Although firemen laid out high pressure hoses in the area, they did not use them in dispersing several thousand white and Negro spectators. Warned by the police the hoses would be turned on if they didn't leave, the on-lookers quickly scattered.[3]

Sparing the hoses was only a temporary courtesy. With each passing day, Birmingham's reaction to the protestors became more ferocious.

After eight days of protests, more than 5,000 arrests, and seventy-two hours of intense negotiations, the city of Birmingham agreed to integrate.

■■

On May 26, 1963, as the Birmingham Campaign began to recede from the headlines in Snyder, Lincoln School held its eleventh annual graduation ceremonies. The activities would span two days *"with baccalaureate services, set for 3 o'clock this afternoon and commencement exercises set for 8 o'clock Tuesday evening.*

"Both functions will take place at the school. [...]

"Music for the baccalaureate services will be presented by the girls chorus, which will sing Bach's 'Jesu, Joy of Man's Desiring', the boys chorus, which will sing 'Climbing Up The Mountain Children', and the full chorus which will sing 'My Task.'

"Principal speaker at the Tuesday commencement exercises will be Dr. Thomas F. Freeman, professor of guidance and special education at Texas Southern University in Houston. [...]

"Gwendolyn Newsome, senior valedictorian, will speak. She will use the class motto 'Striving To Improve' as her theme. The class salutatorian, Raymond Earl Johnson, will give the invocation.

"Langston Powell, eighth grade valedictorian, will give the welcome address. [...]

"Superintendent of Schools T. E. McCollum will make the awards of diplomas and certificates.

"Mrs. Anniece Johnson will provide the music for the processional and recessional at both the commencement exercises and baccalaureate service."[4]

On the evening of June 11th, two weeks after Lincoln School's class of '63 graduated, President Kennedy gathered reporters into the Oval Office to deliver his Report to the American People on Civil Rights. The president abandoned his previous appeals to the law, framing integration as a moral issue. Associated Press coverage of the speech appeared in The Snyder Daily News on the following morning.

"President Kennedy has warned the nation that discrimination against Negroes has lighted 'fires of frustration and discord' that threaten lives and public safety.

"The President outlined a broad legislative program he will propose to Congress next week. He said it would be 'based on the proposition that race has no place in American life or law.'

"'A great change is at hand', he said, 'and our task, our obligation, is to make that revolution, that change, peaceful and constructive for all.' [...]

"'I hope that every American, regardless of where he lives will stop and examine his conscience about this and other related incidents,' said Kennedy.

"'When Americans are sent to Vietnam or West Berlin, we do not ask for whites only," he said. "It ought to be possible, therefore, for American students of any color to attend any public institution they select without having to be backed up by troops.'

"'In short,' Kennedy added, 'every American ought to have the right to be treated as he would wish to be treated, as one would wish his children to be treated. But this is not the case.'

"Kennedy, declaring that America faces 'a moral crisis as a country and as a people,' said he will ask Congress to make a civil rights commitment 'it has not fully made in this century.'

"The president said he will propose legislation that would:

"1. Prohibit stores, hotels, restaurants, and theaters from discriminating against Negroes.

"2. Allow the federal government to take a more active part in court suits aimed at desegregating public schools.

"3. Afford greater protection for the Negroes' right to vote.

"Acknowledging the new laws are not enough, Kennedy said, however, that in too many parts of the country wrongs are inflicted on Negroes because they have no remedies at law and 'unless the Congress acts, their only remedy is the street.' [...]

"In Birmingham, Ala., which was torn by racial strife last month, The Rev. Martin Luther King Jr. disclosed a telegram he sent to Kennedy which praised the President's speech as 'one of the most eloquent, profound, and unequivocal pleas for justice and freedom of all men ever made by any president.' [...]

"'This is not a sectional issue,' said the President. 'Difficulties over segregation and discrimination exist in every city, in every state of the Union, producing in many cities a rising tide of discontent that threatens the public safety.' [...]

"Said Kennedy: 'The fires of frustration and discord are burning in every city, North and South, where legal remedies are not at hand. Redress is sought in the streets, in demonstrations, parades, and protests which create tensions and threaten violence and threaten lives.'

"Kennedy said the crisis cannot be met by repressive police action, left to more demonstrations, or quieted by token moves.

"'It is time to act in the Congress, in your state and local legislative body, and, above all, in all our daily lives.' He said."[1]

■■

Gallatin, Tennessee in the early 19th century was not merely a society with slaves. It was a slave society. And it was into this society that William Read Scurry was born on February 10, 1821.

William's father, Thomas Scurry, ran the Bank of Gallatin. As the first bank established in Sumner County, the Bank of Gallatin was critically important in financing the growth of the slave cotton industry of central Tennessee. After the abolition of the transatlantic slave trade in 1808, enslavers in Gallatin and throughout the American South found other methods of supplying the free labor that their economies demanded.

In his 1999 biography of William Scurry, historian Charles Anderson wrote that the enslaved people of Gallatin were *"marketed like animals, their value based on their age, sex, health, and future prospects for producing healthy babies. Young girls were often placed with the strongest Negro man for breeding purposes and one male slave often bred several young women. Owners who had an especially strong male sometimes 'lent' him to other plantations to breed their young females. Only the most caring slave owners preserved the family unit."*[5]

By the 1830s the largest business in Gallatin, and one of the bank's most important clients, was the slave trading firm of Franklin and Armfield. The firm bought thousands of enslaved Africans each year from "Upper South" states like Virginia and North Carolina, marched them in chains across Appalachia to hubs like Gallatin, then sold them down the Tennessee and Mississippi rivers to buyers in the "Deep South."

Isaac Franklin, cofounder of the firm, amassed a fortune that would be worth billions of dollars at the time of this writing. Fairview, as he called his sprawling cotton plantation near Gallatin, once housed more than 600 enslaved people. The mansion in which Isaac Franklin lived still stands. Franklin and Armfield's main office in Virginia is now the Freedom House Museum, operated by the US National Park Service.[6-8]

In this environment the young William Scurry was introduced to white supremacy and chattel slavery as mere facts of life, indistinguishable from the natural order. After becoming a practicing lawyer as a teenager, he would defend that order for the rest of his life.

Scurry moved to Texas in 1839 at the age of eighteen. In February of 1841 he was appointed Attorney of the 5th Judicial District of the Republic of Texas. By 1845 he was representing Red River County in the 9th (and last) Congress of the Texas Republic.

After Texas gained statehood in 1845, William Scurry advocated for a war with Mexico to open the American West for slave cotton production. His wish was granted in May of 1846. Scurry immediately enlisted in the army and participated in the Battle of Monterrey in September of that year.

In 1850, after returning to civilian life, William Scurry became the editor and part owner of the Austin State Gazette newspaper. According to the Texas State Historical Association, *"editorially it [the State Gazette] promoted states' rights, called for the reopening of the slave trade in Africa, opposed the Compromise of 1850, and blamed the North for the slave problem because of northern reaction to the fugitive-slave laws."*[9]

The federal census of 1850 recorded 58,161 enslaved Africans in Texas. Ten years later the count had more than tripled to 182,556. Their numbers were growing faster than Texas' population as a whole. By 1860 roughly 30.2% of all English-speaking people in Texas were enslaved. About one out of every four Anglo-Texan families owned at least one person. From the establishment of the Austin Colonies in the early 1820s until the end of the American Civil War in 1865, slave cotton generated more wealth than all other industries in Texas combined.[10-12]

The Texas Secession Convention began with a prayer in the early afternoon hours of January 28, 1861. With many Texas legislators boycotting the convention, William Scurry was appointed to represent the peoples of Calhoun, DeWitt, Jackson, and Victoria counties. After five days of deliberation, Scurry and the other convention attendees signed the Texas Ordinance of Secession and published a Declaration of Causes for joining the Confederacy.[13,14]

Scurry's Confederate service began on August 21, 1861. Now a colonel of the 4th Texas Cavalry Regiment, his orders were to ride from Austin to El Paso where his men would join the New Mexico Campaign. After a catastrophic loss at the Battle of Glorieta Pass dashed his hopes of capturing the silver mines of Colorado, William Scurry joined the Red River Campaign and was killed during the Confederate assault at Jenkins Ferry on April 30, 1864.[15]

William Scurry's remains are buried eleven feet from Texas founder Empresario Stephen F. Austin. There are multiple streets, busts, and plaques commemorating Scurry's role in the rebellion. There is no monument to Pottilla, Nat, Deliah, Debra, Eliza, Phoebe, Mary, Jeff, Harra, Jacob, Henry, Sally, "Old Tom", "Yellow Tom", Villies, Lewis, Boyd, or any of the other people bought and sold by William Scurry and his family.

There is much more to the life of William Scurry. But that story has already been written. And none of it happened on the little patch of Comanche land that would eventually bear his name.

Scurry County's only Confederate monument was quietly installed on the north side of the courthouse square on July 3, 1963. Nobody in Snyder requested it, but their new sales taxes were paying for it.[16]

The Scurry marker is a near-perfect example of a new wave of Confederate monuments erected in response to the civil rights movements of the 20th century. The historical text is factually accurate but carefully worded to paint William Scurry, and the Confederacy itself, in exclusively positive terms. While ostensibly a commemoration of the American Civil War, the centrality of slavery to the conflict is neither mentioned nor alluded to on the Scurry monument.

At first glance the stone appears to be a benign historic marker, but a full reading of the text reveals it to be *"A MEMORIAL TO TEXANS WHO SERVED THE CONFEDERACY."* The pink granite slab is one in a set of forty monuments that were scattered across Texas by Governor Price Daniel's Centennial Committee in the early 1960s. Several of them, including the one in Snyder, were placed in cities that did not yet exist at the time of the Civil War. Many of these monuments remain uncontextualized and in public view at the time of this writing. Each one is a subtle rebuke in stone aimed at Texans who worked to end segregation in their communities in the 1950s and '60s.[17]

As of this writing, the Texas Legislature has spent more tax dollars on public symbols of the Confederacy than any other state governing body. The 1960s was their most prolific period.[18]

The William Scurry monument in Snyder, Texas. Erected 1963.

■■

The dam finally broke in the late summer of 1963. The Snyder Daily News speculated that *"the year 1963 may go down in Texas history as the most significant yet in school integration, rivaling the national decision in 1954 when the Supreme Court ruled segregation by race in education unconstitutional.*

"Reason for the Texas significance is the number of schools which have integrated this year. Latest count shows 57 districts mixing or planning to mix white and Negro children in classrooms for the first time. Additionally, four districts announced plans to integrate next year.

"An Associated Press survey shows Texas now has 248 districts which will be integrated by the time school opens this fall out of the 1,440 districts in the state. However, about 600 districts have no Negroes.

"The surge of integration is shown graphically when compared with 1962- when only eight districts desegregated. There may be more newly integrated districts which have

escaped notice. Many announcements of action have been buried obscurely in reports of school board meetings. Also, for the first time to any extent, the general rule of "no integration east of Dallas" has been broken. Numbers of districts as far east as the Louisiana state line will mix Negroes and whites this fall.

"Reasons for the upsurge are numerous. Said one well informed East Texan: 'They're voluntarily integrating the schools because that way they can integrate slowly — a grade at a time. If they held out, the federal courts might demand that they integrate the whole school system in one year.'

"Civil rights advocates object to such a grade-a-year program, pointing out that it means no integration for many Negroes during the 11 more years such a gradual approach takes place. [...]

"The real integration breakthrough took place as one of the final major acts of Will Wilson before he left the attorney general's office. Wilson ruled Dec. 10, 1962, that the 1957 Texas laws designed to stop or slow down integration were unconstitutional. Some schools integrating for the first time this year will do so because of federal court action. Others will desegregate because of anticipation of federal court action. [...]

"Again, some school districts have integrated voluntarily this year with little comment and no pressures."[19]

On August 28, 1963 about 4,000 people joined The March On Austin to protest Governor Connelly's opposition to any new civil rights proposals. Meanwhile, more than 100,000 attended the widely televised March On Washington For Jobs and Freedom where Dr. Martin Luther King Jr. gave the most famous speech of his career at the Lincoln Memorial.

Three days later, the back-to-school bells rang out across Snyder. Students who had begun the first grade immediately after the *Brown v. The Board of Education* decision were now entering high school.[20]

■■

Principal Johnson's eyes gazed through the microphone at some nonexistent object in the middle distance. How do you say it? How do you tell them?

It was November 22, 1963. A Friday. The news began to wash over Snyder at about 12:45 pm and now Daniel Johnson had to tell the students. He pressed his index finger on the little rectangular button and the Lincoln School public announcement system turned on with a little pop.

Coach Albert Lewis silenced the squeaking shoes in the gymnasium when the announcement came that President John Kennedy and Texas Governor John Connally had been shot. The high school students were still in the lunchroom when a weeping Mrs. Powell turned on the television to reveal the horror that had just played out in Dallas.

Lincoln School gymnasium, early 1960s. Courtesy Scurry County Museum

With the details still trickling in, the front page of the Snyder Daily News reported that *"Kennedy, 46, lived about 30 minutes after a sniper cut him down as his limousine left downtown Dallas. Newsmen said the shot that hit him was fired about 12:30 pm (CST). A hospital announcement said he died at approximately 1 pm of a bullet wound in the head.*

"Automatically, the mantle of the presidency fell to Vice President Lyndon B. Johnson, a native Texan who had been riding two cars behind the chief executive. [...]

"Kennedy died at Parkland Hospital where his bullet-pierced body had been taken in a frantic but futile effort to save his life.

"Lying wounded at the same hospital was Gov. John Connally of Texas who was cut down by the same fusillade that ended the life of the youngest man ever elected to the presidency.

"Connolly and his wife had been riding with the president and Mrs. Kennedy.

"The First Lady cradled her dying husband's bloodsmeared head in her arms as the presidential limousine raced to the hospital.

"'Oh, no.' she kept crying.

"Connally slumped in his seat beside the President."[21]

■■

Lyndon Johnson wielded a famously intimidating presence. He was known for his persuasive negotiation skills during his time in the Senate and as Vice President.

On November 27, 1963, five days after the assassination, President Johnson's advisors pleaded with him not to squander his public approval as successor to Kennedy on highly controversial civil rights issues. *"Well, what the hell's the presidency for?"* replied Johnson. He would pin President Kennedy's name on a series of civil rights initiatives, drive them through congress, and dare southern conservatives in his own party to oppose him.

On January 23, 1964, the same day the 24th Amendment abolished poll taxes in federal elections, Lincoln School announced its honor roll.

"Mid-semester awards were presented last week to 39 students at Lincoln School here," noted the Snyder Daily News.

Lincoln School gymnasium. Early 1960s. Courtesy Scurry County Museum.

"The awards, recognizing the honor students in each of the grades, are sponsored by the Lincoln Parent-Teacher Association. William Holt Jr. spoke at the assembly meeting which is designed to give recognition to the honor students. The number of students placed on the honor roll was up from the 29 which had placed on the honor roll at mid-semester."[22]

Five months later, on May 27, 1964, Lincoln High School held it's twelfth annual graduation ceremonies. In anticipation of the event, the Snyder Daily News announced that the services "are planned for 3 p.m. Sunday at the Lincoln gymnasium.

"Speaker at the services will be Howard Adams, Minister of the Avenue L Church of Christ here. [...]

"Commencement services are set for 8 p.m., May 27, at the Lincoln gymnasium.

"The speaker will be the Rev. W.M. Batts, principal of Carverdale High School in Houston. [...] Rev. Batts will be introduced by Daniel L. Johnson, principal of Lincoln School.

"Diplomas and certificates will be awarded by T.E. McCullom, superintendent of Snyder Schools.

"*The welcome address will be given by Vera B. Newsome, eighth grade valedictorian. The presentation of the traditional Senior Gift will be made by Mathel McLaughlin, president of the senior class.*"23

Two days after Lincoln High's eleven seniors got their diplomas, their white neighbors attended a ceremony of their own across town. According to the local paper "*some 160 Snyder High School seniors will receive diplomas tonight at the annual commencement program in the school auditorium. The program will begin at 8 p.m.*"24

■■

After eighty-three days of filibuster from conservatives and constant pressure from the White House, the US Senate finally passed the Civil Rights Act of 1964. The most significant piece of legislation since the Second World War, the Civil Rights Act banned racial segregation in public accommodations and schools and ended the unequal application of voter registration requirements. It also barred discrimination based on national origin, sex, religion, color, or race. Sexual orientation and gender identity would join the list after the *Bostock v. Clayton County* ruling of 2020.

The new Civil Rights Act was being tested before the ink was dry. "*The first test came in Kansas City a minute after the controversial bill became law. [...] A Negro, Gene Young, 13 of Jackson Miss., tried without success to obtain a haircut in the basement barbershop at the Muehlebach Hotel where the Congress Of Racial Equality was holding its national convention.*

"*Members of CORE immediately staged a sit-in at the barbershop and in the hotel lobby until the barbershop closed at its regular time. [...]*

"*Lester Maddox, operator of a restaurant in Atlanta, said he would go to jail before he would serve Negro customers.*

"*In Mississippi, Gov. Paul Johnson said he expected some real trouble there when Negroes seek to desegregate public accommodations.*"25

■■

Snyder ISD began its last segregated school year on August 31, 1964. *"A total of 3,680 students registered on the opening day of the 1964-'65 school year in Snyder schools yesterday,"* said the Snyder Daily News.

"The total is 112 less than on the opening day of school last year. [...]

"There are 692 students in high school. There are 205 in the senior class; 234 in the junior class, and 253 sophomores.

"At Travis Junior High [...] a total of 436.

"Lamar Junior High [...] a total of 423.

"West Elementary [...] 533.

"North Elementary [...] 173.

"Central Elementary [...] 384.

"East Elementary [...] 342.

"Northeast Elementary [...] 233.

"Stanfield Elementary [...] 282.

"Lincoln School: seniors, 5; juniors, 9; sophomores, 8; ninth grade, 8; eighth, 13; seventh, 9; sixth, 18; fifth, 27; fourth 17; third, 27; second, 18; first, 23; for a total of 182."[26]

For the first time since 1902, the people of Scurry County cast their ballots in an election without a poll tax receipt on November 3, 1964. Some 65.82% of Scurry County voters chose Lyndon Johnson over Barry Goldwater.[27]

■■

Lois Powell lugged the cumbersome cardboard cube along the narrow sidewalk. It might as well have been a sail in the relentless Texas wind. Propping the entryway with her shoe, she rotated gracefully through the front door of Lincoln School. The heavy glass and steel door came to rest with a bang and the roaring gale fell silent.

It was the first day of National Library Week and, as Lincoln School librarian, it was Ms. Powell's time to shine. Her library had received a generous gift just one month before graduation. *"Columbia Record Co. gave two sets of 60 records, one for the* main library and one for the branch library at Lincoln School. They range from popular and jazz to classical symphonies and opera."[28]

"The Abraham Lincoln School's Library is a composite of an elementary, junior high, and high school library. The books are arranged as follows: Primary and Kindergarten, which are called "easy books;" Youth and Juvenile books, and adult books. The same system is used for reference books. Subscriptions are maintained to various magazines and several newspapers so that Lincoln students may keep themselves informed on current events and trends. [...]

"Observation indicates that Lincoln students have a decisive advantage over other students, particularly in other cities and towns, since the Lincoln Library is open from 6 p.m. to 9 p.m. three nights each week for the convenience of the students."[29]

The last six students to complete their education at the Abraham Lincoln School of Snyder gathered in the gymnasium and smiled for the cameras of the Snyder Daily News. Preparations had been underway for weeks. "Don Browning, minister at the East Side Church of Christ, will be the speaker at baccalaureate services for Lincoln High School''s seniors," noted the paper.

"The service is set for 3 p.m. Sunday, May 23.

"Mr. Browning, a Snyder native, returned here a year ago to become minister of the East Side church, moving here from Tahoka, where he was minister at the Church of Christ. He graduated from Fluvanna High School in 1955 and holds the bachelor of science degree in Bible from Abilene Christian College, where he is nearing completion of requirements for his masters degree.

"Mr. Browning will be introduced by Daniel L. Johnson, principal of Lincoln School. Mrs. Anniece Johnson will play the processional and recessional music, and special music will be presented by the Lincoln Chorus.

"Immediately following Mr. Browning's sermon, Vera Newsome will sing a solo, "Sometimes I Feel Like a Motherless Child.

"The Lincoln commencement program has been scheduled for Wednesday evening [May 26, 1965]."[30]

LINCOLN'S LAST SENIOR CLASS—These Lincoln High seniors will be the last to receive diplomas at the local Negro school, since students in the Lincoln district will be attending Snyder High next year. From left, front row, are Emma Lorine Garrett, Mary Helen Goosby and Pearlie Jo Scott. Top row, from left, are Billy Norris Cobb, Woodruff L. Powell and Lennon J. Brooks. Powell is the valedictorian of the Class of 1965, and Miss Scott is the salutatorian.

Snyder Daily News. May 23, 1965.

Segregation had come to an end in Snyder's schools. On paper, at least. It had been almost two years since the installation of the William Scurry monument. Eight years since high school classes were first offered at Lincoln. Eleven years since *Brown v. The Board*. Twelve years since the annexation of The Flats. Thirteen years since Lincoln School's construction. Sixteen years since the arrival of Daniel Johnson. Seventeen years since the oil boom. Thirty-nine years since the creation of The Flat. Forty years since the founding of the Dunbar School. Forty-five years since the establishment of Mount Olive Baptist Church. Fifty years since the bombing of Jim Percy's hotel. Fifty-one years since the arrival of Scurry County's African-American community. Eighty-seven years since the beginnings of Snyder, Texas. Eighty-nine years since the naming of Scurry County. Ninety years since western Texas was taken from the Comanche. And one hundred years since the end of the American Civil War.

EPILOGUE
BETTER TO HAVE

In memory of Dan Johnson

Principal of Lincoln School from 1949-50 to 1964-65, who instilled in each of us " it is better to have it and not need, than need it and not have it".

1986 Lincoln School reunion booklet. Courtesy Scurry County Museum.

President Johnson signed the Voting Rights Act of 1965 eleven days after the last high school graduation ceremony at Lincoln. The act outlawed poll taxes, literacy tests, grandfather clauses, and other legal barriers designed to discourage voter participation. States like Texas with long histories of ballot suppression would now be required to get federal approval before amending their voting requirements.

"Passage of the Johnson administration's voting rights bill jeopardizes Texas' system of registering most voters: the poll tax," fretted the Snyder Daily News. *"The bill directs the attorney general to sue at once, challenging the constitutionality of poll taxes in the four states still using them - Texas, Alabama, Mississippi, and Virginia.*

"A federal court, and subsequently the U.S. Supreme Court, could act on such cases before Texas voters get a chance to abolish the poll tax on their own in November 1966. The 50th legislature approved a proposed constitutional amendment doing away with the tax as a voting requirement, but voter action is still needed.

"'It's my duty to defend the laws of Texas, and in the event the U.S. attorney general challenges their validity we will meet him in the courtroom,' said Atty. Gen. Waggoner Carr of Texas."[1]

The Voting Rights Act prevented Texas from imposing new ballot restrictions on its residents until the Supreme Court cases of *Shelby County v. Holder* (2013) and *Brnovich v. Democratic National Committee* (2021) rendered portions of the act unenforceable.

■■

Vernon Clay's senior year of high school would begin in two minutes. He stood on the sidewalk on the north side of Snyder High where the former students of the Abraham Lincoln School were gathered together in a little clump.

They were being watched from all sides. Some of the eyes were merely curious or trying to appreciate the gravity of the moment. Others looked on with burning malice or in patient vigilance for the safety of the newcomers. Regardless of anyone's intent, the first Black students to enter Snyder High School would be closely observed every day from the moment they arrived on campus to the moment they left.

When the first bell sounded on the morning of August 30, 1965, the little cluster of teenagers made their way up the front steps of Snyder High in a single mass. After passing through the glass and steel doors, they paused at the junction of the fine arts and administration wings. There they shared a brief moment of goodbye before scattering themselves into the rush of Snyder's youth.[2,3]

"Racial barriers fell quietly throughout the South," said the Snyder Daily News on the following morning, *"as thousands of Negroes began attending classes with white pupils on the first day of widespread school desegregation accelerated by the 1964 Civil Rights Act.*

"There was no trace of the violent, bitter resistance of earlier years as the trend of quiet change, indicated last year, became a clear-cut pattern in rural and urban areas alike Monday. Few, if any, incidents were reported in the South, and it appeared the era of racial segregation in schools was coming to an end.

"Indicative of the change was Mansfield, Tex. which became a Southern symbol of resistance to school integration less than a decade ago when whites staged mass protests to integration. All was quiet Monday as about 70 Negro junior and senior high school students attended desegregated classes."[4]

Meanwhile, *"a 1963 graduate of Lincoln High School has had his scholarship renewed, another Lincoln graduate has received a new scholarship and five of six of the last graduating class of Lincoln High School will be attending college this fall.*[5]

1965-'66 would be Lincoln's last year as a public school. The high school students were on the other side of town now. The junior high kids were mostly up the street at Travis eating hot food in the same lunchroom where their parents had once received cold leftovers.

Only sixty-nine children came on the first day of school. The last time there had been so few was in 1953 when the building was less than half its current size. The Abraham Lincoln School of Snyder, built to handle 500 but never blessed with even half that many, felt terribly empty in the fall of 1965.[6]

On paper this was integration. Young children were told to report to whichever elementary school was the closest to where they lived. However, due to the way Snyder was built in the first place, the children of The Flats wound up right back at Lincoln.

But the writing was on the wall. On January 12, 1966, Snyder's front page included the headline: *"School Vote Set; Lincoln To Close."*

"The Snyder School Board last night issued the official call for the annual board election, served notice that the Lincoln School building will not be used next fall as a regular classroom facility, and extended Supt. Robert Clinton's contract through the 1967-68 term.

"It was noted that a substantial decrease in enrollment is expected next term in the Central-Lincoln district, and that facilities at the Central Elementary building will be adequate to handle all pupils in the district. During the current term, the Lincoln building houses six grades and the present enrollment is 76."[7]

Four months later, on May 26, 1966, the Snyder Daily News announced that *"over 200 Snyder High School seniors will receive diplomas this evening at the school's commencement program. The graduation rites will begin at 8 p.m. in the SHS auditorium. [...]*

"Ben Brock, SHS principal, will preside at the commencement. Dr. Robert Clinton, superintendent of schools, will present the graduates to Kenneth Wilson, president of the school board, who will award the diplomas."[8]

By virtue of alphabetical order, Vernon Clay became the first African-American student to receive a diploma from Snyder High School. Five days later the local paper reported that *"Dan Johnson, principal of the Lincoln School in Snyder, will receive his Masters Degree in Education June 2 in commencement ceremonies to be held at Eastern New Mexico University in Portales.*

"Johnson has been a certified principal since 1951. He also received lifetime certificates for elementary and high school principal and superintendent from the Commissioner of Education in 1956."[9]

██

Twelve years after the *Brown v. The Board* decision, the student body of Snyder ISD was finally fully integrated. But the desegregation of the faculty did not go as smoothly.

"Snyder School officials were puzzled by reports over the weekend that the Snyder Consolidated Independent School District may not have complied with federal regulations concerning faculty integration.

"At the same time, no official notice of such failure to comply had been received here this morning, although press service wires carried a report late Saturday that Snyder, Abilene, and Coleman schools faced possible withdrawal of federal funds because faculty integration did not meet requirements.

"'We thought we had done more than required,' said Kenneth Wilson, president of the Snyder School Board.

"Pat Falls, assistant superintendent, said the administration believed that all requirements had been met as late as the past week when Dr. Robert Clinton, superintendent, conferred with officials in Washington, D.C. by telephone. Dr. Clinton checked with the officials in the capital before he left for San Francisco where he is currently attending a workshop for school administrators. At that time, Snyder's files in Washington were checked and officials there indicated that everything was in order.

"There were reports late Saturday that official notices should have been received by the three schools no later than last Friday. However, no such notice had arrived in Snyder this morning.

"All teachers who formerly taught in the all-Negro Lincoln School here and who sought contracts here have been placed in jobs with the local school system except one, and the lone exception has been offered a position in the system here and may yet accept.

"There will be no all-Negro school in the Snyder district henceforth, since all operations at the Lincoln School have been halted."[10]

Mary and John Baker, circa 1970. Courtesy Dr. Walter Morris Baker.

■■

John Baker witnessed all of it. With the exception of his Great War service at Camp Bowie in 1918, Mr. Baker lived through the entire experience of legal segregation in Scurry County. Throughout most of that time, he was among the most publicly visible residents of his community and an unofficial cultural ambassador between the two Snyders.

Though it has since been covered over in a facade of bricks, John Baker's home in The Flats still stands across the street from the church to which he dedicated his time and his soul. His remains are buried at Mary Baker's side in the Hillside Memorial Gardens Cemetery on Snyder's southeastern outskirts. Across the street to the west sit the crumbling remains of Hunter Lodge No. 920, founded by Worshipful Master John Baker.

246

Filed safely away in the archive of the Scurry County Museum is, arguably, the most important artifact regarding the Black History of Snyder. It is a letter written by a seventy-six-year-old John Baker on February 14, 1973. In this letter, Mr. Baker explains that *"the Negroes who came out here to work in the Fuller Oil Mill came from Waskom, TX, near the Louisiana line on a 'party ticket'. [...] It took at least 50 persons to qualify for this kind of transportation. The pay was $8.50 per week and housing was furnished."*[11]

Mr. Baker's obituary appeared in the Snyder Daily News on November 23, 1975.

"John Baker, 78, who lived at 1204 34th Street, died at 5 a.m. Saturday in Cogdell Memorial Hospital where he had been a patient for the past month.

"Funeral arrangements were pending at Bell-Seale Funeral Home.

"A native of Waskom, in Deep East Texas, Mr. Baker had been an employee of Snyder National Bank for the past 54 years.

"He was married in 1920 at Marshall to Miss Mary Calvert. She proceeded him in death in 1971.

"Surviving are a brother, Clemmie T. Baker of San Francisco, Calif., and a number of nieces and nephews."[12]

Grave of John and Mary Baker at Hillside Memorial Gardens cemetery near Snyder, Texas.

Abraham Lincoln School reunion. June, 1986. Courtesy Scurry County Museum.

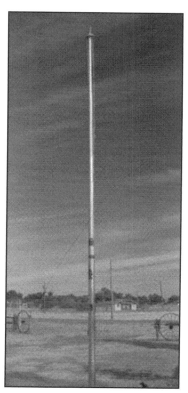

The Abraham Lincoln School flag pole at Scurry County Historic Village.

NOTES

1: Firebrands And Dynamite

1. *Outlawry Should Be Condemned*. The Snyder Signal. July 9, 1915. Pg. 1.
2. Letter by John Baker, written February 14, 1973. Scurry County Museum. Artifact ID: 1975.002.001.
3. Speir, Thomas. *Historic Survey of Waskom, Harrison County, Texas*. East Texas Historical Journal. Vol. 55. Issue 2. Article 6. Fall, 2017.
4. *The Handbook of Texas Online: Cotton Culture*. Texas State Historical Association.
5. *The Handbook of Texas Online: Segregation*. Texas State Historical Association.
6. Sanborn Fire Insurance Map from Snyder, Scurry County, Texas. April, 1911. U.S. Library of Congress.
7. Sanborn Fire Insurance Map from Snyder, Scurry County, Texas. January, 1920. U.S. Library of Congress.
8. *Negro Woman Tried In The Mayor's Court*. The Snyder Signal. April 23, 1915. Pg. 3.
9. *Colored Baptists Organize*. The Snyder Signal. June 25, 1915. Pg. 5.
10. *Snyder is a rapidly growing…* The Snyder Signal. July 9, 1915. Pg. 1.
11. *The Negro Hotel Was Dynamited*. The Snyder Signal. July 9, 1915. Pg. 1.
12. *Negroes Are Leaving Town*. The Corsicana Daily Sun. July 9, 1915. Pg. 1.
13. *Negro Hotel Is Badly Damaged*. The Daily Bulletin (Brownwood). July 8, 1915. Pg. 1.
14. *A Negro Hotel Was Dynamited*. The Bryan Daily Eagle. July 8, 1915. Pg. 1.
15. *Negro Hotel At Snyder Dynamited*. The Daily Ledger (Ballinger). July 9, 1915. Pg. 2.
16. *Negro Hotel Blown Up*. The Houston Post. July 9, 1915. Pg. 4.
17. *Negro Hotel Dynamited*. The San Antonio Express. July 9, 1915. Pg. 4.
18. *Negroes Flee From Snyder*. The San Antonio Express. July 10, 1915. Pg. 4.
19. *Negroes Trekked*. The Temple Daily Telegram. July 10, 1915. Pg. 6.
20. *A Negro Hotel…* The Hutchinson News (Kansas). July 8, 1915. Pg. 8.
21. *Negro Hotel Dynamited*. The Daily Advocate (Victoria). July 10, 1915. Pg. 1.
22. *Snyder Negro Hotel Was Dynamited Today*. The Brownsville Herald. July 9, 1915. Pg. 3.
23. *Negroes Leave Town Following Explosion*. The Brownsville Herald. July 10, 1915. Pg. 3.
24. *Negro Hotel At Snyder Blown Up*. Abilene Daily Reporter. July 8, 1915. Pg. 1.
25. *Negro Hotel Dynamited*. Ardmore Daily Ardmoreite. July 8, 1915. Pg. 1.
26. *Hotel Wrecked*. Galveston Tribune. July 8, 1915. Pg. 2.
27. *Negroes Leave Snyder After Hotel Dynamited*. Wichita Daily Times. July 9, 1915. Pg. 4.
28. *Negroes Are Leaving Town*. Corsicana Daily Sun. July 9, 1915. Pg. 1.
29. *Negro Hotel Blown Up*. Joplin News Herald (Missouri). July 8, 1915. Pg. 3.
30. *Dynamited Negro Hotel*. Laredo Weekly Times. July 11, 1915. Pg. 10.
31. *Hotel For Negroes At Snyder Wrecked*. McKinney Daily Courier-Gazette. July 9, 1915. Pg. 5.
32. *Touching off Bombs Under Negro Houses*. Temple Daily Telegram. July 9, 1915. Pg 1.
33. Sanborn Fire Insurance Map from Snyder, Scurry County, Texas. June, 1927. U.S. Library of Congress.

2: The Limits Laid Out

1. *Negro Laborers Assault White Mill Superintendent Here Monday Nite*. The Snyder Signal. March 19, 1920. Pg. 1.
2. O'Neal, Bill. *The Johnson-Sims Feud: Romeo and Juliet, West Texas Style*. Chapter 7: *Tragedy in Snyder*. University of North Texas Press. 2010.
3. *Workers Under President Woodrow Wilson*. US Department of Labor website. Accessed May, 2022.
4. Scurry County War Memorial. Snyder courthouse square, north lawn.

5. *The Handbook of Texas Online: Snyder, Texas*. Texas State Historical Association.
6. *The Handbook of Texas Online: Cotton Culture*. Texas State Historical Association.
7. McWhirter, Cameron. Red Summer: The Summer of 1919 and the Awakening of Black America. St. Martin's Griffin, 2012.
8. *"A negro rebellion..."* The Snyder Signal. August 1, 1919. Pg. 4.
9. *"Northern people have thought..."* The Snyder Signal. July 25, 1919. Pg. 8.
10. *"A general race war..."* The Snyder Signal. August 1, 1919. Pg. 8.
11. *The Handbook of Texas Online: Longview Race Riot of 1919*. Texas State Historical Association.
12. *Whites Clash With Negroes in Port Arthur.* The Pensacola Journal. July 15, 1919. Pg. 1.
13. *"In Washington City..."* The Snyder Signal. July 25, 1919. Pg. 8.
14. *"White people throughout..."* The Snyder Signal. August 1, 1919. Pg. 3.
15. Hartfield, Claire. *A Few Red Drops: The Chicago Race Riot of 1919*. Clarion Books. 2018.
16. *"Chicago is in the throes..."* The Snyder Signal. August 1, 1919. Pg. 8.
17. *Southern Manhood And The Negro*. The Snyder Signal. August 1, 1919. Pg. 7.
18. U.S. Army Service Card for John Baker. Serial number 4,857,289 (Colored). Form No. 724-2 1/2 A.G.O. March 12, 1920.
19. *Mt. Olive Church In Its 36th Year.* The Snyder Daily News. April 27, 1956. Pg. 10.
20. *To The Citizens Of Snyder And Scurry County*. The Snyder Signal. April 2, 1920. Pg. 3.
21. *The Signal's Attitude As To The Negro Situation*. The Snyder Signal. April 2, 1920. Pg. 1.

3: If Kare Should Interfere

1. *High School Notes*. The Snyder Signal. November 18, 1921. Pg. 1.
2. *The Handbook of Texas Online: Prohibition*. Texas State Historical Association.
3. *The Handbook of Texas Online: Woman Suffrage*. Texas State Historical Association.
4. *Unusual Interest in Thanksgiving Service*. The Snyder Signal. November 25, 1921. Pg.1.
5. *A Communication From Snyder Ku Klux Klan*. The Snyder Signal. December 16, 1921. Pg. 1.
6. *Schools Had Important Role In Development Of County*. The Snyder Daily News. Dec. 9, 1962. Sec. 2, pg. 10 - 11.
7. *Baker Serves For 33 Years.* The Snyder Daily News. March 13, 1955. Pg. 7.
8. *John Baker Dies Saturday*. The Snyder Daily News. November 23, 1975. Pg 1.
9. Sanborn Fire Insurance Map from Snyder, Scurry County, Texas. January, 1920. U.S. Library of Congress
10. *The Handbook of Texas Online: White Primary*. Texas State Historical Association.
11. *The Handbook of Texas Online: Scurry County*. Texas State Historical Association.
12. *Roy Jennings First Colored Citizen To Purchase Property*. The Scurry County Times. December 30, 1937. Sec. 2. Pg. 14.
13. *Resolution*. Scurry County Times. April 17, 1924. Pg. 1.
14. *The Handbook of Texas Online: Ku Klux Klan*. Texas State Historical Association.
15. *The Handbook of Texas Online: Evans, Hiram Wesley*. Texas State Historical Association.
16. *W. S. Arms, Kleagle...* Scurry County Times-Signal. May 8, 1924. Pg 1.
17. *S. W. Arms Speaks In Interest Ku Klux Klan*. Scurry County Times-Signal. May 15, 1924. Pg. 1
18. Klansmen Klanswomen... Scurry County Times-Signal. July 10, 1924. Pg 5.
19. *The Handbook of Texas Online: Ferguson, Miriam Amanda Wallace [Ma]*. Texas State Historical Association.
20. *The Attitude Of The Ku Klux Klan Toward The Negro*. Scurry County Times-Signal. July 17, 1924. Pg 5.
21. *Attention Klansmen*. Scurry County Times-Signal. March 13, 1924. Pg 1.
22. *Klansmen, Klanswomen*. Scurry County Times-Signal. July 10, 1924. Pg 5.
23. *Public Lecture*. Scurry County Times-Signal. September 14, 1924. Pg 3.
24. *Klansmen Joint Meeting*. Scurry County Times-Signal. March 12, 1925. Pg 6.

4: Heartily In Sympathy

1. *A move is on foot...* Scurry County Times-Signal. May 21, 1925. Pg. 6.
2. *Altrurian Club.* Scurry County Times-Signal. October 16, 1924. Pg. 7.
3. Texas Legislative sessions and years. Legislative Reference Library of Texas website.
4. 1925 Constitution of the United States and Texas. Texas Historical Statutes Project. Texas State Law Library.
5. 1925 Penal Code of the State of Texas. Texas Historical Statutes Project. Texas State Law Library.
6. Photo artifact: *"R.S.&P. Depot at Snyder."* Courtesy Roscoe Historical Museum. Roscoe, Texas.
7. *R. S. & P. Official Here.* Scurry County Times-Signal. November 26, 1925. Pg. 5.
8. *School Kept For Colored Section.* Scurry County Times. December 30, 1937. Sec 5. Pg. 10.
9. *Locals.* Scurry County Times-Signal. January 14, 1926. Pg. 7.
10. Recorded interview with Vernest Tippens, May 22, 1984. Scurry County Museum Archive. Tape 74.
11. *Missionary Work In Snyder.* Scurry County Times-Signal. February 11, 1926. Pg. 2
12. Scurry County Records Office, Plat Cabinet A, Slide 80. [Colored Edition renamed Erwin Heights Addition January 6, 1957.]
13. *Committee Disbanded.* Scurry County Times-Signal. April 29, 1926. Pg. 7
14. *We see...* Scurry County Times-Signal. August 12, 1926. Pg. 4
15. *The Times-Signal's Editorial...* Scurry County Times-Signal. August 19, 1926. Pg. 4
16. *Mt. Olive Baptist Church (Colored).* Scurry County Times-Signal. November 4, 1926. Pg. 7
17. *Card Of Thanks.* Scurry County Times-Signal. November 11, 1926. Pg. 6
18. *15,000 Attend Snyder's Mammoth Fourth Of July Barbecue And Picnic.* Scurry County Times-Signal. July 7, 1927. Pg. 1
19. *Schools Had Important Role In Development Of County.* The Snyder Daily News. Dec. 9, 1962. Sec. 2, pg. 10 - 11
20. *Colored Baptist Church Is To Be Dedicated Sunday.* Scurry County Times-Signal. March 29, 1928. Pg. 2
21. *Colored Baptists Dedicate Church.* Scurry County Times-Signal. April 5, 1928. Pg. 1
22. *Real Estate Transfers.* Scurry County Times-Signal. April 19, 1928. Pg. 3
23. *Real Estate Transfers.* Scurry County Times-Signal. June 7, 1928. Pg. 3
24. Charles G. Anderson. *Reflections 1840 - 1990.* Snyder Publishing Company Inc. Pg. 176.
25. *Makers of Snyder: Morse Bantau and Earl Fish.* Scurry County Times-Signal. April 2, 1925. Pg. 1
26. *Makers of Snyder: Richard W. (Dick) Webb.* Scurry County Times-Signal. April 9, 1925. Pg. 1
27. *Makers of Snyder: Tom Boren.* Scurry County Times-Signal. April 16, 1925. Pg. 1
28. *Makers of Snyder: Ernest Taylor.* Scurry County Times-Signal. April 23, 1925. Pg. 1
29. *Makers of Snyder: Joe Strayhorn.* Scurry County Times-Signal. April 30, 1925. Pg. 1
30. *Makers of Snyder: H.L. (Liv) Davis.* Scurry County Times-Signal. May 7, 1925. Pg. 1
31. *Makers of Snyder: George Northcutt.* Scurry County Times-Signal. May 14, 1925. Pg. 1
32. *Makers of Snyder: "Bill" Clyde Schull.* Scurry County Times-Signal. May 21, 1925. Pg. 1
33. *Makers of Snyder: William Porter King.* Scurry County Times-Signal. June 4, 1925. Pg. 1
34. *Makers of Snyder: Howard Garfield Towle.* Scurry County Times-Signal. June 18, 1925. Pg. 1
35. *Makers of Snyder: Henry Rosenberg.* Scurry County Times-Signal. June 25, 1925. Pg. 1

5: 1930 Howling

1. *Gradual Prosperity in 1931 Seen By Civic and Church Leaders.* Scurry County Times-Signal. January 8, 1931. Pg. 1.
2. *Just Like The "Big Boys".* The Scurry County Times. April 14, 1932. Pg. 1.

3. *Highway Work Started.* Scurry County Times-Signal. February 27, 1930. Pg 3.
4. *Innocent Petitioners Stop Work On Road.* Scurry County Times-Signal. March 6, 1930. Pg 3.
5. *Decennial Census of Population and Housing.* United States Census Bureau. 1930.
6. *Colored School Will Have Program May 8; All Are Welcome.* The Snyder News. May 2, 1930. Pg 5.
7. *The Handbook of Texas Online: Sherman Riot of 1930.* Texas State Historical Association.
8. Swanson, Doug J. *Cult of Glory: The Bold and Brutal History of the Texas Rangers.* Penguin Books, 2020. Chapter 17: *"One Riot".*
9. Trent, Sydney. *In Texas, a struggle to memorialize a brutal lynching as resistance grows to teaching historical racism.* The Washington Post. June 3, 2021.
10. *The Month's News.* Scurry County Times-Signal. May 22, 1930. Pg 4.
11. *Notes And Comments.* Scurry County Times-Signal. June 5, 1930. Pg 7.
12. Dedmon, Kylee. *Historical Marker for 1930 Sherman Riot Approved.* KXII Texoma website. February 2, 2022.
13. *Colored Folks West Texas Here June 19.* Scurry County Times-Signal. May 29, 1930. Pg 8.
14. *Colored Folks Will Celebrate Emancipation Day.* Scurry County Times-Signal. June 12, 1930. Pg 3.
15. *Colored Folks Celebrate Day At Wolf Park.* Scurry County Times-Signal. June 19, 1930. Pg 1.
16. *"Juneteenth" was a most quiet...* Scurry County Times-Signal. June 26, 1930. Pg 2.
17. *Justice Loses to Death in Snyder; It Makes a Story.* The Snyder News. June 27, 1930. Pg 1.
18. Pardon book 1926-1930. Texas Board of Pardon Advisers. Volume 1990/134-5. Texas State Library and Archives Commission.
19. Van Winkle, Irene. *TB Hospital for Blacks Gave Hope to Many Who Recovered.* The West Kerr Current. Ingram, Texas. February 21, 2008.
20. *Cattle Price Drops.* Scurry County Times-Signal. July 10, 1930. Pg. 1.
21. The Town Doctor, Doctor of Towns. Scurry County Times-Signal. August 7, 1930. Pg 4.
22. The Town Doctor, Doctor of Towns. Scurry County Times-Signal. August 21, 1930. Pg 4.
23. *Altrurian Women Place "Hobo Box" At Stinson No.1.* Scurry County Times-Signal. January 22, 1931. Pg. 1.
24. *School Taxes To Be Divided In Three Parts.* Scurry County Times-Signal. January 15, 1931. Pg. 1.
25. *Thrift Program To Be Presented By Club Tonight.* Scurry County Times-Signal. January 22, 1931. Pg. 1.
26. *Garden Planting On Scurry Farms Urged By Agent.* Scurry County Times-Signal. January 29, 1931. Pg. 9.
27. Snyder National Bank historic marker (1979). Texas Historical Commission. Northeast corner of 26th St. and Ave. R in Snyder, Texas.
28. Author's interview with Dr. Walter Morris Baker, nephew of John and Mary Baker. August, 2022.
29. *Drouth Loan Funds Should Come Any Day.* Scurry County Times-Signal. February 12, 1931. Pg. 1.
30. *Government Loans Net County $123,000.* Scurry County Times-Signal. May 14, 1931. Pg. 1.
31. *Hundreds Search For Negro Child Lost On Ranch.* Scurry County Times-Signal. July 30, 1931. Pg. 1.
32. *Hunt for Negro Child Convinces Dock White Man Is Friend.* Scurry County Times-Signal. August 6, 1931. Pg. 1.
33. *"A Fine Demonstration".* Lynn County News reprinted in the Scurry County Times-Signal. August 20, 1931. Pg. 4.
34. *We Believe We'll Live Over It.* Scurry County Times-Signal. September 3, 1931. Pg. 4.
35. *Snyder School Board Slashed $6,000 Off 1931-32 Budget.* Scurry County Times-Signal. August 20, 1931. Pg. 1.

36. *"Dear Santa Claus:"*. Scurry County Times-Signal. December 10, 1931. Pg. 5.
37. *Old time pit-cooked barbecue*. The Scurry County Times. April 14, 1932. Pg. 7.
38. *Operating Expenses of the County Reduced*. The Scurry County Times. July 14, 1932. Pg. 8.
39. Leip, David. "Dave Leip's Atlas of U.S. Presidential Elections".
40. *Where Ideas Are Born*. The Snyder News. April 11, 1930. Pg. 1.
41. *Backward, Turn Backward*. The Scurry County Times. May 12, 1932. Pg. 1.
42. *Index of Prices Received And Paid by Farmers 1910-1932*. The Scurry County Times. June 29, 1933. Pg. 1.
43. *And A Happy New Year*. The Scurry County Times. December 29, 1932. Pg. 1.

6: Two Gaunt Horsemen

1. *Current Comment*. The Scurry County Times. July 30, 1936. Pg. 4.
2. Sanborn Fire Insurance Map from Snyder, Scurry County, Texas. January, 1936. U.S. Library of Congress.
3. *Thanksgiving- And Depression*. The Scurry County Times. November 24, 1932. Pg. 4.
4. *Heavy Scurry Liquor Traffic States Democratic Chairman*. The Scurry County Times. February 23, 1933. Pg. 5.
5. *Far-Reaching Events for Scurry County*. The Scurry County Times. June 22, 1933. Pg. 4.
6. *Current Comment*. The Scurry County Times. October 26, 1933. Pg. 4.
7. *The Most Disgraceful*. The Scurry County Times. January 4, 1934. Pg. 4.
8. *Scurry County and Her Front Yard - Across the Atlantic*. The Scurry County Times. March 1, 1934. Pg. 4.
9. *Bank Closed Monday*. The Scurry County Times. June 7, 1934. Pg. 1.
10. *Concert to Be Given By Colored Students*. The Scurry County Times. February 15, 1934. Pg. 1.
11. *Colored Program*. The Scurry County Times. April 12, 1934. Pg. 1
12. *Dunbar School Will Close Friday Night*. The Scurry County Times. April 19, 1934. Pg. 1.
13. *Colored Bout On Fight Card*. The Scurry County Times. March 22, 1934. Pg. 1.
14. *Boxing Program In Bad Way Last Week*. The Scurry County Times. March 29, 1934. Pg. 8.
15. *BOXING*. The Scurry County Times. March 22, 1934. Pg. 5.
16. *Temperature Has An Upward Swing*. The Scurry County Times. July 5, 1934. Pg. 1.
17. *Only .40 Inch Of Rain In June*. The Scurry County Times. July 5, 1934. Pg. 1.
18. *Two Relief Projects Completed In Snyder*. The Scurry County Times. June 21, 1934. Pg. 1
19. *Quick Action On Drouth Relief Set Up*. The Scurry County Times. July 5, 1934. Pg. 1.
20. *The Handbook of Texas Online: White Primary*. Texas State Historical Association.
21. *What About the Negroes?* The Scurry County Times. July 26, 1934. Pg. 6.
22. *Belated Report of Negro Health Week Sent From Lubbock*. The Scurry County Times. November 29, 1934. Pg. 6.
23. *Old Man Weather Unloads Several Unwanted Guests*. The Scurry County Times. February 28, 1935. Pg. 8.
24. *County Gets Taste Of Duststorm That Submerges Plains*. The Scurry County Times. March 7, 1935. Pg. 1.
25. *Good, Evil and Otherwise Rule County Weather*. The Scurry County Times. March 28, 1935. Pg. 8.
26. *Sand Storms As News*. The Scurry County Times. March 14, 1935. Pg. 4.
27. *Wanted: An Inventor*. The Scurry County Times. April 18, 1935. Pg. 4.
28. *Crap Shooters Vs. Soil Wasters*. The Scurry County Times. September 17, 1936. Pg. 4.
29. *AAA Programs Bring County 1934 Cash Totaling $522,000*. The Scurry County Times. January 3, 1935. Pg. 1.
30. *Farmers Get $44,553.50 In 1934 Cotton Checks*. The Scurry County Times. January 3, 1935. Pg. 1.
31. *Shelter Belt To Cross This County*. The Scurry County Times. April 25, 1935. Pg. 1.

32. *Current Comment*. The Scurry County Times. June 6, 1935. Pg. 4.
33. *The Handbook of Texas Online: Dust Bowl*. Texas State Historical Association.
34. *To Baptize Colored Folks at Wolf Park*. The Scurry County Times. August 22, 1935. Pg. 1.
35. *Scurry Could Get $283,000 Through WPA*. The Scurry County Times. August 1, 1935. Pg. 1.
36. *Entire System Is Under One Roof*. The Scurry County Times. December 30, 1937. Sec. 5. Pg. 2
37. *More WPA Projects Okeyed*. The Scurry County Times. September 5, 1935. Pg. 1.
38. *Local Gym To Be Erected As WPA Project*. The Scurry County Times. October 3, 1935. Pg. 1.
39. *Gymnasium At Local School Begun Friday*. The Scurry County Times. November 7, 1935. Pg. 1.
40. *The Tavern Has Dressed Up!*. The Scurry County Times. November 28, 1935. Pg. 5.
41. *Yes, Mr. President*. The Scurry County Times. August 3, 1933. Pg. 7.

7: Accomplished By Vandals

1. Lanehart, Chuck. *Caprock Chronicles: J. Wright Mooar and Snyder's Legendary Buffalo*. Lubbock Avalanche-Journal. January 31, 2021.
2. *J. Wright Mooar Pictured Recently in Connection With Star-Telegram Story*. The Scurry County Times. May 7, 1936. Pg. 1.
3. *The Handbook of Texas Online: Scurry County*. Texas State Historical Association.
4. *The Handbook of Texas Online: Red River War*. Texas State Historical Association.
5. *The Handbook of Texas Online: Buffalo Hunting*. Texas State Historical Association.
6. *The Handbook of Texas Online: Black Codes*. Texas State Historical Association.
7. *The Handbook of Texas Online: Mooar, Josiah Wright*. Texas State Historical Association.
8. *The Handbook of Texas Online: Snyder, TX (Scurry County)*. Texas State Historical Association.
9. *The Handbook of Texas Online: Snyder, William Henry [Pete}*. Texas State Historical Association.
10. Becker, John T. "Jack". *Caprock Chronicles: Picking bison bones for profit*. Lubbock Avalanche-Journal. December 15, 2017.
11. *Decennial Census of Population and Housing*. United States Census Bureau.
12. *The Handbook of Texas Online: Cuney, Norris Wright*. Texas State Historical Association.
13. SJR 3, 27th Regular Session. Legislative Reference Library of Texas.
14. Stone, Brianna. *Why did Texas have a poll tax, and when did it end? Curious Texas investigates*. The Dallas Morning News. September 25, 2018.
15. *Seven Pictures of the Heart of West Texas Centennial Parade*. The Scurry County Times. April 30, 1936. Pg. 1.
16. *Thousands of People Enjoy Huge Pageant*. The Scurry County Times. April 30, 1936. Pg. 1.
17. *AAA Program Brings County $603,965.75*. The Scurry County Times. August 6, 1936. Pg. 1.
18. *1936 Drouth Almost Equals That In 1934; Rainfall 22 Per Cent Normal*. The Scurry County Times. September 10, 1936. Pg. 1.
19. *The Drouth (W.P. Bolin)*. The Scurry County Times. September 10, 1936. Pg. 4.
20. *The Drouth (E.C. Ralston)*. The Scurry County Times. September 10, 1936. Pg. 4.
21. *Many Blocks Will Be Paved Through WPA*. The Scurry County Times. September 3, 1936. Pg. 1.
22. *Gym Dedication Friday at 10:30*. The Scurry County Times. October 8, 1936. Pg. 1.
23. *Snyder Dedicates One of Her Most Beautiful Buildings*. The Scurry County Times. October 15, 1936. Pg. 1.
24. Leip, David. "Dave Leip's Atlas of U.S. Presidential Elections".
25. *Minstrels To Be Presented By Vet Women*. The Scurry County Times. December 10, 1936. Pg. 1.
26. *What Emergency Education Program Is Doing For Texas And Your County*. The Scurry County Times. January 7, 1937. Pg. 5.

27. *Prices Received And Prices Paid By Farmers*. The Scurry County Times. June 24, 1937. Pg. 5.
28. *Mayor Towle Relates How Federal-Aid Projects Have Improved Town*. The Scurry County Times. March 3, 1938. Pg. 3.
29. *Our Hearts Are Burned*. The Scurry County Times. March 17, 1938. Pg. 8.
30. *Smoldering School Building-In Spring Of 1938*. The Scurry County Times. September 7, 1939. Pg. 1.
31. *Start Of School In New Building Stirs Memories Of Horrible Fire*. The Scurry County Times. September 7, 1939. Pg. 3.
32. *School Plans*. The Scurry County Times. March 17, 1938. Pg. 1.
33. *Our Hearts Are Burned*. The Scurry County Times. March 17, 1938. Pg. 8.
34. *Classes Held This Week As Town Rallies*. The Scurry County Times. March 17, 1938. Pg. 1.
35. *$65,455 PWA Grant Assures New School*. The Scurry County Times. September 22, 1938. Pg. 1.
36. *Current Comment By Leon Guinn*. The Scurry County Times. April 14, 1938. Pg. 8.
37. *Colored School Plans Exercises Here Next Week*. The Scurry County Times. April 21, 1938. Pg. 1.
38. *Colored School Will Start Work Monday*. The Scurry County Times. October 6, 1938. Pg. 4.
39. Recorded interview with Vernest Tippens, May 22, 1984. Scurry County Museum Archive. Tape 74.
40. *Hallowe'en Social At Colored School*. The Scurry County Times. October 27, 1938. Pg. 3.
41. *Thanksgiving Plans For Colored School*. The Scurry County Times. November 17, 1938. Pg. 3.
42. *Santa Claus Coming With Candy Aplenty*. The Scurry County Times. December 8, 1938. Pg. 1
43. *Splendid Work for Colored School; All Busy With Studies*. The Scurry County Times. February 9, 1939. Pg. 3.
44. *Jitter-Bug Contest Juneteenth Affair*. The Scurry County Times. June 8, 1939. Pg. 6.
45. *Extreme Precipitation Depths for Texas, Excluding the Trans-Pecos Region*. United States Department of the Interior. United States Geological Survey. Water-Resources Investigations Report 98-4099. Pg 21.
46. *Flood Highlights as Seen by Reporters*. The Scurry County Times. June 22, 1939. Pg. 3.
47. *Correspondents' News Omitted*. The Scurry County Times. June 22, 1939. Pg. 7.
48. *County Counts Flood Ravages*. The Scurry County Times. June 29, 1939. Pg. 1.
49. *More Details About Flood's Ravages Given By Reporter*. The Scurry County Times. June 29, 1939. Pg. 1.
50. *Current Comment By Leon Guinn*. The Scurry County Times. August 31, 1939. Pg. 8.
51. *Snyder Schools Ready To Open In New "Safety" Plant*. The Scurry County Times. September 7, 1939. Pg. 1.
52. *Many Modern Features For School Plant*. The Scurry County Times. September 7, 1939. Pg. 10.
53. *Record Made With Colored School Work*. The Scurry County Times. April 25, 1940. Pg. 8.
54. *Magnolia Has Good Showing In First Well*. The Scurry County Times. September 14, 1939. Pg. 1.
55. *North Sharon Mudge Should Extend Field*. The Scurry County Times. November 2, 1939. Pg. 1.
56. *Large Crowd Attends Final Mooar Rites*. The Scurry County Times. May 9, 1940. Pg. 8.
57. Hunt, James Winford. *Buffalo Days: Stories from J. Wright Mooar*. State House Press, 2005.
58. *Black Tigers Down Anson Nine Sunday For Second Victory*. The Scurry County Times. May 9, 1940. Pg. 4.

8: Don't Raise Cannon Fodder

Notes

1. *Our Schools Don't Raise Cannon Fodder.* The Scurry County Times. September 7, 1939. Pg. 10.
2. *Armistice Day 1939.* The Scurry County Times. November 9, 1939. Pg. 1.
3. *Negro Jailed After Refusal To Register.* The Scurry County Times. November 21, 1940. Sec. 1 Pg. 1.
4. *Snyder School Opens Monday.* The Scurry County Times. September 5, 1940. Sec. 1 Pg. 1.
5. *Times Table: During our new school...* The Scurry County Times. September 5, 1940. Sec. 2 Pg. 1.
6. *Times Table: Never in our generation...* The Scurry County Times. September 5, 1940. Sec. 2 Pg. 1.
7. Leip, David. "Dave Leip's Atlas of U.S. Presidential Elections".
8. *FDR Gets Fine Vote In Scurry.* The Scurry County Times. November 7, 1940. Sec. 1 Pg. 1.
9. *County Gets Many Miles Of Highway Aid.* The Scurry County Times. November 7, 1940. Sec. 1 Pg. 3.
10. *Current Comment by Leon Guinn* The Scurry County Times. December 19, 1940. Sec. 2 Pg. 8.
11. March On Washington pamphlet, 1941. Franklin D. Roosevelt Presidential Library.
12. *The Civil Rights Act of 1964: The Long Struggle for Freedom.* A. Philip Randolph Challenges President Franklin Roosevelt. U.S. Library of Congress.
13. Executive Order 8802. General Records of the United States Government. Record Group 11. National Archives.
14. The Army's Traditional Negro Troop Policy [transcription]. Pg. 48. President's Committee On Equality Of Treatment And Opportunity In The Armed Forces (Vol. 4). Smithsonian National Air and Space Museum Archives. Benjamin O'Davis Jr. Collection.
15. *210 Quarts Beer Taken in Raid by Group Thursday.* The Scurry County Times. April 15, 1943. Pg. 1.
16. *Vacancy at Colored School.* The Scurry County Times. January 7, 1943. Pg. 1.
17. *17-Year-Olds Sought For Service in Navy.* The Scurry County Times. February 18, 1943. Pg. 5.
18. *First Colored WAAC Accepted Saturday.* The Scurry County Times. March 4, 1943. Pg. 1.
19. *Raise A Victory Garden.* The Scurry County Times. April 15, 1943. Pg. 9.
20. *Daily Prayer Offered By Colored Church.* The Scurry County Times. April 8, 1943. Pg. 7.
21. *210 Quarts Beer Taken in Raid by Group Thursday.* The Scurry County Times. April 15, 1943. Pg. 1.
22. *Scholastics to Show Decrease at Snyder.* The Scurry County Times. April 29, 1943. Pg. 6.
23. *These Coons Will Be Seen Next Thursday In Lion's Club's Minstrel.* The Scurry County Times. May 6, 1943. Pg. 1.
24. *Lions Minstrel Ready To Play To Full House At School Tonight.* The Scurry County Times. May 13, 1943. Pg. 1.
25. *Negro Minstrel Staged by Lions Grosses $418 Gate.* The Scurry County Times. May 20, 1943. Pg. 1.
26. *Nite Spot Cafe.* The Scurry County Times. June 17, 1943. Pg. 3.
27. *Juneteenth Ends In Death For Hardrick.* The Scurry County Times. June 24, 1943. Pg. 1.
28. *Sheriff John Lynch Quits Office July 1.* The Scurry County Times. June 24, 1943. Pg. 1.
29. *Letters From Our Readers.* The Scurry County Times. June 24, 1943. Pg. 8.
30. *Letters From Our Readers.* The Scurry County Times. July 1, 1943. Pg. 5.
31. *Anderson Davis Jr. Indicted for Murder By Grand Jury Body.* The Scurry County Times. July 1, 1943. Pg. 1.
32. *Race Problems.* The Scurry County Times. September 30, 1943. Pg. 8.
33. *Current Comment.* The Scurry County Times. November 18, 1943. Pg. 8.
34. *18 More Boys Put In New 1-A Draft Class.* The Scurry County Times. January 14, 1943. Pg. 1.

35. *Draftees Put In New Classes By Board Monday*. The Scurry County Times. February 4, 1943. Pg. 1.
36. *More County Draftees Put In Class 1-A*. The Scurry County Times. February 11, 1943. Pg. 1.
37. *Four Draftees In County Put In 1-A Class By Board*. The Scurry County Times. February 25, 1943. Pg. 1.
38. *37 County Men Put In 4-A By Draft Board*. The Scurry County Times. May 13, 1943. Pg. 1.
39. *Seven Draftees Called for Local Exam by Board*. The Scurry County Times. May 20, 1943. Pg. 1.
40. *Need For Men Reflected In Draft Action*. The Scurry County Times. May 27, 1943. Pg. 1.
41. *More County Draftees Are Placed In 1-A*. The Scurry County Times. June 3, 1943. Pg. 1.
42. *Seven Put In 1-A By County Draft Board*. The Scurry County Times. June 10, 1943. Pg. 1.
43. *105 Selectees Reclassified By Draft Unit*. The Scurry County Times. July 1, 1943. Pg. 1.
44. *19 Put In Class 1-A By County Draft Board*. The Scurry County Times. July 8, 1943. Pg. 1.
45. *52 Draftees Classified By Draft Board*. The Scurry County Times. July 15, 1943. Pg. 1.
46. *59 Classified This Week By Draft Board*. The Scurry County Times. July 22, 1943. Pg. 1.
47. *Large Group Put In 3-A (H) Draft Class*. The Scurry County Times. August 12, 1943. Pg. 3.
48. *11 Placed In Group 1-A By County Draft Board*. The Scurry County Times. August 19, 1943. Pg. 3.
49. *16 Placed In Class 1-A By Draft Board*. The Scurry County Times. September 30, 1943. Pg. 3.
50. *139 Draftees Put In 3-C For Record Class*. The Scurry County Times. October 14, 1943. Pg. 1.
51. *51 Draftees Put In 1-A By Draft Board*. The Scurry County Times. October 21, 1943. Pg. 1.
52. *Unreported Draftees Sought By Draft Unit*. The Scurry County Times. October 28, 1943. Pg. 6.
53. *135 Draftees Classified By Draft Board*. The Scurry County Times. November 25, 1943. Pg. 1.
54. Recorded interview with Vernest Tippens, May 22, 1984. Scurry County Museum Archive. Tape 74.
55. *The Handbook of Texas Online: Texans In World War II*. Texas State Historical Association.
56. *Leads in Drive for Good Will Funds*. The Scurry County Times. September 19, 1940. Sec. 1 Pg. 8.

9: Brewed In The Cauldron

1. *Stop Racial Strife in Time*. The Scurry County Times. November 21, 1946. Sec. 2 Pg. 8.
2. *To the Socialists of Scurry County*. The Snyder Signal. August 11, 1911. Pg. 7.
3. *Socialist Announcement*. The Snyder Signal. December 8, 1911. Pg. 8.
4. *Socialist Announcement*. The Snyder Signal. January 12, 1912. Pg. 4.
5. *The Handbook of Texas Online: Socialist Party*. Texas State Historical Association.
6. *The Handbook of Texas Online: Rebel*. Texas State Historical Association.
7. *The Handbook of Texas Online: Hickey, Thomas Aloysius*. Texas State Historical Association.
8. *Sheriff Strawn Shot; Negro Is Charged*. The Scurry County Times. August 15, 1946. Pg. 1.
9. *Sheriff Strawn Reported To Be Much Improved*. The Scurry County Times. August 22, 1946. Pg. 1.
10. *12 Years To Negro In Sheriff Shooting*. The Scurry County Times. December 5, 1946. Pg. 1.
11. *The Idea Is-*. The Scurry County Times. March 14, 1946. Pg. 2.
12. *The Handbook of Texas Online: Sweatt v. Painter*. Texas State Historical Association.
13. *Negro Enlistments Service Suspended In Pacific Area*. The Scurry County Times. July 25, 1946. Pg. 2.
14. *The Army And The Negro*. The Scurry County Times. July 25, 1946. Pg. 4.
15. *Liquor Fines To Court Action for Week in Snyder*. The Scurry County Times. February 28, 1946. Pg. 4.
16. *Open Pit Barbecue*. The Scurry County Times. May 22, 1947. Sec. 1 Pg. 6.

17. *Liquor Men Arrest Several in Big Raid*. The Scurry County Times. December 12, 1946. Sec. 1 Pg. 1.
18. *The Handbook of Texas Online: Daniel, Marion Price, Sr.* Texas State Historical Association.
19. *Colored School Sets Novel Tacky Party Thursday*. The Scurry County Times. May 1, 1947. Sec. 1. Pg. 5.
20. *Tacky Party Set at Negro School Tonight*. The Scurry County Times. May 8, 1947. Sec. 1. Pg. 6.
21. *Mason Will Speak at Negro Baccalaureate*. The Scurry County Times. May 8, 1947. Sec. 1. Pg. 10.
22. *Negro Davis Gets 10 Years For Cafe Shooting of Cole*. The Scurry County Times. March 25, 1948. Sec. 1. Pg. 1.
23. Harry S Truman, "Special Message to the Congress on Civil Rights," February 2, 1948. Public Papers of the Presidents of the United States. January 1 to December 31, 1948. Washington: United States Government Printing Office, 1964, n. 20.
24. *Civil Rights Program Center of Big Fight In Congress Declares Mahon*. The Scurry County Times. March 18, 1948. Sec. 1. Pg. 10.
25. *Current Comment*. The Scurry County Times. March 25, 1948. Sec. 2. Pg. 8.
26. *Current Comment*. The Scurry County Times. April 1, 1948. Sec. 2. Pg. 8.
27. *Negro Propaganda*. The Scurry County Times. April 22, 1948. Sec. 2. Pg. 8.
28. *Since Governor Jester came out...* The Scurry County Times. June 17, 1948. Sec. 2. Pg. 8.
29. *History Classes See Bill of Sale on Slave*. The Scurry County Times. January 15, 1948. Sec. 1. Pg. 6.
30. *Anderson Davis Nabbed Tuesday Morning by Cops*. The Scurry County Times. January 15, 1948. Sec. 1. Pg. 1.
31. *Big Anderson Davis Pays Two More Fines*. The Scurry County Times. February 19, 1948. Sec. 1. Pg. 1.
32. *Friendship Quilt to Raise Funds for Piano*. The Scurry County Times. April 15, 1948. Sec. 1. Pg. 2.
33. *$54 Raised on Piano For Colored School*. The Scurry County Times. May 13, 1948. Sec. 1. Pg. 1.
34. *Colored Masons Set Installation Services May 9*. The Scurry County Times. April 29, 1948. Sec. 1. Pg. 1.
35. *Visiting Masons Due Sunday For Installation Rites*. The Scurry County Times. May 6, 1948. Sec. 1. Pg. 1.
36. *Schattel Well Producing 20 Barrels Hour*. The Scurry County Times. July 8, 1948. Sec. 1. Pg. 1.
37. *Sun Oil Well Fills All Storage Quickly*. The Scurry County Times. July 15, 1948. Sec. 1. Pg. 1.
38. *West Texas Taps A Big New Oil Pool*. LIFE Magazine. Vol. 27, No. 23. December 5, 1949. Pg. 40
39. *The Handbook of Texas Online: Kelley-Snyder Oilfield*. Texas State Historical Association.
40. *The Handbook of Texas Online: Scurry County*. Texas State Historical Association.

10: To Dam High

1. *West Texas Taps A Big New Oil Pool*. LIFE Magazine. Vol. 27, No. 23. December 5, 1949. Pg. 37-43.
2. *We Don't Want An Oil Boom*. The Scurry County Times. August 12, 1948. Sec. 2. Pg. 8.
3. *Colored Folks Float Wins Prize in Parade*. The Scurry County Times. July 15, 1948. Sec. 1. Pg. 1.
4. *News from the Flat*. The Scurry County Times. July 22, 1948. Sec. 1. Pg. 4.
5. *News from the Flat*. The Scurry County Times. August 5, 1948. Sec. 1. Pg. 6.
6. *News from the Flat*. The Scurry County Times. July 29, 1948. Sec. 1. Pg. 6.
7. *Snyder People Urged To Provide Housing*. The Scurry County Times. July 22, 1948. Sec. 1. Pg. 8.

8. *The Philadelphia Story: Truman-Barkley*. The Scurry County Times. July 29, 1948. Sec. 2. Pg. 3.
9. *Notice of Sale of School Property*. The Scurry County Times. August 26, 1948. Sec. 1. Pg. 7.
10. Bartels, Bernhard. *96 And Going Strong*. The Canyon Reef Oil Boom. Pg. 136-139. CreateSpace Independent Publishing Platform (January 11, 2016).
11. *Faculty For Snyder Schools Complete With One Exception*. The Scurry County Times. September 9, 1948. Sec. 1. Pg. 1.
12. *News from the Flat*. The Scurry County Times. October 14, 1948. Sec. 1. Pg. 7.
13. *Major Gas Lines Extensions Show Growth of City*. The Scurry County Times. September 30, 1948. Sec. 1. Pg. 1.
14. *"Harlem Upbeat"*. The Scurry County Times. October 21, 1948. Sec. 1. Pg. 8.
15. Leip, David. "Dave Leip's Atlas of U.S. Presidential Elections".
16. Hooper, Shelton. *From Buffalo...to Oil: History of Scurry County, Texas*. Scurry County Historical Survey Committee. Chapter 3. Pg. 45.
17. *Schools Had Important Role In Development Of County*. The Snyder Daily News. Dec. 9, 1962. Sec. 2, pg. 10 - 11.
18. *Decennial Census of Population and Housing*. United States Census Bureau.
19. Anderson, Charles G. *Reflections 1840 - 1990*. Snyder Publishing Company Inc. Pg. 320 - 321.
20. *Mt. Olive Church In Its 36th Year*. The Snyder Daily News. April 27, 1956. Pg. 10.
21. *$10 Million School Plant Is Built Here Within A Decade*. The Snyder Daily News. October 11, 1959. Pg. 46.
22. Waite, Charles V. *Price Daniel: Texas Attorney General, Governor, And Senator*. Texas Tech University Doctorate Dissertation In History. August, 1999. Pg. 58.
23. *Dr. H.G. Towle, Mayor for 20 Years, Dies*. The Snyder Daily News. November 12, 1950. Sec. 1. Pg. 1
24. *Miss Ivan Perry's...* The Snyder Daily News. December 24, 1950. Sec. 2. Pg. 2.
25. *Plans for New High School Are Approved*. The Snyder Daily News. February 14, 1951. Sec. 1. Pg. 1.
26. *School Board Passes Plans For Buildings*. The Snyder Daily News. March 14, 1951. Sec. 1. Pg. 1.
27. *Contracts for Administration Building and School Are Let*. The Snyder Daily News. June 13, 1951. Pg. 1.
28. *Enrollment is increased 22*. The Snyder Daily News. September 23, 1951. Sec. 1. Pg. 1.
29. *Names Chosen For City's 4 New Schools*. The Snyder Daily News. October 10, 1951. Pg. 1.
30. *School Enrollment At 3,271 Students Here*. The Snyder Daily News. November 21, 1951. Sec. 1. Pg. 2.
31. *Prepare For New Bridge*. The Snyder Daily News. May 4, 1952. Sec. 1. Pg. 1.
32. *Negro School Half Completed*. The Snyder Daily News. November 25, 1951. Sec. 1. Pg. 7.
33. *High School Will Almost Be City In Itself On Completion*. The Snyder Daily News. May 29, 1952. Sec. 1. Pg. 9.
34. *Cafeterias In Seven Schools Ready To Start September 5*. The Snyder Daily News. August 26, 1952. Sec. 1. Pg. 8.
35. *First Day at Central Primary*. The Snyder Daily News. September 7, 1952. Sec. 2. Pg. 1.
36. *Expansion Of Schools Is Not Completed*. The Snyder Daily News. January 4, 1953. Sec. 2. Pg. 7
37. *Team From Lincoln School Takes Firsts In League Contest*. The Snyder Daily News. April 15, 1953. Sec. 1. Pg. 5.
38. *County And School Agree On Road; Continuing Contracts*. The Snyder Daily News. May 13, 1953. Sec. 1. Pg. 2.
39. *Promotion At Lincoln School*. The Snyder Daily News. May 26, 1953. Sec. 1. Pg. 2.

40. *New High School Is Causing Some Shifts In The System Here.* The Snyder Daily News. July 26, 1953. Sec. 1. Pg. 3.
41. *New Ordinances Are Protested Last Night, None Is Passed.* The Snyder Daily News. November 3, 1953. Sec. 1. Pg. 1.
42. *Lincoln School Teams Take Win By Lack Of Competition.* The Snyder Daily News. March 4, 1954. Sec. 1. Pg. 6.
43. *Negro Education Discussed At School Board Here Last Night.* The Snyder Daily News. March 9, 1954. Sec. 1. Pg. 2.

11: Keep The Peace

1. *Price Daniel Raps Ruling On South Schools.* The Snyder Daily News. May 18, 1954. Sec. 1. Pg. 1.
2. *Local Men See No Problem As Segregation Is Ended.* The Snyder Daily News. May 18, 1954. Sec. 1. Pg. 1.
3. *Lincoln School Promotion Set.* The Snyder Daily News. May 25, 1954. Sec. 1. Pg. 2.
4. *Negroes Seek Help In June 19 Celebration.* The Snyder Daily News. May 30, 1954. Sec. 2. Pg. 5.
5. *School System Is A Major Industry.* The Snyder Daily News. August 15, 1954. Sec. 1. Pg. 6.
6. *New Courses Planned For High School.* The Snyder Daily News. August 15, 1954. Sec. 1. Pg. 6.
7. *Enrollment Increase Of Over 350 Is Due.* The Snyder Daily News. August 15, 1954. Sec. 1. Pg. 1.
8. *Seven Are Added To Teaching Staff.* The Snyder Daily News. August 15, 1954. Pg. 1.
9. *School Health System Emphasizes Education.* The Snyder Daily News. August 15, 1954. Sec. 1. Pg. 6.
10. *Lincoln Boys Enroll For Shop Course.* The Snyder Daily News. October 24, 1954. Sec. 1. Pg. 4.
11. *Big Classroom Shortage Here Involves Elementary Schools.* The Snyder Daily News. October 24, 1954. Sec. 1. Pg. 9.
12. *Enrollment Is 400 In Excess Of Capacity.* The Snyder Daily News. October 24, 1954. Sec. 1. Pg. 9.
13. *Enlarged Facilities Planned Throughout School System.* The Snyder Daily News. October 24, 1954. Sec. 1. Pg. 9
14. *Who Can Vote On Saturday.* The Snyder Daily News. October 24, 1954. Sec. 1. Pg. 9
15. *Turnout At Polls Sets Record Here.* The Snyder Daily News. October 31, 1954. Sec. 1. Pg. 1.
16. *Negro Pupils Here Showing Increased Interest In Studies.* The Snyder Daily News. February 13, 1955. Sec. 2. Pg. 6.
17. *Entries From Lincoln Place.* The Snyder Daily News. March 28, 1955. Sec. 1. Pg. 2.
18. *Desegregation May Be Postponed In Texas.* The Snyder Daily News. August 21, 1955. Pg. 12.
19. *Prisoners Guarded In Mississippi Jail.* The Snyder Daily News. September 5, 1955. Pg. 2.
20. *School Opens Here Friday.* The Snyder Daily News. September 1, 1955. Pg. 1
21. *Salk Polio Vaccines Are Released.* The Snyder Daily News. September 1, 1955. Pg. 1
22. *Report On School Classrooms Given.* The Snyder Daily News. November 11, 1955. Pg. 1
23. *Work Almost Finished On School Here.* The Snyder Daily News. November 9, 1955. Pg. 1
24. *Silver Tea Planned At Lincoln.* The Snyder Daily News. February 15, 1956. Pg. 3.
25. *Scholarship Silver Tea.* The Snyder Daily News. February 23, 1956. Pg. 3.
26. *Boycott Faces Transit Firm.* The Snyder Daily News. December 5, 1955. Pg. 1.
27. *Negro Pupils Show Increased Interest.* The Snyder Daily News. March 11, 1956. Sec. E Pg. 8.
28. "The Southern Manifesto". Congressional Record, 84th Congress Second Session. Vol. 102, part 4 (March 12, 1956). Washington, D.C.: Governmental Printing Office, 1956. 4459-4460.

12: A Forgotten Era

1. Anderson, Charles G. *Reflections 1840 - 1990*. Snyder Publishing Company Inc. Pg. 320 - 321.
2. *First Place Certificates Brought Back*. The Snyder Daily News. April 9, 1956. Pg. 6
3. *Vote Set On New Park Facilities*. The Snyder Daily News. April 19, 1956. Pg. 2
4. *Two Added To Faculty At Lincoln*. The Snyder Daily News. September 5, 1956. Pg. 2
5. Waite, Charles. *Price Daniel, Texas Democrats, and School Segregation, 1956-1957*. East Texas Historical Journal. Vol. 48. Issue 2. Article 10. October, 2010.
6. *A Divided Sentiment*. The Snyder Daily News. May 30, 1956. Pg. 4.
7. *Official Mobbed During Dispute Over Integration*. The Snyder Daily News. August 31, 1956. Pg. 1.
8. *New Effigy Strung Up*. The Snyder Daily News. August 31, 1956. Pg. 1.
9. Swanson, Doug J. *The Horrible Truth of Love Field's Texas Ranger Statue*. D Magazine. June, 2020.
10. *Negro Youth Likes School In Ft. Worth*. The Snyder Daily News. August 31, 1956. Pg. 2.
11. Swanson, Doug J. *Cult of Glory: The Bold and Brutal History of the Texas Rangers*. Pg. 329-333.
12. *The Handbook of Texas Online: Mansfield School Desegregation Incident*. Texas State Historical Association.
13. *3 Negroes Stopped By Texarkana Picket Line*. The Snyder Daily News. September 7, 1956. Pg. 1.
14. *Shots Fired Over Church*. The Snyder Daily News. September 7, 1956. Pg. 1.
15. *Cross Burns In Texarkana*. The Snyder Daily News. September 9, 1956. Pg. 8.
16. *Two Added To Faculty At Lincoln*. The Snyder Daily News. September 5, 1956. Pg. 2.
17. *School Issue Is Discussed*. The Snyder Daily News. September 19, 1956. Pg. 1
18. *School Board Sets Meeting In Cafeteria*. The Snyder Daily News. September 25, 1956. Pg. 1.
19. *Tentative School Plans Are Okayed*. The Snyder Daily News. October 10, 1956. Pg. 1.
20. *Dear Santa…* The Snyder Daily News. December 20, 1956. Pg. 2.
21. *Gifts Given To Children*. The Snyder Daily News. December 23, 1956. Pg. 2.
22. *Work Is Launched On Lincoln School*. The Snyder Daily News. January 3, 1957. Pg. 9.
23. *Johnson Is Installed In District Post*. The Snyder Daily News. March 18, 1957. Pg. 7.
24. *Segregation Will Continue In Dallas*. The Snyder Daily News. August 15, 1957. Pg. 7.
25. Anderson, Charles G. *Reflections 1840 - 1990*. Snyder Publishing Company Inc. Pg. iv-v.
26. Anderson, Charles G. *Confederate General William R. "Dirty Neck Bill" Scurry*. Snyder Publishing Company Inc. Pg. viii.
27. *Chronicling Texas history*. The Snyder News. June 27, 2018.
28. *School Job Delayed*. The Snyder Daily News. August 15, 1957. Pg. 7.
29. *Guard Holds Back Negroes*. The Snyder Daily News. September 4, 1957. Pg. 1.
30. *Lincoln Organizes Football Program*. The Snyder Daily News. September 17, 1957. Pg. 5.
31. *Little Rock Is Shocked*. The Snyder Daily News. September 24, 1957. Pg. 1.
32. *Enrollment 250 Above Last Year.* The Snyder Daily News. December 12, 1957. Sec. B Pg. 1.
33. *Lincoln School Sets First High School Commencement*. The Snyder Daily News. May 25, 1958. Sec. B Pg. 7.

13: Where Parents Read

1. *Lincoln P-TA Holds First Session Here*. The Snyder Daily News. September 14, 1958. Pg. 6.
2. *Our View- Pepper And Salt Class*. The Snyder Daily News. September 2, 1958. Pg. 6.
3. *Nearly 3,800 Pupils Enroll In Schools*. The Snyder Daily News. September 2, 1958. Pg. 1.
4. *Branch Of Library Set*. The Snyder Daily News. September 7, 1958. Pg. 2.
5. *The Texas Almanac Online: Elections of Texas Governors, 1845-2010*.
6. *No New Integration Seen In Texas*. The Snyder Daily News. August 30, 1959. Sec. B. Pg. 5.

7. *School Enrollment Tops 4,000 Mark.* The Snyder Daily News. September 6, 1959. Pg. 3
8. *$10 Million School Plant Is Built Here Within A Decade.* The Snyder Daily News. October 11, 1959. Sec. 6 Pg. D. (Microfilm page 46)
9. *Decennial Census of Population and Housing.* United States Census Bureau.
10. Records, Texas State Historical Survey Committee. Archives and Information Services Division, Texas State Library and Archives Commission. Boxes 808-1 - 808-11.
11. *Lunch Counters Remain Closed.* The Snyder Daily News. February 9, 1960. Pg. 7.
12. *Observance at Lincoln School Held.* The Snyder Daily News. February 14, 1960. Pg. 2.
13. 1,500 Negroes Plan Sitdown To Back San Antonio Edict. The Snyder Daily News. March 14, 1960. Pg. 2.
14. Seals, Donald Jr., "The Wiley-Bishop Student Movement: A Case Study in the 1960 Civil Rights Sit- Ins," The Southwestern Historical Quarterly, Volume 106, July 2002 - April, 2003, Ron Tyler, editor.
15. *Schools Meet Demands Of Busy Decade By Expanding.* The Snyder Daily News. June 12, 1960. Sec. 7 Pg. 3.
16. Leip, David. "Dave Leip's Atlas of U.S. Presidential Elections".
17. *Achievements Of Negro Are Cited.* The Snyder Daily News. February 19, 1961. Pg. 6.
18. *Lincoln Is Tops In Meet.* The Snyder Daily News. May 28, 1961. Pg. 3.
19. *Texans Start Paying Sales Tax Tomorrow.* The Snyder Daily News. August 31, 1961. Pg. 1.
20. Waite, Charles. *Price Daniel, Texas Democrats, and School Segregation, 1956-1957.* East Texas Historical Journal. Vol. 48. Issue 2. Article 10. October, 2010.
21. National Park Service website. Vicksburg National Military Park. History and Culture: The Texas State Memorial.
22. Frazier, Dr. Donald S. *The Deadly Hills at Vicksburg.* The Texas Historical Foundation. May 20, 2016.
23. *Texas monument rededicated.* The Vicksburg Post. May 25, 2001.
24. *Work begins to repair erosion near Texas Monument.* The Vicksburg Post. May 25, 2001.
25. *Relic hunters tear up park's Railroad Redoubt.* The Vicksburg Post. May 12, 2007.
26. *School Budget Discussed, Bids Are Opened At Session.* The Snyder Daily News. June 20, 1962. Pg. 1.
27. *Enrollment Shows Slight Gain Here.* The Snyder Daily News. September 7, 1962. Pg. 1.
28. *Lincoln School Moves Ahead.* The Snyder Daily News. December 20, 1962. Sec. B. Pg. 1.
29. *Lincoln Principal On League Council.* The Snyder Daily News. January 11, 1963. Pg. 2.
30. Speri, Alice. *"Deadly Heat" in U.S. prisons is killing inmates and spawning lawsuits.* The Intercept. August 24, 2016
31. McGaughy, Lauren. *"It's hell living there": Texas inmates say they are battling COVID-19 in prisons with no A/C.* The Dallas Morning News. July 31, 2020.
32. Hicks, Tyler. *"'Slowly Cooked Alive': Many Texas Prisons Still Don't Have Air Conditioning.* The Dallas Observer. July 18, 2022.

14: A Great Change

1. *JFK Charts Civil Rights Legislation.* The Snyder Daily News. June 12, 1963. Pg. 2.
2. *Lincoln High Debaters Win First Place.* The Snyder Daily News. April 22, 1963. Pg. 2.
3. *Judge Says Pupils Will Stay In Jail.* The Snyder Daily News. May 3, 1963. Pg. 1.
4. *Lincoln School Exercises Are Set Today And Tuesday.* The Snyder Daily News. May 26, 1963. Pg. 10.
5. Anderson, Charles G. *Confederate General William R. "Dirty Neck Bill" Scurry, 1821-1864.* Snyder Publishing Company. July, 1999. Pg. 13-32.
6. Natanson, Hanna. *They were once America's cruelest, richest slave traders. Why does no one know their names?* The Washington Post. September 14, 2019.
7. Rothman, Joshua D. *The Men Who Turned Slavery Into Big Business.* Atlantic Magazine. April 20, 2021.
8. Franklin and Armfield Office. US National Park Service official website.

9. *The Handbook of Texas Online: Austin State Gazette*. Texas State Historical Association.
10. *The Handbook of Texas Online: Slavery*. Texas State Historical Association.
11. Campbell, Randolph B. *An Empire For Slavery: The Peculiar Institution in Texas, 1821-1865*. Louisiana State University Press, 1991. Chapter 4: The Economics of slavery in Texas.
12. *Decennial Census of Population and Housing*. United States Census Bureau.
13. *A declaration of the causes which impel the State of Texas to secede from the Federal Union*. Texas State Library and Archives Commission.
14. *Texas Ordinance of Secession*. Texas State Library and Archives Commission.
15. Anderson, Charles G. *Confederate General William R. "Dirty Neck Bill" Scurry*. Snyder Publishing Company Inc. Pg. 83-121.
16. *Historical Marker*. The Snyder Daily News. July 4, 1963. Pg. 1.
17. Records, Texas State Historical Survey Committee. Boxes 808-1 - 808-11. Texas State Library and Archives Commission. Archives and Information Services Division.
18. The Southern Poverty Law Center website: Public Symbols of the Confederacy.
19. *Racial Barriers Tumbling In Texas School Districts*. The Snyder Daily News. August 25, 1963. Pg. 4.
20. *School Clothes Made Ready By Joe Graham Cleaners*. The Snyder Daily News. August 31, 1963. Pg. 6.
21. *Assassin Slays President, Wounds Governor Connally*. The Snyder Daily News. November 22, 1963. Pg. 1.
22. *Lincoln Honor Roll Students Recognized*. The Snyder Daily News. January 26, 1964. Pg 2.
23. *Baccalaureate And Commencement Programs Set At Lincoln School*. The Snyder Daily News. May 24, 1964. Pg 10.
24. *Graduation Exercises Here Tonight*. The Snyder Daily News. May 29, 1964. Pg 1.
25. *New Law Immediately Tested*. The Snyder Daily News. July 3, 1964. Pg 1.
26. *3,680 Start School Here*. The Snyder Daily News. September 1, 1964. Pg 1.
27. Leip, David. "Dave Leip's Atlas of U.S. Presidential Elections".
28. *Records Received*. The Snyder Daily News. April 25, 1965. Sec. B. Pg 1.
29. *Library At Lincoln Is Kept Busy*. The Snyder Daily News. February 28, 1965. Sec. B. Pg 6.
30. *Service For Lincoln's Seniors Set*. The Snyder Daily News. May 23, 1965. Pg 7.

Epilogue: Better To Have

1. *Poll Tax In Jeopardy*. The Snyder Daily News. August 6, 1965. Pg 1.
2. Author's interviews with Vernon Clay. June 2020 - March 2023.
3. *Welcome, Teachers*. The Snyder Daily News. August 29, 1965. Sec. B. Pg. 1.
4. *South Quietly Ends School Segregation*. The Snyder Daily News. August 31, 1965. Pg 11.
5. *Lincoln Grads In College*. The Snyder Daily News. September 14, 1965. Pg 2.
6. *Schools Have 3,611 Pupils*. The Snyder Daily News. August 31, 1965. Pg 1.
7. *School Vote Set; Lincoln To Close*. The Snyder Daily News. January 12, 1966. Pg 1.
8. *SHS Graduation Slated Tonight*. The Snyder Daily News. May 26, 1966. Pg 1.
9. *Johnson To Get Degree*. The Snyder Daily News. May 31, 1966. Pg 7.
10. *Report Puzzles School Officials*. The Snyder Daily News. July 18, 1966. Pg 1.
11. Letter by John Baker. Scurry County Museum Artifact 1975.002.001.
12. *John Baker Dies Saturday*. The Snyder Daily News. November 23, 1975. Pg 1.

f5d39648-c832-4c31-b19a-222ce6f3fdd5R01